Developing Software for the QUALCOMM BREW Platform

RAY RISCHPATER

Apress™

Developing Software for the QUALCOMM BREW Platform
Copyright ©2003 by Ray Rischpater

ISBN (pbk): 1-59059-116-X

Printed and bound in the United States of America 12345678910

Distributed to the book trade in the United States by Springer-Verlag New York, Inc., 175 Fifth Avenue, New York, NY, 10010 and outside the United States by Springer-Verlag GmbH & Co. KG, Tiergartenstr. 17, 69112 Heidelberg, Germany.

In the United States, phone 1-800-SPRINGER, email orders@springer-ny.com, or visit http://www.springer-ny.com. Outside the United States, fax +49 6221 345229, email orders@springer.de, or visit http://www.springer.de.

For information on translations, please contact Apress directly at 2560 Ninth Street, Suite 219, Berkeley, CA 94710. Phone 510-549-5930, fax 510-549-5939, email info@apress.com, or visit http://www.apress.com.

The source code for this book is available to readers at http://www.apress.com in the Downloads section.

Contents at a Glance

Contents

About the Author

Ray Rischpater is a software engineer and writer who has focused on mobile computing since 1995. During that time, he has developed countless applications for Fortune 500 companies using handheld computers and wireless interfaces for enterprise and commercial deployment. This includes the first handheld Web server on a commercially available platform and the development of several of the first handheld Web browsers available, including those for the Apple Newton and Palm Powered platforms. He's the author of seven books and 48 articles on mobile and wireless computing.

When not aggressively pursuing his avocation as a full-time geek and evangelist of the geek lifestyle, Ray spends time with his family hiking, camping, and providing public service using amateur radio.

Ray is a member of the IEEE and is currently employed as a staff engineer at Rocket Mobile, where he develops Web-based applications and services for the QUALCOMM BREW platform and other mobile wireless platforms.

About the Technical Reviewer

Shane Conder is a software engineering professional specializing in wireless BREW applications. He spends his precious free time road tripping and traveling, and he's an avid amateur radio hobbyist. He lives in Santa Cruz, California, with his fiancée, Lauren, and six rabbits named Bit, Nibble, Heap, Qubit, Stack, and Null.

Acknowledgments

IT SEEMS THAT with each passing book I write, I widen my debt to others. Writing any book is a collaborative effort, but the input and feedback I've received in developing this one far surpasses any other I've had the pleasure of attempting.

Primarily, I'm indebted to my family, Rachel and Jarod, for their ongoing support as I continue to juggle writing, work, and my responsibilities as a husband and father. For you, Rachel, my soul mate, I owe you the world. And Jarod, my son, thank you for your Tuesdays and Thursdays of infinite patience as your daddy sat hunched beside you on the couch, typing away and pausing occasionally to read you another page (often of what he was writing and not what you were reading!).

Of course, I am again indebted to the staff at Apress for their contribution throughout this book. As always, Kim Wimpsett was there with excellent editorial input and an eye for consistency and detail that I only wish I could have. Simon Hayes, Jim Sumser, and Nate McFadden shepherded the book along the course from idea to manuscript to the tome you now hold, patiently enduring my notion of a schedule as a mere skeleton on which to hang the occasional delivery. Of course, there were countless others at Apress who gave their support; most unfortunately go thankless and unacknowledged. Rest assured that I'm well aware of your efforts, and I'm deeply grateful to your contributions in making this book what it is today.

Shane Conder, my technical editor, is both a first-rate developer and a true friend. I owe him tremendous thanks in providing his input and wisdom pertaining to the QUALCOMM BREW platform and in carefully scrutinizing each page and testing each application before errors slipped through. His deep knowledge of QUALCOMM BREW is reflected in this book through a number of well-crafted points and corrections, and in many cases his suggestions paved the way for a better discussion of some of the more challenging aspects of learning the QUALCOMM BREW platform. Of course, any errors that remain rest on my shoulders, not his.

In many ways, this book didn't just have one technical editor but rather six. From the early drafts of the first chapter, my colleagues at Rocket Mobile—most of whom were either actively developing applications for the QUALCOMM BREW platform or anxious to learn the platform—harangued me for draft chapters and were more than willing to offer input and corrections in return. These are people with whom I've shared offices, projects, and time, often for many years, and I'm thankful not just for the time they invested in this work but my ongoing professional and personal relationships with them. For Erik Browne, Graham Darcey, Konstantin Kraz, Spencer Nassar, and Charles Stearns, my thanks go to you as contributors second and as friends first. I'd also like to take a moment and thank

Dr. William Confer of Auburn University, who provided valuable feedback and positive encouragement during the final editing phases of the project.

A special thanks is also due to my manager at Rocket Mobile, Wayne Yurtin, who openly supported this book with corporate contacts, frequent comments, and the opportunity to include large segments of RocketMileage as a sample application accompanying this book. It's rare to have the opportunity to offer the source code to a commercially available application (outside of open source) to the public, and his open-mindedness and respect for the greater QUALCOMM BREW development community is worthy of note.

Introduction

ANALYSTS AND PUNDITS alike have been pointing to the promise of a revolution in wireless telephony for several years. The increasing number of so-called "convergent" devices—smart phones with keyboards, Personal Digital Assistants (PDAs) with cellular radios, or hybrid PDA phones—clearly heralds the onset of a new way of viewing computing and communication.

QUALCOMM, the inventor and leading manufacturer of Code Division Multiple Access (CDMA) technology, has introduced the QUALCOMM BREW platform to permit software developers like you and me to deliver high-quality applications to wireless subscribers everywhere. QUALCOMM BREW consists of the client layer, which is a thin layer of Application Programming Interfaces (APIs) that resides atop the chip set in many of today's wireless handsets, and a back-end delivery system for carriers, which consolidates software deployment, delivery, and payment with the handset and subscriber's billing system. The QUALCOMM BREW platform is available on more than two million handsets today. Furthermore, more than 50 percent of handset users regularly purchase applications with their QUALCOMM BREW–enabled handsets, and the platform is available from major carriers in several countries, including Verizon Wireless, AllTel, and U.S. Cellular in the United States, China Unicom in China, Vivo in Brazil, KDDI in Japan, Telstra in Australia, and KTF in South Korea.

With mobile handsets expected to surpass other kinds of data connectivity by 2005, and with QUALCOMM BREW leading the pack for mobile wireless application development and deployment, now is the time for you to begin developing applications for the QUALCOMM BREW platform.

Who Needs to Read This Book

If you're a software developer interested in bringing your application to the latest crop of smart phones running QUALCOMM BREW, this book is for you. Because of the wide variety of application developers and possible applications for the QUALCOMM BREW platform, I make only a few assumptions about your experience. You should be familiar with programming in C and comfortable with the basics of application development on at least one platform. I don't, however, expect that you have previous experience developing applications for wireless terminals. If you do—or if you've already used the QUALCOMM BREW platform to develop and deploy applications—you still have much to gain because I present many advanced concepts about application development for the platform.

Although you can write applications for QUALCOMM BREW using C++, I've chosen to use only C throughout this book, both because the vast majority of BREW applications are written in C and because many C++ features don't mesh well with the paradigms of programming for the platform. Consequently, you don't need to know C++ to read this book, but some concepts may be familiar to you if you've used it in the past.

If you're responsible for other aspects of software deployment for the QUALCOMM BREW platform, such as project management or quality assurance, several chapters of this book, especially the first two chapters and the last chapter, will be of interest to you.

What You Will Find in This Book

I wrote this book with the assumption that you've never written applications for the QUALCOMM BREW platform. Consequently, the book tells a story, starting with the how, why, and wherefore of the QUALCOMM BREW platform, and then builds from there to show you how to construct user interfaces, an application framework, storage, and network subsystems when building your application.

Chapter 1, "Introducing the QUALCOMM BREW Platform," does just that, showing you why you should be developing applications for the platform if you're not already. In addition, it compares the platform with other platforms such as Sun's Java 2 Micro Edition and shows the strengths and weaknesses of each.

Chapter 2, "Designing for the QUALCOMM BREW Platform," takes a step back from the platform itself and helps you understand how applications for the platform are likely to be different from those you've designed and built before.

Chapter 3, "Developing for the QUALCOMM BREW Platform," provides an overview of the various tools you use when constructing your application. Although it doesn't replace the excellent QUALCOMM BREW Software Developer's Kit (SDK) User's Guide that accompanies the QUALCOMM BREW SDK, it presents enough information that, after reading it, you'll be ready to follow along with the sample code throughout the book.

Chapter 4, "Handling Events," describes the fundamental event-driven model that powers the QUALCOMM BREW platform and presents the underpinnings of a state machine framework that you can use to build your own applications. As you learn how to construct and use the state machine, you'll also see your first useful sample application. This application, SlideShow, lets you present prototype user interfaces for your application to stakeholders during your application design.

Chapter 5, "Interacting with the User," presents an overview of the various user interface controls you can use when developing for the QUALCOMM BREW platform. As you read this chapter, you'll learn how each of these controls fits into the event model of your application and see how to add support for controls to the state machine framework introduced in the previous chapter to make managing user interface controls easy.

Chapter 6, "Streaming Data," shows you how the QUALCOMM BREW platform uses streams to carry data from memory, the embedded file system, and remote servers and conserve memory while enabling the presentation of rich multimedia such as pictures and sounds.

Chapter 7, "Storing Data," shows you the other means for data storage on the platform: databases. The QUALCOMM BREW platform provides a robust interface for storing records of associated fields in flash memory, letting you save data sets on the embedded file system within your application.

Chapter 8, "Drawing Graphics," presents the various graphics interfaces and presents the enhancements that have been added as the platform has matured. You'll learn how to use the display interface for simple graphics, the more advanced graphics interface for complex graphics, and the sprite engine for sprite-based animations and games. Two sample applications demonstrate these interfaces, giving you ample code with which to experiment as you learn about the interfaces at your disposal.

Chapter 9, "Playing with Sounds," lets you add sound support to the applications presented in the previous chapter, showing you the three different interfaces you can use to add sound to your application. Because the QUALCOMM BREW platform is designed to provide rich support for multimedia, this chapter also presents the latest interfaces that will support not just audio playback but other kinds of real-time media, such as video and audio capture.

Chapter 10, "Networking Your Data," introduces the various interfaces available to you to utilize the wireless network in your application. The platform includes support for the Transmission Control Protocol/Internet Protocol (TCP/IP) that powers the Internet, as well as an interface that implements the Hypertext Transfer Protocol (HTTP), so your applications can move data between the handset and remote servers anywhere on the Web.

Chapter 11, "Controlling the Handset," introduces a bevy of interfaces that lets you integrate various handset functions such as position determination, telephony, ringer tones, and the built-in address book. These interfaces distinguish the platform from virtually every other mobile platform on the market, giving you unprecedented control of the wireless handset.

Chapter 12, "Certifying Your Application," goes over the last crucial part of developing your application: third-party certification and distribution to wireless carriers. This chapter looks at what you can do ahead of time to increase the chances that your application will pass third-party certification on your first attempt and examines how you distribute your application once it receives certification.

If you're already familiar with the QUALCOMM BREW platform, feel free to skip around. You may want to start by skimming bits in Chapters 4 and 5, where I present the application framework on which all of the sample applications in this book are built. In fact, the same framework is available in the source code that accompanies this book (available from the Downloads section of the Apress Web site at http://www.apress.com/), and you're welcome to use this framework in developing your own applications. Throughout this book, I've taken pains to point out when QUALCOMM BREW interfaces are different between versions of the platform so you'll be up to speed with the latest developments on the platform.

Finally, if you want to see the QUALCOMM BREW platform in action within a shipping application, you may want to start with the source code available from the book's Web site and have a look at the source code to RocketMileage, an automotive expense tracking application that's commercially available.

A Word on Presentation

As with other technical books, it helps to distinguish between what's meant for people to read and what's meant for computers to read.

Any text in this book that looks like this is either a fragment of code or a variable name. Whole listings of code are set in the same style, with line numbers:

```
1: typedef struct _Node
2: {
3:    /// Next node
4:    struct _Node *m_pNext;
5:    /// Pointer to data for this node
6:    void *m_pData;
7:    /// Pointer to any additional data for this node.
8:    void *m_pMetaData;
9: };
```

Most of the sample code uses comments that conform to the doc++ syntax, available from http://docpp.sourceforge.net/. Because doc++ provides a great way to mark up your source code and to automatically generate documentation about its interfaces and use, I highly recommend you investigate it. Moreover, because a great deal of the code I present is meant for you to use immediately in your applications, you can download the doc++ application from the aforementioned site and immediately build an online reference to the source code you find in this book.

The saying goes that a picture is worth a thousand words. I've tried to use illustrations in this book for two purposes: to show you the screen of the various sample applications I present throughout the book and to describe relationships between the interfaces provided by the QUALCOMM BREW platform. To do the latter, I use the Unified Modeling Language (UML). UML provides a powerful way to represent different aspects of systems in a compact notation clearly and intuitively.

Getting the Latest Resources

Throughout the book, you'll be using developer tools and resources for the QUALCOMM BREW platform. After reading this introduction, your first stop should be the QUALCOMM BREW Web site at http://www.qualcomm.com/brew/ to download the SDK, and your second stop should be the Apress Web site at http://www.apress.com/ to download the sample applications that accompany this book.

Looking Ahead

QUALCOMM BREW mixes the best of tried-and-true development technologies with a revolutionary method of real-time application deployment to wireless handsets. In January 2003, QUALCOMM announced that the combined royalties paid out to all developers had exceeded a million dollars per month, and adoption of the platform continues. It's time to sit down, dig in, and begin planning how you can bring your application to the QUALCOMM BREW platform and share in its success!

CHAPTER 1

Introducing the QUALCOMM BREW Platform

THE **QUALCOMM BINARY** Runtime Environment for Wireless (BREW) platform is an exciting step forward in mobile application development. Within the QUALCOMM BREW platform there's a powerful set of Application Programming Interfaces (APIs) that you use with C or C++ to build your application for wireless handsets. Once you complete your application, you can submit it to QUALCOMM for external validation and from there to wireless carriers around the world for your customers to purchase and enjoy.

This chapter gives you a quick overview of the QUALCOMM BREW platform, including what it can and can't do and why carriers, handset manufacturers, and developers have been keen to adopt the platform. After examining the platform from a marketing perspective, the chapter sketches the architecture of the QUALCOMM BREW application, as well as gives you a thumbnail view of how to organize a QUALCOMM BREW application. Finally, the chapter closes with your first sample application written for QUALCOMM BREW—the now-famous HelloWorld program.

Seeing the QUALCOMM BREW Platform for the First Time

If you've never used a QUALCOMM BREW–enabled handset, the first thing you should do is go get one and play with it. Books such as this one can't fully capture the experience of using a QUALCOMM BREW–enabled handset, but it'll try.

Most QUALCOMM BREW–enabled handsets look like regular cell phones and have the following features in common:

- A multiline color, grayscale, or monochrome display used by the handset for both telephony operations and QUALCOMM BREW applications

- A directional keypad or arrow keys to navigate a selection cursor up, down, left, and right

- A selection key

- Alphanumeric entry support through either multitap (where you press a number key one or more times to navigate through successive letters) or other mechanisms such as Tegic's T9 predictive keyboard

- A means to launch QUALCOMM BREW applications, either via a configuration menu or a dedicated key on the handset

In addition, most newer QUALCOMM BREW–enabled handsets support the third-generation wireless networks (often called *express networks*) and on-handset global positioning for emergency response and location applications.

What differentiates these handsets from most other programmable handsets—including those running the Palm Powered and Microsoft Pocket PC for Smartphone platforms—is that they are priced to be competitive with today's wireless handsets rather than with handheld computers. This helps ensure the rapid adoption of QUALCOMM BREW–enabled handsets by consumers—even consumers who may not immediately want to run an application on their handset.

You can launch a QUALCOMM BREW application (called an *applet*) using a phone control to bring up the application menu, which looks something like Figure 1-1.

NOTE *Both the mechanism for launching the QUALCOMM BREW application menu and the appearance of the BREW application menu can differ from handset to handset. Many QUALCOMM BREW–enabled handsets offer a button labeled with a carrier-dependent logo, such as the Verizon Wireless Get It Now logo, and others use a menu option or sequence of keys. Similarly, the appearance of the QUALCOMM BREW application menu may differ slightly from what you see in Figure 1-1.*

Figure 1-1. The QUALCOMM BREW application menu in action

You can obtain new QUALCOMM BREW–enabled applications by using the Mobile Shop application, which wirelessly obtains a list of the latest applications and lets you purchase them for immediate use on the phone. When you launch an application such as RocketMileage, the application consumes the entire screen (as shown in Figure 1-2), and you can freely interact with the application. If you receive a telephone call or Short Message Service (SMS) message while you're using the application, the handset pauses your application and shows a dialog box that lets you choose to accept the call or message or continue using the application.

Figure 1-2. The RocketMileage application

Choosing the QUALCOMM BREW Platform

Making the decision to develop applications for the QUALCOMM BREW platform hinges on three factors: the wireless carriers your application targets, the market your application targets, and the flexibility QUALCOMM BREW provides you with as a developer. Equally important, you should understand why you might *not* want to use QUALCOMM BREW to develop your application. The following sections take a closer look at each of these issues.

Why Carriers Choose QUALCOMM BREW

Wireless carriers face two challenges directly affecting their profits: decreasing Average Revenue Per User (ARPU) and increasing subscriber demand. Competition between wireless carriers (and legislation in some countries) continues driving down what carriers can charge their customers, even as carriers must continue to invest to upgrade their infrastructures to support increasing demand. Paradoxically, however, the increased revenue from new customers doesn't fully offset the costs carriers incur when upgrading their networks to handle the additional customer demand.

Consequently, carriers are in the awkward position of needing to drive additional demand for existing services in the hopes of raising ARPU and increasing profits. By opening the wireless network to third-party applications, carriers want software developers to provide value-added applications that increase subscriber network use and raise ARPU.

Initial attempts to spur demand by offering third-party applications have met with limited success for several reasons. First, few handsets are available for any one carrier that can run third-party applications. These handsets, often called *smart phones* or *wireless terminals*, are a hybrid handheld computer (often running Palm OS, Windows Pocket PC, or Symbian OS) and wireless handset that typically costs several times more than a phone. Second, these smart phones are difficult to use, often with limitations on battery life and with user interfaces more similar to computers than phones. Third, installing third-party applications on these devices is an arcane process generally requiring a computer and separate cable (even the first generation of Java-enabled handsets suffer this drawback) so that out of the small fraction of subscribers that *use* one of these handsets, even fewer actually *use* them more than they use a traditional wireless handset.

QUALCOMM BREW has features that meet each of these drawbacks. First, QUALCOMM BREW is lightweight; it's essentially a thin veneer over a telephone's native operating system, and it often provides interfaces to hardware features of today's handsets (such as media decoding) that are implemented in silicon on the device. Consequently, QUALCOMM BREW is available on even the least expensive wireless handsets, making it easy for carriers to offer QUALCOMM BREW to subscribers with little or no added cost. Second, both QUALCOMM BREW itself and the handsets on which it's available are primarily wireless handsets. These devices bear little resemblance to traditional computing devices, making them comfortable to nearly all users. Finally, QUALCOMM BREW provides an end-to-end software distribution platform for carriers and consumers. As you'll see in the next section, you have access to third-party applications when using a QUALCOMM BREW–enabled handset. When you purchase an application, the application is wirelessly transferred to your phone, and the cost of the application is added to your phone bill. The QUALCOMM BREW platform handles the necessary billing, maintains a secure transaction between handset and server, and even provides developers with royalty checks from carriers on a regular basis from application sales.

Why Developers Choose QUALCOMM BREW

So why should *you* choose QUALCOMM BREW? If you're looking to develop and deploy applications for wireless handsets, QUALCOMM BREW provides several advantages.

First, QUALCOMM BREW is likely the most widely distributed platform for handset software development in the world. Within the first year of QUALCOMM BREW's introduction to the market, QUALCOMM BREW was in the hands of more than a million users. Moreover, it's seeing rapid and widespread adoption in the United States and abroad, often replacing older smart phones in the process. This is largely because when carriers offer QUALCOMM BREW handsets, they generally do so across all price points, making QUALCOMM BREW available on all handsets. Consequently, the applications you write are likely to be available to all subscribers for a wireless carrier as soon as a carrier adopts QUALCOMM BREW.

Second, QUALCOMM BREW uses concepts and programming languages familiar to the experienced software developer. You write your applications in C or C++ using the BREW APIs, test them in a simulator on your desktop computer, and download them directly to the handset for testing. Although this is similar to development for other platforms including Sun's Java 2 Micro Edition (J2ME) for handsets and the Palm Powered platform for handsets, there are fewer hurdles because the APIs and tool chain remain largely unchanged for QUALCOMM BREW.

Third, QUALCOMM BREW is truly a write-once, run-anywhere platform because the APIs have been established by QUALCOMM and are available on *all* platforms. In other words, it's not a community process with different manufacturers providing various extensions, as is common with J2ME, the Palm Powered platform, and Microsoft Pocket PC Smartphone edition. Most of the QUALCOMM BREW APIs are available on all handsets, and few handset vendors extend the QUALCOMM BREW APIs in unconventional ways.

Why Developers Choose Other Platforms

Before closing this section, you should understand why you might *not* want to choose QUALCOMM BREW for your application. Obviously, if your customers use a cellular network that doesn't support QUALCOMM BREW, it makes little sense to write your applications using QUALCOMM BREW. If you're porting business logic from another application—say, one in Java or one running the Palm Powered platform for a handheld computer—it may make sense for you to use a super phone running the same platform, rather than trying to port your entire application to QUALCOMM BREW. This is especially true if you're writing a *vertical application* (an application targeted to a particular market), where you can control your customers' hardware configuration and require a specific wireless carrier and wireless handset.

NOTE *At the time of this book's publication, vendors including Insignia and IBM have demonstrated J2ME Mobile Information Device Profile (MIDP) runtimes for the QUALCOMM BREW platform. By the time you read this, it's quite likely that the J2ME MIDP will be available for QUALCOMM BREW on at least some handsets and you'll be able to run your J2ME MIDP applications on QUALCOMM BREW–enabled handsets with no difficulty. If this comes to pass, you'll have yet another alternative for deploying applications on QUALCOMM BREW: either native applications in C or C++ using the QUALCOMM BREW APIs or traditional J2ME MIDP midlets running atop a third-party Java virtual machine that uses QUALCOMM BREW.*

Understanding the QUALCOMM BREW Platform

When you first open the QUALCOMM BREW Software Development Kit (SDK), you may be daunted by all of the new terms, APIs, and conventions. Although it's easy to get confused—especially if you're the type who dives into something without looking at the documentation—it's not as difficult as it looks to grasp the fundamentals.

Confusion usually centers around three aspects of QUALCOMM BREW: understanding the relationship between modules, applications, and classes; understanding Module Information File (MIF) and resource files; and understanding the application delivery process. Learning about each of these topics now makes it far easier for you to understand other aspects of the QUALCOMM BREW platform later.

Understanding the Relationship Between Modules, Applications, and Classes

A *module* is a chunk of executable code in QUALCOMM BREW, much like a shared library on other platforms. Modules contain definitions of classes, or the implementations of interfaces you use to build applications. Many of these classes are loaded from the handset's Read-Only Memory (ROM) on demand when your application needs to use them; however, you can define your own classes to use in your application. When you do so, you can also choose to share these classes with other developers; in this case, the module is called an *extension* because the handset obtains it online when the classes are required.

As on most other object-oriented platforms, your *applet* (QUALCOMM BREW's name for applications) itself is a class—specifically, a subclass of the

IApplet class. It must implement the interface defined by the IApplet class to process events the system sends in response to system and user interface events. Note, too, that because an application is simply a class, a module can contain more than one applet.

Every class—be it a system class, one of your classes, or an applet—must have a unique class identifier (or *class ID*). A class ID is a 32-bit integer and is allocated by QUALCOMM as a service to registered developers at the QUALCOMM BREW extranet (available from http://www.qualcomm.com/brew/). When obtaining an interface to a class, you must use its class ID to request the interface from the system shell, the only interface loaded when your applet first runs. (An exception to this is the IShell, IModule, and IDisplay interfaces; your application will receive instances of these interfaces when it executes.)

NOTE *When you create your unique class ID using the extranet, the extranet will offer to let you download a BREW ID (BID) file, which contains a C-style definition of your class ID. You'll need to use this BID file when creating your application, so be sure to set it aside in your project directory.*

You build modules in two ways when developing your applet. During most of your development, you use Microsoft Visual Studio to build Dynamically Linked Libraries (DLLs) you invoke through the QUALCOMM BREW handset simulator. Periodically you build your modules using the ARM compiler and QUALCOMM tool chain, resulting in module files (which end in .mod and are sometimes called *MOD files*) that you transfer to your handset for on-device testing.

Understanding MIF and Resource Files

In addition to your applet's module file, your applet needs an MIF to describe the applet to the handset's runtime. As the handset starts up, it reads each applet's MIF to determine the applet's name, icons, and class ID. The MIF also contains additional information, such as the author of the application and a set of flags delineating various kinds of behaviors the application performs (such as file system access or network transactions). You build MIFs using the BREW MIF Editor, a component of the QUALCOMM BREW SDK.

In many of your applets, you want to include strings, icons, and dialog boxes. You can include these items in your application using the BREW Resource Editor, which lets you add items to your application. Once you use the BREW Resource

Editor to add items to your application, it will create a C header file and a resource file (called a *bar* file, short for *BREW Application Resource* file) for your application.

Chapter 3, "Developing for the QUALCOMM BREW Platform," discusses both of these tools in greater detail.

Understanding the Application Delivery Process

Deploying your QUALCOMM BREW application is quite different from deploying traditional shrink-wrapped applications for existing desktop and handheld platforms. Because your application will run on wireless handsets that are expected to never fail, your application must meet a high standard of quality. Moreover, the deployment process must be different to accommodate the over-the-air application download features of QUALCOMM BREW.

To meet these goals, you must submit your completed application to QUALCOMM for validation. To do this, you must first become a registered QUALCOMM BREW developer (discussed fully in the "Becoming an Authenticated QUALCOMM BREW Developer" section). Next, you need to use the QUALCOMM BREW tools to cryptographically sign a snapshot of the module, resource file, and MIF. You electronically submit these, along with your user manual and test plan, to QUALCOMM for verification.

In turn, QUALCOMM validates your application and provides you with the validation results. If your application passes the testing, QUALCOMM assigns your application a unique part number and certifies it as a *TRUE BREW* application. You may then offer your application—by referring to its part number, not by submitting new binaries!—to wireless carriers such as Verizon Wireless to offer to its customers.

As customers purchase your application, your carrier's BREW Mobile Shop tracks customer purchases, charging customers' regular wireless service bills accordingly. Quarterly you receive payments aggregated by QUALCOMM for your application sales, and you can check your sales by part number using the QUALCOMM extranet at any time.

Creating Your First Application

By now, you're probably wondering exactly what a QUALCOMM BREW application looks like from the inside out or at least how you can get started writing applications for QUALCOMM BREW. So let's stop the chatter about what QUALCOMM BREW is about and see a QUALCOMM BREW application in action!

Becoming an Authenticated QUALCOMM BREW Developer

Although it's not imperative that you do so immediately, it's helpful to become an authenticated QUALCOMM BREW developer as soon as you start developing for QUALCOMM BREW. By doing so, you receive a number of advantages, including the ability to run applications on test handsets and obtain unique class IDs for your applications.

To become an authenticated developer, visit http://www.qualcomm.com/brew/ and follow the links through the developer support section to the Become an Authenticated Developer page. You'll need to apply for a VeriSign certificate, complete the BREW Independent Solutions Vendor (ISV) development form, and register with National Software Testing Labs (NSTL), which is the validation firm QUALCOMM uses to test your applications prior to giving them TRUE BREW certification.

Installing the QUALCOMM BREW SDK

Although you don't need to be authenticated to begin QUALCOMM BREW development, you *do* need the QUALCOMM BREW SDK. It's available from the QUALCOMM BREW Web site at http://www.qualcomm.com/brew/. You need to install Microsoft Visual Studio first and then download and install the QUALCOMM BREW SDK.

Installing the SDK is easy; it's packaged as an installer for Microsoft Windows. It includes the headers and libraries you'll need as well as the documentation, sample applications, and the BREW Emulator for Microsoft Windows, which you need to test your application on your desktop computer.

NOTE   *Throughout this book, I refer to the BREW 2.0 SDK, including the BREW 2.0 SDK tool chain, even though many of the examples operate correctly on QUALCOMM BREW 1.0 and 1.1. Where a specific version of QUALCOMM BREW is required, I note it in the text that accompanies the example.*

If you've become an authenticated QUALCOMM BREW developer, you should also go to the QUALCOMM BREW extranet (available from http://www.qualcomm.com/brew/) and download the tools available to authenticated developers. These tools include the applications you need to install, test, and execute your application on a wireless handset.

Writing Your First Application

With the tools installed, it's time to write your first application. Let's start with the simple HelloWorld application that launches and draws the words *Hello World* on the display.

 CAUTION *Although you can build applications with Microsoft Visual Studio .NET or Microsoft Visual Studio 6.0, the following instructions are for Microsoft Developer Studio 6.0. Be sure to check the documentation included with Microsoft Visual Studio .NET for further details.*

To create the HelloWorld program, follow these steps:

1. Go to the QUALCOMM BREW developer extranet and create a class ID named *HELLOWORLD* for your application. If you haven't created a developer account yet, you can borrow the class ID from the QUALCOMM HelloWorld example by copying the file helloworld.bid to your project directory and naming it *hello.bid.*

2. Use Microsoft Paint or another paint application to create an icon for your application. Icons should be no more than 26-by-26 pixels and should be saved as uncompressed bitmaps (Microsoft Windows BMP). Be sure that the icons you create are black and white for black-and-white phones and 8-bit color for color phones. Of course, you can also borrow one of the sample icons from the QUALCOMM BREW SDK during this step. In either case, save the icon in your project directory.

3. Launch Microsoft Visual Studio.

4. Launch the BREW Wizard by selecting File ➤ New ➤ Projects ➤ BREW Application Wizard.

5. Choose a destination for your project and name it *hello.*

6. Click OK.

7. Because your application only draws to the screen, leave all of the options under What Support Would You Like to Include? unchecked and click Next.

8. Launch the MIF Editor by clicking the MIF Editor option to create an MIF for your application.

9. Within the MIF Editor, select the BID file you created in the first step by clicking Browse for BID File.

10. By Name, enter *Hello* as the application name.

11. By Applet Type, select Tools.

12. Select the icon you created in the second step by clicking Browse.

13. Save the MIF using File ➤ Save As and naming it *hello.mif.* (If you're only going to run this in the emulator, you don't need to worry about selecting an MIF type option.)

14. Exit the MIF Editor using File ➤ Exit.

15. Return to Microsoft Visual Studio and click Finish. Then click OK.

16. Under the File View, open the Hello.c file and replace its contents with the contents of Listing 1-1.

NOTE *The source code for this applet (and all of the sample applications from this book) is available at the Apress Web site (*http://www.apress.com/*) in the Downloads section, so you can simply use Microsoft Visual Studio to load the Hello.dsw project.*

Listing 1-1. The HelloWorld Applet

```
 1: /**
 2:  *  @name Hello.c
 3:  *
 4:  *  @author Ray Rischpater
 5:  *  Copyright (c) 2001 - 2002 Ray Rischpater.
 6:  *  Portions copyright (c) 2001 - 2002 QUALCOMM, Inc.
 7:  *  @doc
 8:  *  A sample application that draws Hello World
 9:  */
10: #include "AEEModGen.h" // Module interface definitions
11: #include "AEEAppGen.h" // Applet interface definitions
12: #include "AEEDisp.h"   // Display interface definitions
```

```
13: #include "hello.bid"    // Applet class ID
14:
15:
16: /*
17:  * Private function prototypes
18:  */
19: static boolean HelloWorld_HandleEvent( IApplet * pi,
20:                         AEEEvent eCode,
21:                         uint16 wParam,
22:                         uint32 dwParam );
23:
24: /**
25:  * Create an instance of this class. This constructor is
26:  * invoked by the BREW shell when the applet is launched.
27:  *
28:  * @param AEECLSID clsID: class ID of the class being requested
29:  * @param IShell *pIShell: a pointer to the BREW shell
30:  * @param IModule *po: a pointer to the current module
31:  * @param void **ppObj: a pointer to the created applet
32:  * @return AEE_SUCCESS on success, with the applet in *pobj.
33:  */
34: int AEEClsCreateInstance( AEECLSID clsID,
35:                 IShell * pIShell,
36:                 IModule * po,
37:                 void ** ppObj )
38: {
39:   boolean result;
40:   *ppObj = NULL;
41:
42:   // If it's this class being requested...
43:   if( clsID == AEECLSID_HELLOWORLD)
44:   {
45:     // Use the BREW helper function to
46:     // create an instance of this class
47:     result= AEEApplet_New( sizeof(AEEApplet),
48:                         clsID,
49:                         pIShell,
50:                         po,
51:                         (IApplet**)ppObj,
52:                         (AEEHANDLER)HelloWorld_HandleEvent,
53:                         NULL);
54:   }
55:   return result ? AEE_SUCCESS : EFAILED;
56: }
57:
```

```
58: /**
59:  * Handles incoming events from the shell.
60:  *
61:  * @param IApplet *pi: pointer to this applet.
62:  * @param AEEEvent eCode: event to handle
63:  * @param int wParam: word argument associated with event
64:  * @param uint32 dwParam: double word arg associated with event
65:  * @return TRUE if the event was handled, FALSE otherwise.
66:  */
67: static boolean HelloWorld_HandleEvent( IApplet *pi,
68:                       AEEEvent eCode,
69:                       uint16 wParam,
70:                       uint32 dwParam )
71: {
72:   AECHAR szBuf[] = {'H','e','l','l','o',' ',
73:                 'W','o','r','l','d','\0'};
74:   AEEApplet * pMe = (AEEApplet*)pi;
75:   boolean handled = FALSE;
76:
77:   // Decide what to do with the incoming event.
78:   switch (eCode)
79:   {
80:     // The application is launching.
81:     case EVT_APP_START:
82:       // Clear the display.
83:       IDISPLAY_ClearScreen( pMe->m_pIDisplay );
84:       // Display string on the screen
85:       IDISPLAY_DrawText( pMe->m_pIDisplay, // What
86:                 AEE_FONT_BOLD,             // What font
87:                 szBuf,                     // How many chars
88:                 -1, 0, 0, 0,               // Where & clip
89:                 IDF_ALIGN_CENTER | IDF_ALIGN_MIDDLE );
90:       // Redraw the display to show the drawn text
91:       IDISPLAY_Update (pMe->m_pIDisplay);
92:       handled = TRUE;
93:
94:     // Application is closing
95:     case EVT_APP_STOP:
96:       handled = TRUE;
97:
98:     default:
99:       break;
100:   }
101:   return handled;
102: }
```

As you can see from Listing 1-1, the code is pretty straightforward. Hello.c consists of two functions: the applet constructor `AEEClsCreateInstance` and the event handler `HelloWorld_HandleEvent`.

Invoked by the QUALCOMM BREW shell, `AEEClsCreateInstance` is the entry point of your application. It uses the helper function `AEEApplet_New` (found in AEEAppGen.c) to create an instance of your applet. This function creates an instance of the IApplet class that references your application, registering your event handler so that the QUALCOMM BREW shell can send your application system events as they occur. This function also stashes aside several important object instances in your application instance, such as a reference to the QUALCOMM BREW shell and a reference to the display.

NOTE *The AEEAppGen.c file contains a set of utility functions and the necessary wrapper to enclose your application inside an instance of the IApplet class, which is the root class for all applications. Similarly, the AEEModGen.c file contains a set of utility functions and the necessary wrapper to enclose a module inside an instance of the IModule class. Under normal circumstances, you won't need to change either of these files; however, as you learn more about QUALCOMM BREW, it's instructive to take a look at them.*

The application's event handler, `HelloWorld_HandleEvent`, needs to handle only two events: `EVT_APP_START`, which the shell sends when the application first launches, and `EVT_APP_STOP`, which the shell sends when the application ends. The event handler accepts the shell's event and arguments of the event, as well as a reference to your applet instance. In turn, the event handler handles events appropriate to the application and returns `TRUE` if the application has handled the event or `FALSE` otherwise, giving the system an opportunity to manage events that your application ignores.

Although the event handler passes a pointer to your application instance, it's of type `IApplet`, not the more specific `AEEApplet` that describes your applet. In fact, as you'll see in later chapters, you often add fields to your applet structure to carry application globals (because QUALCOMM BREW doesn't support global variables), so it's more convenient to cast the `IApplet` reference as a pointer to your application, as on line 74.

The `EVT_APP_START` event gives your application an opportunity to perform any launch-time initialization, such as creating instances of other classes, displaying the initial copyright screen, and so on. This sample application simply draws the welcome message on lines 83–92. First, it clears the display using the

IDISPLAY_ClearScreen method of IDisplay, the class that encapsulates display-related functions. It extracts a reference to the handset's display from the application instance, where the BREW function AEEApplet_New previously saved it. Next, it uses the IDisplay method IDISPLAY_DrawText to draw the message on the screen. This function lets you specify not just what text it should draw, but where it should be drawn and the bounds of the clipping rectangle that surrounds the text. It also uses two flags, IDF_ALIGN_CENTER and IDF_ALIGN_MIDDLE, to tell the display to ignore the coordinates specified and instead draw the text displayed on the center of the display. After drawing the text, it calls IDISPLAY_Update to flush the display changes to the display and mark that the application has handled the EVT_APP_START event by setting the function's return value to TRUE.

Handling application termination—which the shell indicates by sending the EVT_APP_STOP event—is much easier. Because you don't have any variables or initialized objects, you simply mark that you've handled the event and pass the result back to the system.

That's all there is to it! Of course, this is a somewhat artificial example—not only did it make minimal use of QUALCOMM BREW's capabilities, but it didn't even break up the event handler into separate functions by event, which you'll want to do in most applications. Nonetheless, this applet gives you a good idea of what goes into a simple BREW applet.

Testing Your First Application

For at least half your software development cycle, you build and test your applet using the QUALCOMM BREW Emulator, a Microsoft Windows–hosted application that lets you run your QUALCOMM BREW applets with Microsoft Visual Studio.

When you build your applet with Microsoft Visual Studio, it creates a DLL that the emulator loads when you run your application. Building your application with Microsoft Visual Studio is easy; simply select Build ➤ Set Active Configuration, choose either the Debug or Release version, and then build your application using the Build ➤ Build menu item (or pressing the F7 key).

TIP   *You can use the debug and release settings to conditionally include debugging code within your code by testing the _DEBUG compiler macro. Doing this is a great way to provide debugging scaffolding within the QUALCOMM BREW Emulator while still creating relatively clean versions of your applet for demonstration purposes.*

Once you build your application, you need to configure the emulator to find both your applet's DLL and your applet's MIF. Unfortunately, this is trickier than it sounds because the emulator expects your file system to be organized in the same way that a QUALCOMM BREW–enabled handset is. This places some rather bizarre restrictions on your filenames and directory structure. For best results, you should always do the following:

- Name your applet's project directory—or the target directory where you'll be placing your built DLLs—the same as your DLL name. In this chapter's example, the hello.dll file resides in the project directory, which is named *hello*.

- Place your MIF file in the same directory as your applet DLL.

- If you're testing multiple applets, you'll need to either keep all of the project directories in one directory or copy each applet's DLL to the same directory.

- If you're testing multiple applets at once, place all of your MIFs in the same directory.

If you follow these steps, you'll find that using the emulator is far easier. To run the applet in the emulator, follow these steps:

1. Launch the application using the Build ➤ Start Debug ➤ Go menu item in Microsoft Visual Studio.

2. When Microsoft Visual Studio asks what application to run the DLL in, select the QUALCOMM BREW Emulator.

3. Within the emulator, choose the Tools ➤ Settings item.

4. On the Initial Applet Directory line, choose the directory *above* your project directory.

5. Within the emulator, choose the Tools ➤ Settings item.

6. Check the Specify MIF Directory line.

7. On the Initial MIF Directory line, select the directory that contains your application's MIF—in this example, your project directory itself.

8. Click OK.

9. Use the emulator's arrow and Select keys to choose your application.

Once you follow these steps, you'll see the screen shown in Figure 1-3.

Hello World

Figure 1-3. The HelloWorld application running in the emulator

Running Your Application on Your Handset

Getting your application running on a QUALCOMM BREW–enabled handset initially seems more time consuming than useful, but it's important for you to do so as soon as you can because nothing beats running your applet on its target hardware. Testing your applets on the real hardware often and thoroughly helps you uncover implementation problems that you don't find in the emulator and helps keep you from using Microsoft Windows–specific functions in your application.

Unfortunately, getting your application to run on a handset isn't a trivial task because you need to work with the QUALCOMM staff to obtain developer access to your wireless handset. Before you can run any applications that aren't available through Mobile Shop on your wireless handset, you must do the following:

1. Sign up as a QUALCOMM BREW–authenticated developer, as described in the previous "Becoming an Authenticated QUALCOMM BREW Developer" section.

2. Be sure you've obtained a unique class ID for your applet, as discussed in the section "Writing Your First Application."

3. Buy a QUALCOMM BREW–enabled wireless handset. Although you don't need to activate the handset with a wireless carrier if your application doesn't need to access the wireless network, you should do so anyway so you can explore the other applications available through Mobile Shop. When you buy your handset, be sure to buy a serial data cable if one isn't included; you'll need one to download your application to the handset.

4. Follow the instructions on the QUALCOMM BREW extranet from the link at `http://www.qualcomm.com/brew/` and send your handset to QUALCOMM to enable developer testing support. QUALCOMM uses a proprietary in-house tool to configure your handset so that you can download your application to the handset via the data cable.

5. While you're waiting for QUALCOMM to return your handset (this typically takes a few business days), download the QUALCOMM BREW application loader from the QUALCOMM BREW extranet. This application includes support for both downloading files to your handset and running a console-style debugging log that you can use to monitor your application as it runs on the handset.

6. Use the QUALCOMM extranet to create a signature file (also called a *SIG file*) for your handset. The SIG file is a unique, cryptographically signed file that contains information from QUALCOMM and your handset's unique Electronic Serial Number (ESN).

Although all of this may sound like a needless headache—especially in comparison with competing smart phone platforms—these obstacles serve a necessary purpose. By restricting handsets so that only QUALCOMM-authenticated developers can run applications and requiring a SIG file for each handset, QUALCOMM maintains the integrity of the BREW download mechanism. Furthermore, it's nearly impossible for consumers to pirate applications, defeat network security, or tamper with the flash file systems on their handset. This insurance both increases the overall security of the wireless network (crucial to maintaining the trust of wireless carriers) and improves the consumer experience because consumers don't have easy access to tools that could render their handset inoperable if misused. Fortunately, you need to complete these steps only once for each handset you use when testing your application.

While you wait for QUALCOMM to return your handset, you can obtain one of the available tool chains to compile applications for QUALCOMM BREW–enabled handsets. Currently, you have several choices, all well documented on the QUALCOMM BREW Web site. These tool chains include a version of ARM's C and C++ compiler for the ARM chipset, which is at the core of the QUALCOMM BREW platform. If you're only dabbling with BREW, ARM offers a free, time-limited trial of its ARM compiler chain, or you can purchase a full tool chain from ARM. For more information about either, see `http://www.qualcomm.com/brew/developer/developing/armbrewpack.html`.

NOTE *At the time of this book's publication, QUALCOMM has promised to document and deliver support for using the GNU C Compiler (GCC) to compile modules for QUALCOMM BREW–enabled handsets. As you explore tool chain products for QUALCOMM BREW, be sure to check with QUALCOMM's Web site for the latest details about using GCC.*

Once you download and install your tool chain, you use a make file such as the one Microsoft Visual Studio creates when you choose AddIn Toolbar ➤ GenerateARMMakeFile. The make file uses the ARM tools to compile your sources, link them together, and convert the resulting binary file to a QUALCOMM BREW module.

TIP *If GenerateARMMakeFile doesn't work for you, close your project and open it once.*

Once you build your application for the handset, you should have three files: hello.mod, which contains your applet's object code; hello.mif, your applet's MIF file; and your SIG file. To transfer your applet to your handset, follow these steps:

1. Rename a copy of your SIG file to *hello.sig*. (You can keep the original SIG file to reuse with other applets.)

2. Create an empty folder and name it after the application, *Hello*.

3. Copy the SIG, MIF, and module files to the directory you created in the previous step.

4. Connect your handset to your computer using its data cable.

5. Launch the QUALCOMM BREW Application Loader application.

6. In response to the OEM Layer DLL Lookup dialog box, select the port to which you connected your handset and click OK.

7. Choose Module ➤ New and click Browse to select the folder you created in the second step. Enter the application name *Hello* in the lower line.

8. Click OK to transfer your applet to your phone.

That's all there is to it! After you transfer these files to your handset, you need only transfer the MOD file on subsequent builds (unless, of course, you change your MIF).

Once you transfer your applet's files to your handset, you may run the applet just as if you had downloaded it from Mobile Shop by using your phone's interface to bring up the QUALCOMM BREW application menu and select it using the direction pad.

Summary

In this chapter, you learned the following key points:

- From the developer perspective, the QUALCOMM BREW platform is a lightweight set of APIs that sits atop QUALCOMM's hardware for wireless handsets, letting you write applications in C or C++ that take advantage of the handset's features.

- Carriers are choosing the QUALCOMM BREW platform because it enables them to provide third-party applications easily and securely.

- Developers are choosing the QUALCOMM BREW platform because it lets them write applications for consumer wireless handsets.

- The QUALCOMM BREW platform includes Mobile Shop, a carrier-side application that lets consumers download your application and pay for it on their existing wireless service bill. In turn, you can monitor sales using QUALCOMM's extranet and receive regular payments for the copies of your application that consumers purchase.

- Within QUALCOMM BREW, your application is an *applet* that inherits an interface from the IApplet class. You can also write *extensions*—software libraries encapsulated as classes for applications that you and others write.

- You can begin writing your applet using a Microsoft Windows–hosted SDK consisting of Microsoft Visual Studio and the QUALCOMM SDK.

- To develop and deploy applets on wireless handsets via Mobile Shop, you must become a QUALCOMM BREW–authenticated developer via QUALCOMM's extranet at http://www.qualcomm.com/brew/. Becoming an authenticated developer enables you to obtain a copy of the ARM compiler necessary to build your application for the handset and enable handsets to run your application.

Designing for the QUALCOMM BREW Platform

ALL GOOD PROGRAMS start with a design. Moreover, the best programs start with a good design. By starting with a good design for your QUALCOMM BREW applications, you can streamline both your software development and your software deployment.

The design phase of your development cycle for QUALCOMM BREW applications is especially important given the high reliability that wireless carriers require of *any* QUALCOMM BREW application. As part of your application deployment, you must submit your application for third-party testing and include several pieces of your design documentation, as you'll see in this and subsequent chapters. By starting your development with a good design, you provide a firm foundation for your application.

Starting with a Design

Design is a crucial part of software development. Even when you don't set aside a specific period of time for design, you inevitably spend time during your application development performing tasks that constitute design. Determining how an application's interface should look; selecting individual components, algorithms, and data structures; and defining external interfaces are all part of what you do as you design your application.

Understanding the Importance of Design

When this chapter refers to *design*, it means all of these tasks, as well as the process of actually *capturing* your design decisions as you make them. For large software projects, this is crucial because often an application's implementation remains available far longer than the individual developers who built the application. Thus, documenting an application's design is essential because often only the application's source code and design decisions are available when others must change the application.

What is not as obvious is that capturing design decisions for small applications—especially those for wireless systems including QUALCOMM BREW—is as important as for larger applications. This is because of two key factors.

First, documenting your design decisions is a proven way to help improve the quality of your application by enhancing team communication and ensuring a shared vision for your application's appearance and implementation. Making the time to record your documentation decisions in advance helps you set them down while they're fresh in your mind and gives you time to update them and share them with others as you work. In fact, many studies have shown that even for small projects, making the time for an explicit design phase is not only cost effective but can actually *reduce* the cost of applications *vis-à-vis* developing similar applications with no clearly demarcated design phase.

Second, your wireless application will be rigorously examined and tested by a variety of third parties, including QUALCOMM's external certification agency and each wireless carrier that resells your application. As part of this verification, you're expected to submit documentation detailing your application's user interface flow, external dependencies, and other information in the form of a *test plan* that explains to others what your application does, how it does it, and under what conditions it might not work correctly. All of these are questions you must answer as you develop your application; thus, you should capture the information before you set out and then revise it to match the changes you make as you go along. (Chapter 12, "Certifying Your Application," discusses the certification process in detail.)

Capturing the Design

To a large extent, *how* you capture your design decisions is less important than capturing them. In general, if you or your organization has a system that meets simple criteria, you're probably in good shape when you start writing applications for QUALCOMM BREW. You can capture your decisions in formal design documentation, marketing requirements documentation, user interface specifications, functional specifications, test plans, and the like or in a more informal series of documents and living examples such as user interface prototypes in PowerPoint or on the handset itself using mock-up screen shots, Unified Modeling Language (UML) diagrams, and the like.

At a minimum, your design should capture the following information:

- How your application will interact with the user, including screen layouts, valid data inputs, and invalid data inputs

- How your application will interact with other components, including extensions and back-end network resources

- How your application will store persistent data

- The fundamental components of your application, such as modules or classes for data storage, network Input/Output (I/O), computation, and rendering

- How these fundamental components will interact with each other

Making the decisions you must record in your design requires a combination of experience, experimentation, and trial and error. It's not uncommon to write small prototype applications when you design your application to test parts of your implementation. For example, you could write a prototype to mock up parts of your user interface to show potential customers or write a bit of code to determine whether specific computations are feasible on the phone.

A key ingredient to your design is your application's user interface: what the user expects from your application, how your user will use your application, and how your application presents itself to the user. To do this, you need to see your application from the users' perspective, a difficult prospect at best.

Understanding the User

You face unique challenges when designing and developing the interface for mobile applications. Not only are wireless handsets grossly different from desktop (or even handheld!) computers, but when you use a wireless handset, you have different expectations as to how it should behave than when you use a desktop or handheld computer.

Understanding the Mobile Paradigm

As you develop your mobile applications, you must always keep in mind that your users are in motion. When you use a wireless handset, you're seldom sitting still with all of your attention focused on a single task. You may be walking around, talking with others, or riding in a vehicle.

Being mobile when you use a handset directly impacts both an application's appearance and its use. Obviously, input must be simple: Not only are phone keypads tedious to use for long entries, but it's difficult to hit numerous keys with one finger while moving. Similarly, application output must be clear and concise because you can't spare attention reading a complex user interface while mobile.

Because of these specific factors, your application must be simple and easy to use. Moreover, your application must accommodate the device itself, using high-contrast colors visible in all lighting for color handsets, using sharp black-and-white text on grayscale displays, and requiring a minimum of alphanumeric input. Use menus—with numeric shortcuts—whenever possible to give users an easy way to make choices and selections rather than having to enter text.

Your application must meet specific interface criteria set out by QUALCOMM, too. Every application must begin with a descriptive splash screen that uniquely identifies the application. This splash screen should automatically disappear after a few seconds or as soon as the user presses any key. Similarly, QUALCOMM has specific interface requirements for specific keys; for example, the Clear key should always take you to the previous screen, and the Select key should always accept an entry, bringing you to the next screen or feature in the application.

Capturing the User Interface

A key part of your design is your application's user interface. An application rich in features with a poor user interface typically fares far worse on the market than a simple application with an easy-to-use interface. Designing a user interface takes patience, organization, and a good understanding of your customers' needs.

A good way to start the design and capture your application's user interface is through *use case analysis*, in which you use UML to diagram what uses individuals—called *actors*—will have for your application. Each actor is a set of users, such as consumer, network administrator, or the like, with common characteristics. Each use encapsulates a specific operation, such as "enter purchase" or "determine average fuel consumption."

A benefit to creating use cases is that once you note each use case, you can begin identifying common parts of each use case and flesh out the components of the user interface that each use case shares. From there, it becomes relatively easy to establish the components of your application, guiding you to the application's overall composition. With these use cases, your design can turn to two separate tasks: determining the appearance of the user interface and documenting the application's individual components.

Determining the actual appearance of the user interface is a matter of common sense, experience, trial and error, and user testing. At the least you should plan to show sketches of your interface ideas to potential users and other shareholders; if you can, be prepared to construct mock-up demonstrations that either run on the handset or on the desktop. You can keep the prototypes and sketches throughout the process to help document your user interface as you develop your application.

Understanding the RocketMileage Application

RocketMileage, the sample application referred to throughout this book, is a car mileage and service tracking applet for QUALCOMM BREW. Certified by National Software Testing Labs (NSTL), it's available on the Verizon Wireless network for the Motorola T720 and other handsets. The following sections show how to use the techniques described in this chapter to design RocketMileage.

Applying Use Cases to RocketMileage's Design

It's easy to go overboard planning the feature set for an application, especially a relatively small one such as a mileage calculator. As you begin planning your application, you may find yourself adding features that seem interesting to use and implement willy-nilly. If left unchecked, this can spell disaster, yielding an application that's confusing to use and difficult to maintain. For that reason, I created use cases during the initial design of RocketMileage to determine what features of RocketMileage were truly necessary.

As I fleshed out the application, I realized that Verizon Wireless was targeting specific markets for QUALCOMM BREW using its Get It Now advertising campaign. Consequently, my application focuses around two actors that mesh well with the markets Verizon targets. By doing this, I hope to leverage Verizon Wireless's marketing campaign, as well as provide an application useful to the customers Verizon Wireless has attracted with its campaign. My first actor is the quintessential consumer, interested in tracking mileage and automotive service details. My other actor is a mobile professional who finds their phone indispensable and uses the application more to track automotive expenses related to their profession. Figure 2-1 shows a use case diagram outlining *all* the possible features that came to mind for the application during a brainstorming session.

Obviously, implementing *all* of these use cases for an application on a cell phone would be absurd. Not only would the resulting application be almost impossible to use, but some of these features would be expensive and time consuming to implement. Instead, I eliminated many use cases, choosing to implement only those of use to both actors or those with clear market value to one of the actors. Figure 2-2 shows the use cases actually implemented.

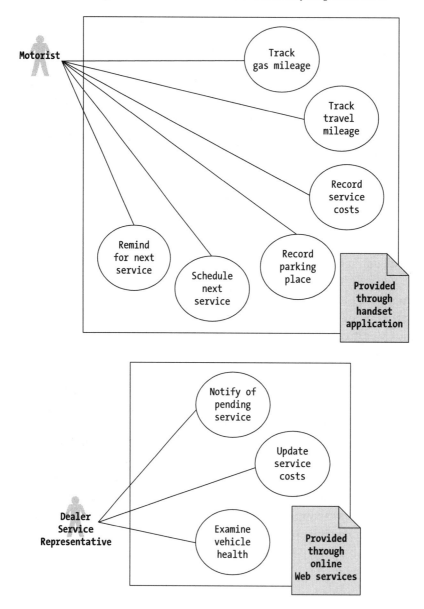

Figure 2-1. Possible use cases for RocketMileage

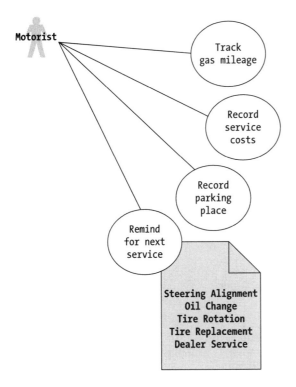

Figure 2-2. Selected use cases for RocketMileage

Once I identified the use cases RocketMileage should implement, I easily identified common components. For example, almost all of the use cases require an actor to enter the current odometer reading; so, clearly implementing a single input dialog box to accept an odometer entry for all points in the user interface makes far more sense than writing ones for each use case. Figure 2-3 shows a more detailed use case analysis, detailing many of the operations in common between the different use cases.

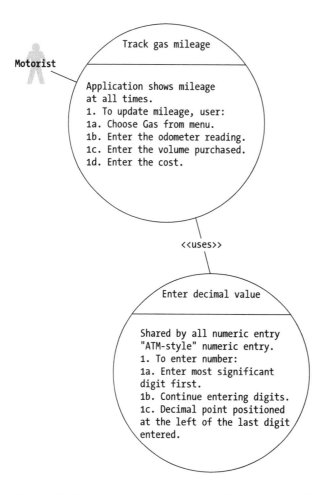

Figure 2-3. Operations common to multiple use cases for RocketMileage

Describing the RocketMileage Interface

With a better understanding of how people will use RocketMileage, it's time to step back and describe how the application works. You can do this in two steps: sketching sample screen shots and preparing an application description document, which you can include with your application submission to NSTL (see Chapter 12, "Certifying Your Application").

It's easy to mock up screen shots for your QUALCOMM BREW application. You can start by using the QUALCOMM BREW Emulator and sample applications. Simply take several screen shots of the sample applications and use the components as starting points to build the interface of your application. For example, I have a Microsoft Paint file that contains snippets of menus, input lines, and icons, and I can quickly assemble them in bitmap files to get an idea of what my application will look like. Create small bitmap images of your application screens—120-by-130 pixels for a color screen such as the one on the Motorola T720 or 88-by-99 pixels for a monochrome screen such as the screen on the Kyocera QCP-3035. You can also use snippets of BREW interface components and text (10-point Arial closely resembles the fonts on many screen phones in both size and appearance). Figure 2-4 shows several representative screen shots from the prototyping phase of RocketMileage's development.

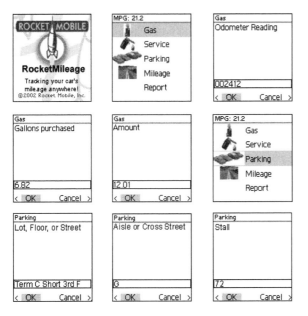

Figure 2-4. Screen concepts from the early design phase of RocketMileage

You can show these screen shots to potential customers, arranging them in the order they will appear to implement a specific use case. Another thing that helps is to put them in a Microsoft PowerPoint presentation, so you can flip through them as if they were an application running on your computer.

In fact, you can do one better—Chapter 4, "Handling Events," shows an application you can use to navigate between bitmaps on your handset. By using this application with your screen concepts, you can give potential users first-hand experience with how your application will appear. In turn, they can give you valuable feedback, helping you tune your interface to meet their needs before you start writing your application.

To refine your application, you can also write an application description. This description is similar to a functional specification in that it describes the features your application must implement, but not how it implements them. The application description is a required documentation component you must include when you submit your application for validation and distribution, so it helps to get this out of the way as soon as possible.

At this point, your application description should contain the following information:

- **Application purpose**: In a single paragraph, this should state what your application does, who your anticipated users are, and how your users will use your application. It should also provide an end-user marketing feature list.

- **Catalog information**: This section states your application's name, your application's tag line, and your anticipated application pricing.

- **System-level information**: This section states your application's title on the phone and shows its icons, your company name, your application copyright, and the privileges your application will require.

- **Application user-level architecture diagram**: This section shows a state machine diagram of your application, documenting the flow between each application screen. You can begin this diagram by organizing your use case diagrams and fill it out using your screen prototypes.

Decomposing RocketMileage into Components

In examining RocketMileage's use cases, several obvious points of decomposition are clear:

- Odometer entry

- Dollar amount entry

- Service detail information

You can generalize these even further, for example, noting that the odometer and amount entry screens are both simply numeric entry screens with different prompt text.

On larger projects, identifying common components gives you a handle on the dependencies between components. Once you identify which components rely on other components, you can assign independent components to different developers, letting your team do some development in parallel.

One thing I'm still missing is some notion of the data that RocketMileage must store. Fortunately, a look at the various input screens suggests two separate data sets, one for mileage and service and one for parking.

Most records you enter are gas mileage records or service records, and they all have five common components:

- Date and time of event. Although the user doesn't need to enter this information, the application should still store it.

- The next time and odometer reading at which the event should occur.

- Odometer reading at the time of event.

- Dollar cost of event.

- Both gas mileage and service records have an additional component—a number. Gas mileage records must store the number of gallons consumed, and service records must store the odometer reading for the next service.

Merging this information, you have a record consisting of a type identifier (kind of service including gas mileage, oil, tune up, tire rotation, or other service), a date and time, an initial odometer reading, a next date and time and odometer reading, a cost, and a second number that's either the amount of gas purchased or the odometer reading for the next service. To accommodate the description field in services falling into the Other category, you can simply tack on a null-terminated C string. In fact, with a bit of tweaking, the same fields can store the cost of parking (simply by ignoring the additional numeric field) and trip mileage (by ignoring the cost field). So, the actual data structure looks like Listing 2-1.

Listing 2-1. RocketMileage Data Structure

```
 1: typedef enum _EMileageEntryType
 2: {
 3:   ME_Gas,
 4:   ME_Oil,
 5:   ME_Tire,
 6:   ME_Tuneup,
 7:   ME_OtherService,
 8:   ME_Parking,
 9:   ME_Mileage
10: } EMileageEntryType;
11:
12: typedef struct _TMileageEntry
```

```
13: {
14:    EMileageEntryType m_type;
15:    uint32  m_nTime;
16:    uint32 m_nDueTime;
17:    uint32 m_nMiles;
18:    uint32 m_nDueMiles;
19:    uint32 m_nOther;
20:    uint32 m_fCost; // dollar cost for event
21: } TMileageEntry;
```

As you'll see in Chapter 7, "Storing Data," you can use a series of functions and macros to abstract access to each of the fields in TMileageEntry, making it easy to change the data structure if the need arises.

Because the remaining data are all singletons (for example, the application needs to store only *one* miles-per-gallon calculation), the remaining data can be stored in the application preferences.

Summary

With all of these details taken care of, you can begin the process of actually coding your application. Before you see how to do that, however, it's time to dive more deeply into the QUALCOMM BREW platform itself.

In the next chapter, you get the 30,000-foot view of QUALCOMM BREW so that you can begin writing your own applications as well as understand the internals of RocketMileage as you look at each of the major QUALCOMM BREW interfaces in upcoming chapters.

Developing for the QUALCOMM BREW Platform

MY PARENTS WERE fond of giving me obscure advice when I was young. Working on the house, my father would lavish me with instructions such as "Always use the right tool for the job." In the kitchen, my mother frequently reminded me that sharpened knives were both easier to use and safer in the kitchen than dull ones.

Thirty years later, this advice remains as relevant in front of the keyboard as it is around the house. Fortunately, QUALCOMM provides a suite of tools that makes developing your application easier. Equally important, the QUALCOMM BREW environment contains the interfaces you need to quickly develop your application. In this chapter, you'll see an overview of the interfaces available to your application, as well as learn more about the desktop tools you can use to develop your applications.

Getting Started with Development

Developing applications for QUALCOMM BREW requires you to have a firm grasp of two fundamental concepts: application flow in QUALCOMM BREW and the class interfaces that QUALCOMM BREW makes available to your application. Because these themes are crucial to the QUALCOMM BREW application development, the following sections explore these themes, and later chapters return to them throughout this book.

Understanding Application Flow

As you first saw in Chapter 1, "Introducing the QUALCOMM BREW Platform," your QUALCOMM BREW application is *event driven*; that is, your application is invoked by and responds to events sent by the platform. These events include not just user interface events from controls but also events indicating that your application should start and stop in response to external actions such as a received Short Message Service (SMS) message or the user launching the application.

Consequently, the center of your application is a single function called an *event handler* that receives events from the system's *event pump*, which monitors system activity and converts relevant incidents (such as key presses, application launches, and so forth) into events. In turn, your application examines the incoming event, determines if it's relevant to your application, and does something if it finds the event relevant. If your application doesn't do anything with the event, it should share it with any system interfaces it's using, such as controls, before returning it.

Before your application can receive events from the system, it must register your event handler with the system. Because your application is actually an instance of a class and your event handler is actually a method of your application's class, you must add a reference to your class's dispatch table that points to your event handler. Although this isn't difficult, it's one of several setup actions every application must take, so QUALCOMM has provided a helper function that does all of your class setup, including registering a pointer to your event handler.

All of this magic happens when your application launches. As the shell attempts to launch an application, it executes each class's AEEClsCreateInstance function. Your application's AEEClsCreateInstance function should test the incoming class ID and, if it matches your class ID, create an instance of itself. Typically, you do this simply by calling the QUALCOMM BREW helper function called AEEApplet_New, which does the behind-the-scenes magic of allocating memory for your class, setting up its dispatch table, and returning an instance of your class. Listing 3-1 shows a simple AEEClsCreateInstance function.

Listing 3-1. The AEEClsCreateInstance *Function*

```
1: int AEEClsCreateInstance( AEECLSID clsID,
2:                           IShell * pIShell,
3:                           IModule * po,
4:                           void ** ppObj )
5: {
6:   boolean result;
7:   *ppObj = NULL;
8:
9:   // If it's this class being requested...
10:   if( clsID == AEECLSID_MYCLASSID )
11:   {
12:     // Use the BREW helper function to
13:     // create an instance of this class
14:     result = AEEApplet_New( sizeof( AEEApplet ),
15:                             clsID,
16:                             pIShell,
17:                             po,
```

```
18:                        (IApplet**)ppObj,
19:                        (AEEHANDLER) HandleEvent,
20:                        NULL );
21:    }
22:    return result ? AEE_SUCCESS : EFAILED;
23: }
```

In object-oriented terms, you can think of the aggregate of all of the
AEEClsCreateInstance functions as an object factory, responsible for creating
a specific instance of a class. Your application's implementation of
AEEClsCreateInstance is a class method, invoked by the system when a new
class instance is requested by another application such as the shell application
launcher.

> **NOTE** *Whether you're writing an application or an extension (an imple-
> mentation of a class to share with other applications), the startup
> process is the same (although extensions don't have event handlers). As
> you gain experience with the platform, it's instructive to skim the
> AEEAppGen.c and AEEModGen.c files that contain the helper functions
> described in this chapter. By doing so, you significantly increase your
> understanding of the QUALCOMM BREW platform.*

Once your event handler is registered in your application's dispatch table, the
system's event pump calls your event handler once for each event in its queue.
Typically, your event handler must respond to at least four events:

- The EVT_APP_START event, which your application receives after registering
  its event handler to instruct it to begin executing. Your application should
  allocate memory and objects necessary for its execution and begin running
  in response to this event.

- The EVT_APP_STOP event, which your application receives when it must quit,
  either in response to a specific keystroke such as the handset's End Call key
  or another action. Your application should free all allocated resources
  (memory and object instances) in response to this event.

- The EVT_APP_SUSPEND event, which your application receives when it must
  suspend execution because of an incoming telephone call, SMS message, or
  other handset activity. Your application should save its current context and
  free any unnecessary resources in response to this event.

- The EVT_APP_RESUME event, which your application receives when it may resume operation after an incoming telephone call, SMS message, or other handset activity. Your application should resume execution from the point saved when the EVT_APP_SUSPEND event was received, re-creating any freed resources in the process.

There are at least 28 other events (see Table 3-1 for a list of the most common events), and you can define your own events as well. Each event comes with two arguments, a 16-bit integer and a 32-bit integer. Events use these arguments to communicate specific details about the event, such as the control the event relates to, a pointer to a string containing more information about the event, and so forth. The event handler accepts the event, its arguments, and a pointer to the application receiving the event and returns TRUE if it handles the event and FALSE if it doesn't.

Table 3-1. Commonly Used QUALCOMM BREW Events

EVENT DEFINITION	wParam	dwParam	MEANING
EVT_APP_START			Application started
EVT_APP_STOP			Application stopped
EVT_APP_SUSPEND			Application suspended
EVT_APP_CONFIG			Alternate application launch: show configuration screen
EVT_APP_HIDDEN_CONFIG			Alternate application launch: show hidden configuration screen
EVT_APP_BROWSE_URL		const AECHAR *szURL	Called after EVT_APP_START to show Uniform Resource Locator (URL) indicated at szURL
EVT_APP_BROWSE_FILE		const AECHAR *szName	Called after EVT_APP_START to browse the file indicated at szFile
EVT_APP_MESSAGE		const char *szMsg	Application-directed SMS message received; contents at szMsg as null-terminated ASCII string

Table 3-1. Commonly Used QUALCOMM BREW Events (Continued)

EVENT DEFINITION	wParam	dwParam	MEANING
EVT_KEY	Key code		Application key (key pressed and released)
EVT_KEY_PRESS	Key code		Application key down
EVT_KEY_RELEASE	Key code		Application key released
EVT_KEY_HELD	Key code		Application key held
EVT_COMMAND	Custom	Custom	Application custom control code
EVT_CTL_TAB	dir	IControl *pCtl	Application Tab; dir == 0 left tab, dir == 1 right tab, in control at pCtl
EVT_ALARM	uCode		Shell alarm corresponding to uCode
EVT_NOTIFY		AEENotify *pNotice	Shell notification

Listing 3-2 shows an application's event handler.

Listing 3-2. A Sample Event Handler

```
1: static boolean HandleEvent( IApplet *pi,
2:                    AEEEvent eCode,
3:                    uint16 wParam,
4:                    uint32 dwParam )
5: {
6:   AEEApplet * pMe = (AEEApplet*)pi;
7:   boolean handled = FALSE;
8:
9:   // Decide what to do with the incoming event
10:   switch (eCode)
11:   {
12:     // The application is launching
13:     case EVT_APP_START:
14:       // Do whatever startup is necessary
15:       handled = TRUE;
16:       break;
```

```
17:
18:     // Shell needs to interrupt application
19:     case EVT_APP_SUSPEND:
20:       // Relinquish all resources possible, suspend any callbacks
21:       handled = TRUE;
22:       break;
23:
24:     // Shell returns control to application
25:     case EVT_APP_RESUME:
26:       // Redraw UI, resume any timers or callbacks
27:       handled = TRUE;
28:       break;
29:
30:     // Application is closing
31:     case EVT_APP_STOP:
32:       // Free any used memory, release any instances, exit
33:       handled = TRUE;
34:       break;
35:
36:     default:
37:       break;
38:   }
39:   return handled;
40: }
```

NOTE *Not all QUALCOMM BREW–enabled handsets return all events in all circumstances. For example, early Kyocera handsets don't return* EVT_KEY_HELD *events when you hold down a key.*

Thus, the simplest application consists of two functions: the entry point AEEClsCreateInstance and an associated event handler. Together, these functions comprise an application's executable, but what about its data?

The QUALCOMM BREW platform, like many lightweight application platforms, doesn't support global variables. This is both a blessing and a curse. Without global variables, your application is easier to debug and maintain; however, you're left with the uncomfortable question of where to stash application-specific data that you don't want to pass around on the stack between functions. (Respecting the stack is especially important on small platforms, too, where a device's stack may be only a few kilobytes.)

NOTE *The inability to support global variables can have some peculiar effects on your application implementation! Because the C compiler stores static module-scope and function-scope variables in the same manner as global variables, there's no support for them either. Consequently, you should be careful to avoid defining static variables in either modules or functions. Failure to do so won't impair your application's execution within the QUALCOMM BREW Emulator, but it'll cause bizarre problems when your application executes on a wireless handset.*

Instead, you should plan on defining an *application structure*, which contains your application's variables, such as the application state and pointers to QUALCOMM BREW interfaces your application uses while it's running. Your application structure should begin with a member of the type AEEApplet, which contains the basic information every class descending from the IApplet interface must contain. After the AEEApplet member, you're free to declare any other member variables you want. In turn, a pointer to your application structure is created in AEEApplet_New, where the function initializes the AEEApplet fields (including the reference to your event handler). Once AEEApplet_New returns, memory for your application structure has been allocated, and you're free to use it as you want. Similarly, your event handler receives a pointer to your application structure (even though the prototype for the event handler treats the incoming application structure as an AEEApplet pointer), which you can then cast to the appropriate type to access your application structure.

NOTE AEEApplet_New *initializes the contents of the* AEEApplet *structure in your application structure by casting the freshly created application pointer to an* AEEApplet *pointer and accessing the necessary fields. Consequently, you must be sure your application structure has as its first element an* AEEApplet *member (and not a pointer to an* AEEApplet *structure!) or your application will fail in mysterious and inexplicable ways.*

Listing 3-3 unifies the AEEClsCreateInstance and HandleEvent functions with a simple application structure that contains only an AEEApplet member and a couple of integers.

Listing 3-3. The AEEClsCreateInstance *Function*

```
1: typedef struct _CApp
2: {
3:    AEEApplet a;      // this applet's class info
4:    uint32 m_launchTime, m_nEvents;     // some application-specific data
5: } CApp, *CAppPtr;
6
7: int AEEClsCreateInstance( AEECLSID clsID,
8:                           IShell * pIShell,
9:                           IModule * po,
10:                          void ** ppObj )
11: {
12:    boolean result;
13:    *ppObj = NULL;
14:
15:    // If it's this class being requested...
16:    if( clsID == AEECLSID_MYCLASSID )
17:    {
18:      // Use the BREW helper function to
19:      // create an instance of this class
20:      result = AEEApplet_New( sizeof(CApp),
21:                              clsID,
22:                              pIShell,
23:                              po,
24:                              (IApplet**)ppObj,
25:                              (AEEHANDLER) HandleEvent,
26:                              NULL );
27:    }
28:    return result ? AEE_SUCCESS : EFAILED;
29: }
30:
31: static boolean HandleEvent( IApplet *pi,
32:                             AEEEvent eCode,
33:                             uint16 wParam,
34:                             uint32 dwParam )
35: {
36:    CAppPtr  pMe = (CAppPtr )pi;
37:    boolean handled = FALSE;
38:
39:    // Decide what to do with the incoming event
40:    switch (eCode)
41:    {
42:      // The application is launching
```

```
43:    case EVT_APP_START:
44:      pMe->m_launchTime = GETTIMESECONDS();
45:      pMe->m_nEvents = 1;
46:      handled = TRUE;
47:      break;
48:
49:    // Shell needs to interrupt application
50:    case EVT_APP_SUSPEND:
51:      handled = TRUE;
52:      break;
53:
54:    // Shell returns control to application
55:    case EVT_APP_RESUME:
56:      handled = TRUE;
57:      break;
58:
59:    // Application is closing
60:    case EVT_APP_STOP:
61:      DBGPRINTF( "Application ran for %ld seconds.",
62:                  GETTIMESECONDS() - pMe->m_launchTime );
63:      DBGPRINTF( "Application received %ld events.",
64:                  pMe->m_nEvents );
65:      handled = TRUE;
66:      break;
67:
68:   default:
69:      break;
70:   }
71:   pMe->m_nEvents++;
72:   return handled;
73: }
```

The sample application simply times how long the application runs and counts the number of events it receives during its lifetime, storing the intermediate results in a simple application structure named CApp. There are two key changes from the previous listings in this chapter. First, instead of initializing an AEEApplet when calling AEEApplet_New on lines 20–26, the application now creates a CApp structure. Because AEE_AppletNew takes the size of a region to allocate and presumes the first element in the region is an AEEApplet, AEEApplet_New correctly initializes the IApplet specific variables within the CApp it creates. In a similar vein, the HandleEvent function now receives a pointer to the application structure, disguised as a pointer to an IApplet. To make reading the code easier, the first thing to do is cast the incoming application instance to a pointer in the application's structure so that you can easily access your application variables.

The meat of this sample application is in three places: lines 44–45, line 71, and lines 61–64. The first segment, lines 44–45, simply initialize the application's variables, storing the current time in seconds and counting the first event. This operation is analogous to an instance member initializing its member variables and in larger applications is often written as a separate application. Line 71 simply increments the variable responsible for counting the number of events. Finally, lines 61–64 use the DBGPRINTF function (which prints debug messages to either the Microsoft Windows output window or to a debugging console shown using the QUALCOMM BREW Logger) to display both the number of seconds the application was running and the number of events the application received. In a larger application, this functionality—along with the destruction of dynamically allocated resources created during the application's execution—occurs here, often as an invocation to a separate function. This function is in essence the application class destructor, which is the last function the application executes before it terminates.

Understanding QUALCOMM BREW Interfaces

Like most object-oriented platforms, the interfaces in QUALCOMM BREW descend from a common parent. As you see in Figure 3-1, the inheritance tree is quite flat, reflecting the specific nature of each BREW interface.

All interfaces descend from IBase, the base class responsible for supplying the object reference counting mechanism that all objects use for managing memory. The IBase interface defines two methods, IBASE_AddRef and IBASE_Release. IBASE_AddRef merely increments an object's reference count, indicating that it's in use and shouldn't be freed, and IBASE_Release decrements an object's reference count, freeing an object and its associated resources when the reference count is equal to zero.

A key interface you'll use a lot is the IShell interface, which provides a grab bag of miscellaneous system functions, including a factory to create instances of other classes. You use the ISHELL_CreateInstance method to obtain instances of other classes, providing it with the ID of the desired class and a pointer to a pointer that will contain the result. For example, deep in the bowels of AEEApplet_New, you can find this line:

```
1: ISHELL_CreateInstance( pIShell,
2:                        AEECLSID_DISPLAY,
3:                        (void **) &pme->m_pIDisplay);
```

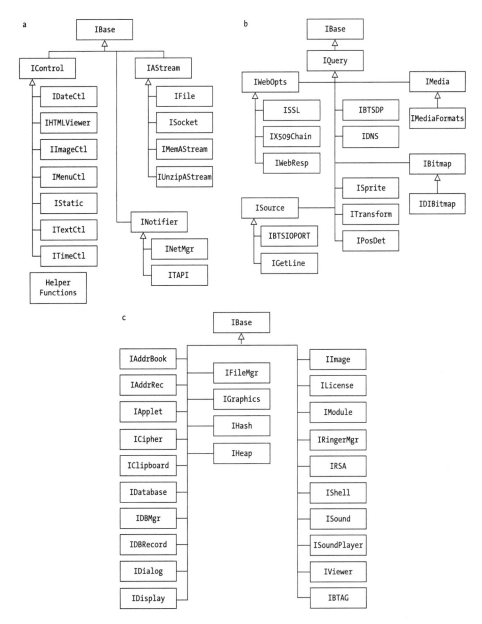

Figure 3-1. The QUALCOMM BREW class hierarchy

If you take the time to nose around the various header files, you'll find that pIShell is a pointer to an IShell instance and that pme->m_pIDisplay is defined as a pointer to an IDisplay instance. Thus, this call to ISHELL_CreateInstance creates an instance of IDisplay, placing the result at &pme->m_pIDisplay. In turn, the caller can use this display interface to access the screen to determine its dimensions, to draw bitmaps, and so forth.

TIP ISHELL_CreateInstance *signals success or failure in two ways. On success, it returns* TRUE *and a pointer to the desired object as the third argument; on failure, it returns* FALSE *and places* NULL *in the specified pointer. You can test either return value to determine whether your request has succeeded or failed.*

Other methods of IShell include methods to load text and binary resources from resource files, set timers and alarms, determine device characteristics, and manipulate times and dates. Throughout the coming chapters, you'll see many applications of the IShell interfaces, and chances are that if you don't see a particular interface that does what you want, you can find a method or two in IShell that does what you want.

In addition to the IShell interfaces, QUALCOMM BREW provides a number of helper functions. Under the hood, a few are macros, and most are methods of a module that provide these helper functions. Fortunately, you don't have to worry about the details—you have immediate access to functions such as ANSI C library string functions, wide string manipulation functions, memory management, and so forth. Most of these are named the same as their C library functions, but their names are in all-capital letters. See Table 3-2 for a list of the most commonly used ones.

NOTE *When writing your application, be sure to use the QUALCOMM BREW helper functions and not the C standard library variants, unless you're certain that the code you're writing will only execute in the emulator. The tools you use for building applications for the handset don't have provisions for the standard C library, so you can't call them from your application on the handset.*

Table 3-2. QUALCOMM BREW Helper Functions

HELPER FUNCTION	C STANDARD LIBRARY EQUIVALENT
ATOI	atoi
DBGPRINTF	printf
FREE	free
INET_ATON	inet_aton
INET_NTOA	inet_ntoa
MALLOC	malloc
MEMCMP	memcmp
MEMCPY	memcpy
MEMMOVE	memmove
MEMSET	memset
REALLOC	realloc
SPRINTF	sprintf
STRCAT	strcat
STRCHR	strchr
STRCMP	strcmp
STRCPY	strcpy
STRDUP	strdup
STRLEN	strlen
STRNCPY	strncpy
STRSTR	strstr

There is also a slew of BREW-specific helper functions, such as ones that let you initialize and cancel callbacks, convert color values, and manipulate BREW-specific data structures. As with the various IShell interfaces and the classes themselves, you'll encounter them throughout this book (after all, that's what this book is about!).

NOTE *If you're anxious to get a head start and look at the utility functions (perhaps you're looking at porting an existing application or are just plain curious), refer to the relevant sections of the QUALCOMM BREW API Reference, part of the QUALCOMM BREW Software Development Kit (SDK).*

Pundits will note—quite rightly—that QUALCOMM BREW lacks several aspects of true object-oriented environments such as Smalltalk or even mixed environments such as C++ or Java. For example, all of the fundamental types and most of the BREW data types are data types, not objects. Take character strings, for instance: QUALCOMM BREW lets you manipulate character strings using the traditional C char data type, as well as the QUALCOMM BREW–specific AECHAR type to support multiple-byte character strings. Moreover, the functions you use to manipulate these strings are just that: helper functions, not methods you can apply to a particular object. In fact, the platform includes data types for many kinds of data, including points, rectangles, function callbacks, and the results of many functions. Most of these data types are transparent; that is, you can directly access members without using functions or macros. A few, however, include helper functions, and you should be in the habit of using these functions in the event that the data type's representation changes in a future version of QUALCOMM BREW.

Another key difference between the QUALCOMM BREW platform and other object-oriented environments, such as Java 2 Enterprise Edition (J2EE) or Microsoft Foundation Classes (MFC) is that you can't readily create derived classes from the QUALCOMM BREW interfaces. These interfaces are best seen as final in the Java sense: An interface's member variables and implementation are private to QUALCOMM BREW, but not for external modification. In most cases, this doesn't cause trouble as long as you approach your application's design and implementation with that in mind.

Using the QUALCOMM BREW Developer Tools

As you develop your application, you rely on QUALCOMM's developer tools to package your application for testing and distributing on the handset.

Using the QUALCOMM BREW MIF Editor

Every application—in fact, every module—requires a Module Information File (MIF) that describes the module's name, icon, class ID, corporate author, exported classes (if any), and dependencies on other classes.

Most of the time, you'll only need to use the first two tabs of the editor to identify your application. In the Applets tab, shown in Figure 3-2, you describe your application, setting your application's class ID, name, application type, and icon.

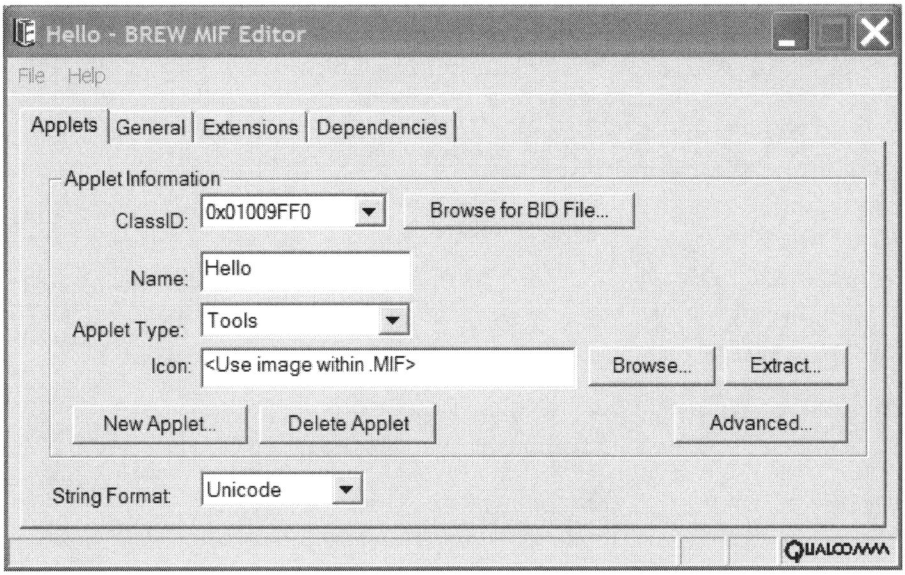

Figure 3-2. The QUALCOMM BREW MIF Editor, the Applets tab

You can either manually enter your application's class ID or select the Brew ID (BID) file you downloaded from the QUALCOMM developer extranet. Because a module can contain more than one applet, the classID entry is a pull-down menu; you can add additional applet class IDs by clicking the New Applet button. Below the ID, you enter the application name, which the handset displays in the application launcher along with the icon that you choose using the Icon entry line and the Browse button. The Applet Type menu lets you specify what kind of application your applet is; although it's not currently used, carriers or the handset can categorize applications based on the type you specify here.

Under the General tab, shown in Figure 3-3, you enter your company's name and the copyright string, which the handset shows when you enter the handset's application management screen, such as the Get it Now application on QUALCOMM BREW–enabled handsets on the Verizon Wireless network. You must also specify what (if any) privileges your application requires, such as privileges to access raw TCP/IP sockets or the local flash file system.

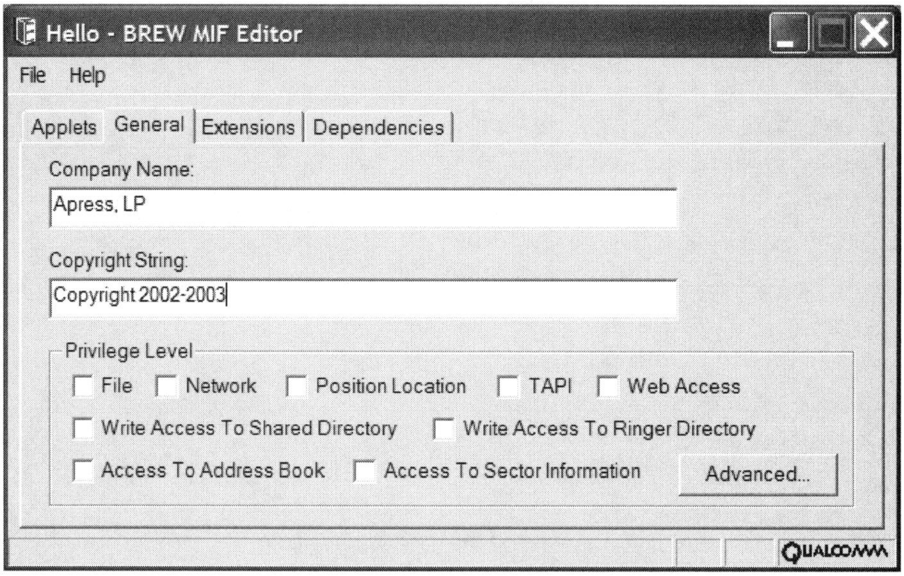

Figure 3-3. The QUALCOMM BREW MIF Editor, the General tab

The privileges you can give your application are as follows:

- **File**: Permits your application to read from and write to the local file system in its local directory using the `IFileMgr` and `IFile` interfaces.

- **Network**: Permits your application to use raw TCP/IP sockets via the `INetMgr` and `ISocket` interfaces.

- **Position Location**: Permits your application to determine the handset's position (if known) using the `ISHELL_GetPosition` method.

- **TAPI**: Permits your application to access the Telephony Application Programming Interface via the `ITAPI` interface.

- **Web Access**: Permits your application to access the Web via Hypertext Transfer Protocol (HTTP) using the IWeb interface.

- **Write Access to Shared Directory**: Permits your application to use the IFileMgr and IFile interfaces to write to the handset's shared directory.

- **Write Access to Ringer Directory**: Permits your application to use the IFileMgr and IFile interfaces to write to the handset's ringer directory.

- **Access to Address Book**: Permits your application to use the IAddrBook interface to manipulate the handset's built-in address book.

- **Access to Sector Information**: Permits your application to determine the cellular sector information via the IPositionDet interface.

Note that you should be sure to maintain the principle of *least privilege* when selecting privileges in your application's MIF. This principle states that your application should assert only those privileges it needs to operate correctly. By following the principle of least privilege, you ensure that in case of an application error your application doesn't violate the system's integrity by performing potentially dangerous actions.

The third and fourth tabs describe how your module interacts with other modules. In the Extensions tab, shown in Figure 3-4, you list the class IDs of any interfaces your module exports; other applications can use these interfaces by making a call to IShell_CreateInstance and passing the desired class ID. (If your module is an application, you should not export its class ID, however.) You can also list MIME types so that other applications can use the ISHELL methods to invoke media viewers based on the MIME types you support. In the Dependencies tab, shown in Figure 3-5, you list the class IDs of external modules—not those internal to BREW, but extensions you license from other developers—so that the handset can ensure that all of the components your application requires are available when it executes.

An MIF aggregates all of its contents. For example, when you add an icon (or an image or thumbnail image, through the dialog box you access by clicking the Advanced button on the first tab), the images are added to the MIF. Thus, if you want to use the information in another file, you need to use the corresponding Extract button to recover the information in a separate file.

As you'll see in subsequent sections, what you name your MIF is very important. Your MIF must be named the same as your module—the Dynamic Linked Library (DLL) and Module (MOD) files—so that the system can correctly associate the module information with the module.

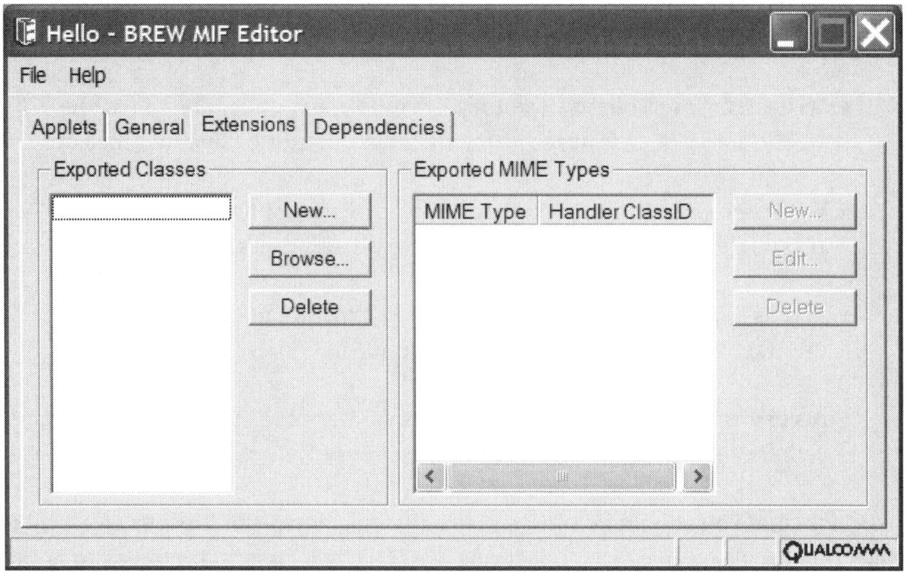

Figure 3-4. The QUALCOMM BREW MIF Editor, the Extensions tab

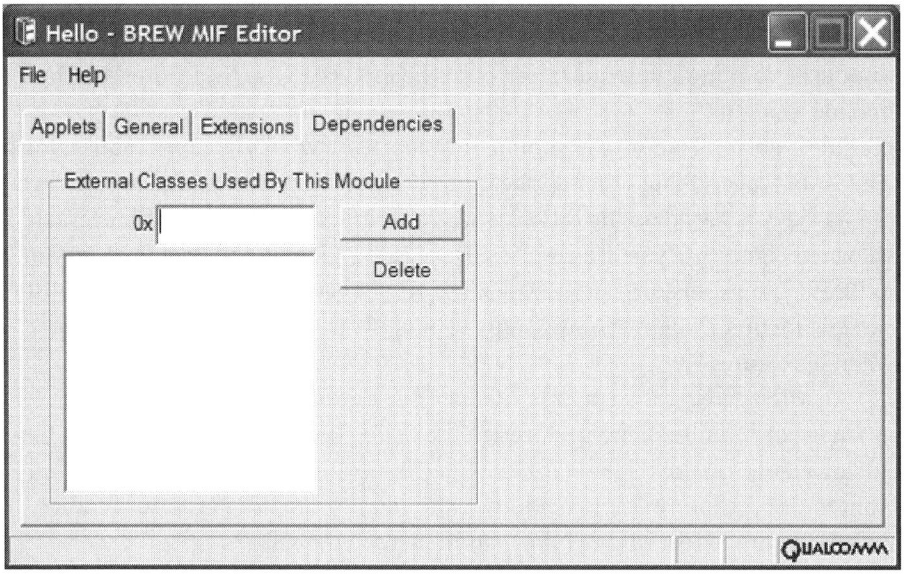

Figure 3-5. The QUALCOMM BREW MIF Editor, the Dependencies tab

Using the QUALCOMM BREW Resource Editor

Although applications don't need resources, all but the simplest of applications (such as the one you created in Chapter 1, "Introducing the QUALCOMM BREW Platform") use them to store text, images, and occasionally even user interface dialog boxes. Figure 3-6 shows the QUALCOMM BREW Resource Editor.

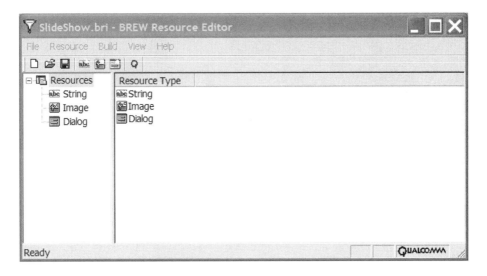

Figure 3-6. The QUALCOMM BREW Resource Editor

Most often you simply will be adding or editing an existing resource. To edit a resource, you can double-click it in the right pane; to add a new resource, either choose the appropriate action from the Resource menu or click the appropriate button along the top of both panes. You'll see a panel like that shown in Figure 3-7 (the appearance is slightly different depending on whether you're editing text, an image, or a dialog box resource). You'll enter both the resource and a name for the resource; the name you enter identifies the resource in the corresponding header file the editor creates when you build the resource file.

Once you enter (or edit) the application's resources, you need to build the resource file and the associated header file. The resource editor really doesn't edit these files in place; rather, it edits a file that describes the contents of the resource file. The resource editor maintains the list of contents in the file you edit, the BREW Resource Information file (BRI file), and produces the BREW Archive file (BAR file) and the resource header that contains the IDs and names of each of the resources. In turn, you include the resulting header file in your application and Microsoft Visual Studio project, and then you include the BAR file with the module file when you run the application on the handset or in the emulator.

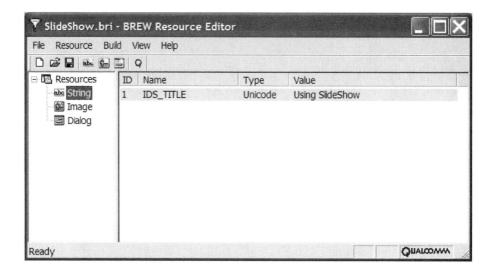

Figure 3-7. Editing a resource

Unlike MIFs, you can create more than one resource (BAR) file and name these files anything you like. In most cases, it makes the most sense to create a single file that contains all of your resources; however, you may find other reasons—as in the next chapter—to break your resources into multiple files.

Using the QUALCOMM BREW Emulator

The QUALCOMM BREW Emulator is your workhorse when you're debugging. It emulates the handset on your workstation, letting you debug your application as a Windows DLL using the Microsoft Visual Studio environment. Figure 3-8 shows the QUALCOMM BREW Emulator.

As you see in Figure 3-8, the emulator gives you a graphic presentation of the handset it's emulating. You can use your mouse to interact with the handset's control by moving the cursor over a button and clicking, or you can interact with the emulator's control by moving the cursor up to the menu bar and choosing a menu item.

You can control the basic appearance and operation of the emulator via the Tools menu. Typically, you'll use the Settings dialog box—shown in Figure 3-9 and available by selecting Tools ➤ Settings—to choose which phone the emulator should emulate and indicate the specific directory for your application and MIF.

Figure 3-8. The QUALCOMM BREW Resource Editor

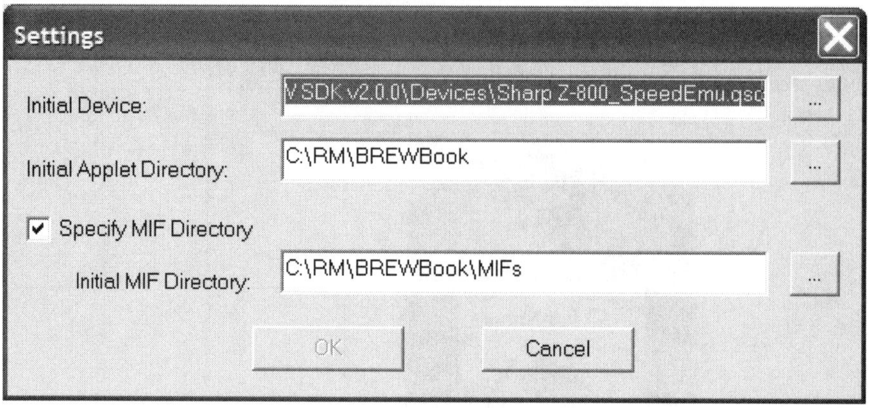

Figure 3-9. The emulator's Settings dialog box

The emulator represents different handsets using *skins*, which are similar to but not the same as the notion of skins for popular media player applications. QUALCOMM provides skins for commercially available handsets, and you can create your own for specific purposes using the QUALCOMM BREW Device Configuration Editor (see the next section). You can load a different skin using the ellipsis (...) button next to the Initial Device field in the Settings dialog box. Skins from QUALCOMM come in two flavors: those that emulate the phone's user interface and those that emulate both the phone's user interface and performance, using software delays to simulate the slower processing on the handset.

You also use the Settings dialog box to specify the location of your application and your application's MIF. Setting these directories is tricky—not because of the user interface but because the emulator accurately emulates how the phone's flash file system works. When selecting the directory for your application, you must choose the directory *above* the directory that contains your application's module (as a DLL, of course). Moreover, the directory containing your module *must* be named the same as the module itself. Your MIF can be anywhere you like, but typically you'll keep it close to your project directory.

For example, when developing the examples for this book, I created a BREW Book root directory for all of the examples. Inside this directory, I created a directory for each example application, such as Hello, RocketMileage, and so forth. Inside each of these directories was the module for each application: The Hello directory contains the source code and Hello.DLL, the RocketMileage directory contains RocketMileage.DLL, and so forth. The BREW Book directory also has another directory, MIFs, that contains each of the MIFs for the applications in the book: Hello.MIF, RocketMileage.MIF, and all of the other MIFs. This parallels the directory structure on the handset, where each application has its own directory named after that application's module, and the MIFs reside in the root directory of the handset.

Using the emulator, you can also adjust the emulator's network performance speed, which is handy if you want to see how your application is likely to perform on a real handset. You can also simulate telephone events, such as an incoming telephone call or BREW-directed SMS message, to test how your application handles suspend and resume events or SMS reception. You can also simulate positioning input by either connecting an external Global Positioning System (GPS) receiver or by taking the captured output of a GPS receiver in a file and directing the emulator to load the file. In turn, the emulator uses this positioning information to provide data for the `IPositionDet` interface and `ISHELL_GetPosition` method.

Despite all of these features, it's important to recognize that the emulator is just that: an *emulator*. It's not the handset, and it's impossible to do all of your testing in the emulator. Be prepared to do frequent builds for the handset using the ARM QUALCOMM BREW Builder, and exercise your application on handsets as often as you can. Not only will you get a better feel for how your application appears and behaves, but you can find and correct defects on the handset more quickly this away.

TIP *Don't leave handset testing to the end of your project, especially when you're first learning how to develop for the QUALCOMM BREW platform. You can easily make mistakes—such as using Windows Application Programming Interfaces (APIs)—in the emulator that you won't catch until you run your application on the handset. If you wait until the last minute to test your application on the handset, it may be too late to fix these problems without delaying your application's launch.*

Using the QUALCOMM BREW Device Configuration Editor

At times, you may need to alter how a particular emulator skin behaves. Perhaps you've received confidential information about a soon-to-be-announced handset and need to test your application for that device before you can get one to use. Or, perhaps you want to force a particular kind of failure, such as a low memory condition, while using the Microsoft Developer Studio debugger. To do this, you can use the QUALCOMM Device Configuration Editor, shown in Figure 3-10.

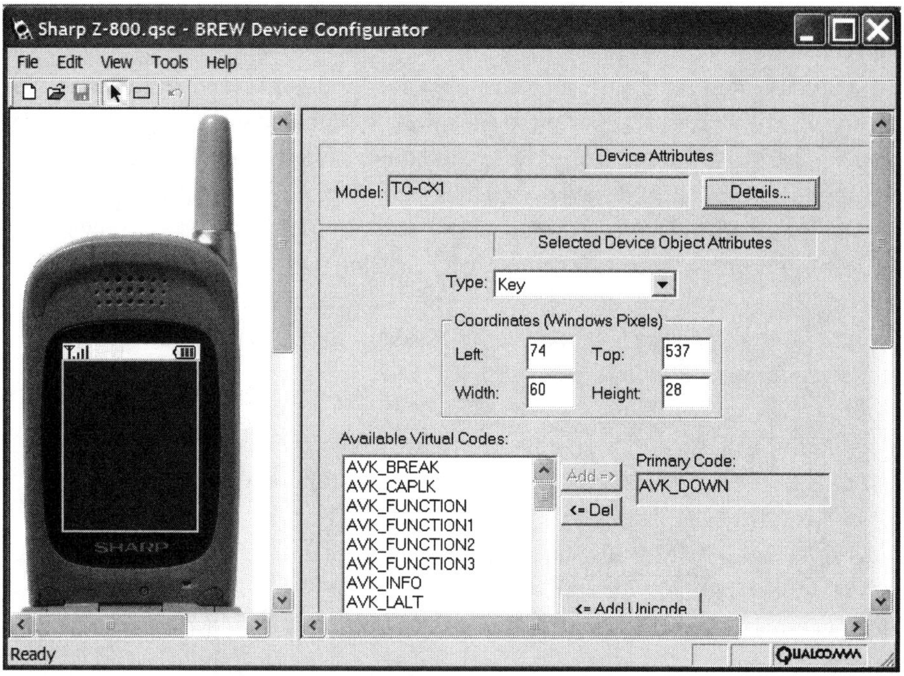

Figure 3-10. The QUALCOMM BREW Device Configuration Editor

Because it's unlikely that you'll need to make major changes to a device configuration without needing to consult QUALCOMM's documentation, the following sections only hit the highlights of using the editor.

The editor lets you specify a bitmap that models the appearance of the handset you want to emulate. On the bitmap, you must mark both where the emulator should draw the screen and the location of each button, along with specifying the key code for each key. For each region of the bitmap you mark, you specify whether it is a display or a key and then describe the other characteristics of the object, such as its aspect ratio or key code.

Using the QUALCOMM BREW Application Loader

You use the QUALCOMM BREW Application Loader to install your application on a developer handset for testing (see Figure 3-11). The QUALCOMM BREW Application Loader provides an Explorer-style window that lets you browse the QUALCOMM BREW section of the handset's file system, letting you copy files to and from the handset. (You can't copy some files, such as the files for applications you purchase using your carrier's download application, from the handset.)

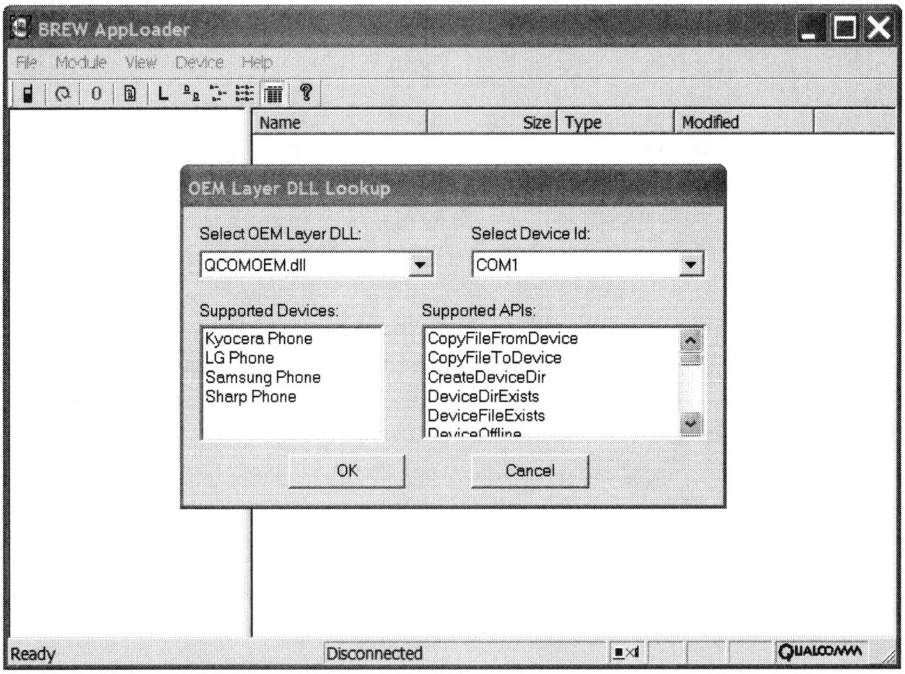

Figure 3-11. The QUALCOMM BREW Application Loader

NOTE *You can only load your application on handsets that have been enabled for developer use with the QUALCOMM BREW Application Loader. Because different handsets have different ways of enabling developer access, you should check the QUALCOMM BREW extranet before trying to use the QUALCOMM BREW Application Loader with your handset and application, as discussed in the previous chapter.*

To use the QUALCOMM BREW Application Loader, you first need to obtain a signature file—commonly called a *SIG file* because its filename ends in *.sig*—from http://www.qualcomm.com/. When you install your application, you'll copy your application's module, signature, resource, and module information files to the handset. To do this, follow these steps:

1. Connect your handset to an unused port on your workstation using the handset vendor's data cable. (You may need to install the driver that comes with the cable to use it.)

2. Launch the QUALCOMM BREW Application Loader.

3. Select the serial port you connected your handset to in step 1.

4. Click OK in the dialog box you see in Figure 3-11.

Your workstation and handset will communicate via a proprietary protocol, and you'll see the browser window in Figure 3-12. You can use the explorer to open directories, create new directories, and copy files to or from the handset. To install your application, simply copy its MIF to the root of the file system (either by using the right-click menu commands or by dragging and dropping the file to the window's right pane). Then create a folder with the same name as the module, and copy the module and any other required files into that folder. (You may need to turn the handset off and then on again so that the handset can detect the newly installed application.) Note that the folders with numeric names are applications you've purchased using your wireless service's BREW Delivery Service such as Get it Now on Verizon Wireless, and you shouldn't change those directories or their contents or you'll render the applications within them useless.

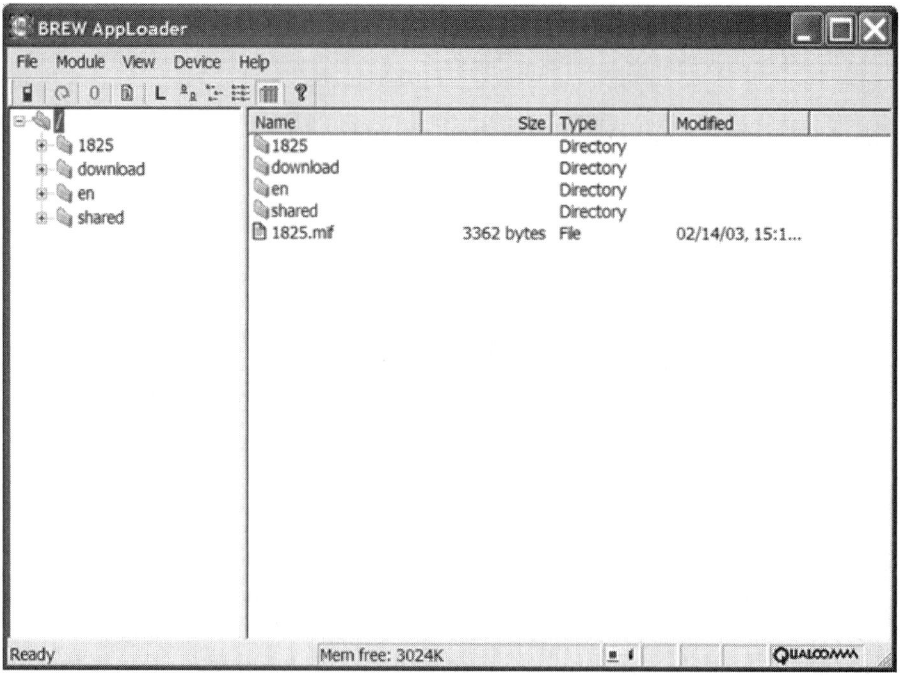

Figure 3-12. Exploring with the application loader

TIP   *Many developers have reported problems with the QUALCOMM BREW Application Loader when disconnecting the handset while the application is loading. It's best to disconnect from your handset using the application loader's leftmost button in the button bar or by quitting the application loader before you unplug or reset the handset.*

Using the QUALCOMM BREW Logger

The QUALCOMM BREW Logger lets you monitor the output of debug print statements on the handset. This is just like how the Microsoft Visual Studio output window (or the output window of the emulator) lets you view information printed by the DBGPRINTF function in your application. Although not as useful as a source-level or assembly-level debugger, it's the only on-device debugging tool you have. Figure 3-13 shows the QUALCOMM BREW Logger and the options you can set.

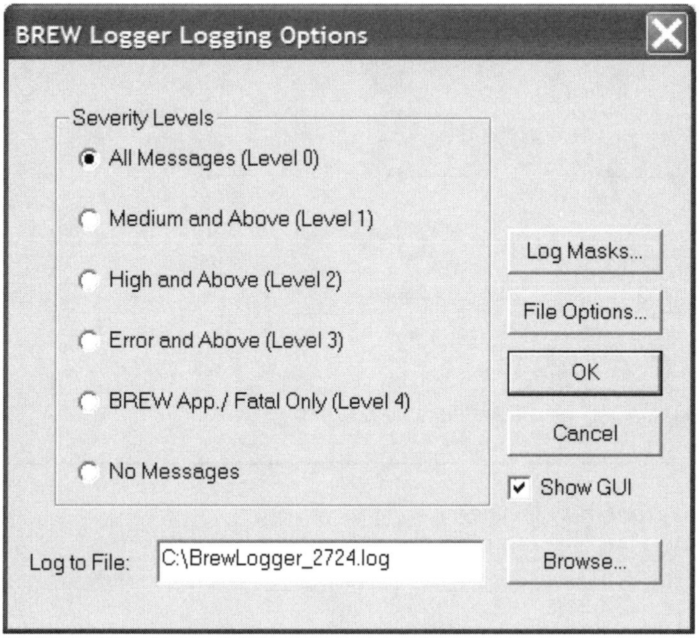

![BREW Logger Logging Options dialog. Severity Levels group with radio buttons: All Messages (Level 0) selected, Medium and Above (Level 1), High and Above (Level 2), Error and Above (Level 3), BREW App./ Fatal Only (Level 4), No Messages. Buttons: Log Masks..., File Options..., OK, Cancel, and a checked Show GUI checkbox. Log to File: C:\BrewLogger_2724.log with Browse... button.]

Figure 3-13. The QUALCOMM BREW Logger

You connect your handset to the logger the same way you do to the application loader—in fact, once you connect the handset to one application, it's connected to the other, so you can easily build your application, install it, test it, review the log, make a change, and rebuild and install it again for another run. Once you've connected your handset, you connect to the handset's logger by clicking the cell phone icon, start logging by clicking the start/stop logging button, and then view the log by clicking the icon with an eye. (You can also perform these operations by using the application's menus, but the button bar is easier.)

When you view the log, you'll see the window shown in Figure 3-14. This window includes the first characters of each log message, along with the time at which each log message occurred. You can use this information with debugging scaffolding in your application to trace application flow, perform rudimentary profiling of application performance, and examine variables during a program run.

TimeStamp	Message	FileName	Line Number	Level
02/24/03 12:30:04.7772..	FS_OPEN=nvm/brew/en/oat.bar	*dbgprintf*	0	4
02/24/03 12:30:04.7799...	Reading from non-existent file	fs_ops.c	2119	3
02/24/03 12:30:04.7972..	FS_OPEN=nvm/brew/oat.bar	*dbgprintf*	0	4
02/24/03 12:30:04.7990..	Reading from non-existent file	fs_ops.c	2119	3
02/24/03 12:30:04.8272..	FS_OPEN=nvm/brew/en/oat.bar	*dbgprintf*	0	4
02/24/03 12:30:04.8300..	Reading from non-existent file	fs_ops.c	2119	3
02/24/03 12:30:04.8450..	FS_OPEN=nvm/brew/oat.bar	*dbgprintf*	0	4
02/24/03 12:30:04.8531..	Reading from non-existent file	fs_ops.c	2119	3
02/24/03 12:30:04.8622..	*** AppMgr: (oat.bar) error ***	*dbgprintf*	0	4
02/24/03 12:30:04.8640..	ISHELL_SETTIMER	*dbgprintf*	0	4
02/24/03 12:30:04.8690..	+++++AEE_DISPATCH=1++	uihsig.c	136	3
02/24/03 12:30:04.9013..	CAPPMGR_ADDMENUITEM	*dbgprintf*	0	4
02/24/03 12:30:04.9040..	ISHELL_SETTIMER	*dbgprintf*	0	4
02/24/03 12:30:04.9063..	+++++AEE_DISPATCH=1++	uihsig.c	136	3
02/24/03 12:30:04.9363..	CAPPMGR_ADDMENUITEM	*dbgprintf*	0	4
02/24/03 12:30:04.9422..	FS_OPEN=nvm/brew/en/mshop.bar	*dbgprintf*	0	4
02/24/03 12:30:05.0449..	BLTDIB=8,-16	*dbgprintf*	0	4
02/24/03 12:30:05.0722..	FS_OPEN=nvm/brew/en/appmgr.bar	*dbgprintf*	0	4
02/24/03 12:30:05.1490..	IMENUCTL_ADDITEMEX	*dbgprintf*	0	4
02/24/03 12:30:05.1522..	PLAY ASSOCIATED SOUND FILE A...	*dbgprintf*	0	4
02/24/03 12:30:05.1540..	CAPPMGR_RESIZEMENU	*dbgprintf*	0	4
02/24/03 12:30:05.1881..	+++++AEE_DISPATCH=2++	uihsig.c	136	3
02/24/03 12:30:05.1900..	OEMDISP_UPDATE=19069780,29,0	OEMDisp.c	533	3
02/24/03 12:30:05.2300..	+++++AEE_DISPATCH=1++	uihsig.c	136	3
02/24/03 12:30:05.4122..	BLTDIB=4,-32	*dbgprintf*	0	4
02/24/03 12:30:05.4463..	OEMDISP_UPDATE=19069780,29,0	OEMDisp.c	533	3
02/24/03 12:30:05.4872..	+++++AEE_DISPATCH=0++	uihsig.c	136	3

Figure 3-14. Sample output from the logger

TIP *As with the application loader, developers have reported problems with the QUALCOMM BREW Logger when disconnecting the handset while the application is loading. It's best to disconnect from your handset using the application loader's leftmost button in the button bar or by quitting the application loader before you unplug or reset the handset. Moreover, the QUALCOMM BREW Logger only shows the first 67 bytes of a string logged with* DBGPRINTF.

Summary

In this chapter, you learned the following:

- QUALCOMM BREW provides an object-oriented toolkit for developing applications on the handset.

- Your application must register itself with the system to receive events generated by the system's event pump. These applications signal your application's launch, user and system interaction with your application, and your application's termination.

- The IShell interface offers a bevy of functions for managing system interfaces (including timers), managing resources, and obtaining device characteristics.

- You use the ISHELL_CreateInstance method to create instances of other system interfaces within your application.

- The QUALCOMM BREW platform includes many of the standard C library functions, along with QUALCOMM BREW–specific data types to represent characters and other data.

- You use the QUALCOMM BREW MIF Editor to create the MIF that describes your application, specifying its class ID, icon, name, and other details such as the privileges it requires to execute correctly.

- You use the QUALCOMM BREW Resource Editor to collect and package string, image, and dialog box resources for your application.

- You use the QUALCOMM BREW Emulator to demonstrate your application on your workstation or to debug your application using the Microsoft Visual Studio debugger.

- You use the QUALCOMM BREW Application Loader to install your application on a developer handset for testing using the handset, the QUALCOMM extranet–provided SIG file, and a data cable.

- You use the QUALCOMM BREW Logger to view the output of `DBGPRINTF` statements on your workstation from the handset via a serial cable.

CHAPTER 4

Handling Events

AT THE CORE of every QUALCOMM BREW application is its event loop, which accepts incoming user and system events, dispatches them to the application's user interface controls, and does whatever the application needs to do. Consequently, your understanding of QUALCOMM BREW's event model is a fundamental step in being able to write your application.

In this chapter, you'll learn about QUALCOMM BREW's events and how your application should handle them. It discusses the structure of events, the kinds of events your application must be prepared to handle, and how your application should share events with user interface elements. It then offers an application framework that helps you manage events; you can use this framework to build your own applications. The chapter also details how you can use the framework construct SlideShow, an application that presents bitmaps for user interface prototypes.

Understanding the Event Model

As described in the previous chapter, the system sends your application events by calling your application's *event handler*, which receives each event, processes it, and returns control to the system.

Unlike most systems, your application doesn't poll for events; instead, the system invokes your application in response to events. This difference is crucial because your application must do its background processing as it handles each event. Unlike larger computing platforms, such as Microsoft Windows CE and the real-time operating systems used by many embedded devices, QUALCOMM BREW is a single-threaded environment. Consequently, you must do your processing as you receive events and be sure to yield as much time to the underlying system by keeping the work you do when handling events as brief as possible. In that manner, QUALCOMM BREW resembles simpler handheld operating systems, such as Palm OS.

Processing an Event

The shell sends your application events by invoking its event handler method, a method of IApplet that you override during your application's instantiation. If you're using the QUALCOMM-supplied AEEAppGen.c file, the AEEApplet_New function does this on your behalf.

NOTE *The AEEAppGen.c file actually registers its own method as the event handler for your applet and then invokes your event handling function as part of its execution.*

Your application's event handler is a function that must match the following prototype:

```
1: boolean HandleEvent( IApplet * pi,
2:                       AEEEvent eCode,
3:                       uint16 wParam,
4:                       uint32 dwParam);
```

The first argument, pi, is a pointer to your application's instance. In all but the simplest of cases, you'll need to cast this pointer to a structure that carries your application's data because QUALCOMM BREW applications can't have global variables. Instead, as shown in the previous chapter, it's easy to emulate this behavior by using members in an application structure that matches the shell's expectation of the contents of an IApplet structure.

The second argument, eCode, is the event your application can process. Your HandleEvent function will be called once for each event it receives and has the choice of processing the event for its own purpose or ignoring the event. If your event handler processes the event, it should return TRUE; this signals to the shell that the event has been managed. If it returns FALSE, the shell will attempt to process it on your application's behalf.

The remaining arguments, wParam and dwParam, can contain additional information about the event. For example, when you press a key on the handset, the shell passes a code identifying the key in the argument wParam. Similarly, when your application receives a Short Message Service (SMS) message, your event handler will receive a pointer to the message's contents in a buffer at the address specified in dwParam.

Typically, your event handler becomes a massive switch statement, testing the incoming event code against the kinds of events you want to handle. If you're not careful, this can turn into a bunch of nested switch statements or, worse yet, a massive `switch` statement with scores of `if` statements within each `case`. This can quickly render a well-written application unmanageable as your logic grows more complex. (The next section shows you one way to better organize the structure of an event handler.)

Handling System Events

At a minimum, your application must handle four system events that pertain to the following:

- The shell sends your application the `EVT_APP_START` event after registering your application.

- The shell sends your application the `EVT_SUSPEND` event when it must suspend your application to perform another operation, such as presenting an incoming SMS message or phone call. You should free as many system resources as you can before returning control to the system, including memory and object instances.

- The shell sends your application the `EVT_RESUME` event when your application can continue executing after receiving an `EVT_SUSPEND` event.

- The shell sends your application the `EVT_APP_STOP` event when your application should quit, such as when you press the End Call button or when you call `ISHELL_CloseApplet` to tell the shell to close your application.

Your application may also need to manage other system events, such as the following:

- The `EVT_APP_CONFIG` event, sent by the shell when you invoke an application's configuration options from the application launcher

- The `EVT_APP_MESSAGE` event, sent by the shell when the handset receives an SMS message directed at your application

- The `EVT_ALARM` event, sent by the shell when an alarm set by your application fires

- The `EVT_NOTIFY` event, sent by other classes when you register your application as wanting notifications for class-specific events such as network activity

You can also define your own events by using event codes with values greater than EVT_USER. You can then post events to your application using the function ISHELL_PostEvent, like this:

```
1: b = ISHELL_PostEvent( pIShell, classid, eCode, wParam, dwParam );
```

where pIShell is a valid pointer to the shell, classid is the class ID of your application, and the arguments eCode, wParam, and dwParam represent the event to post. After the call executes, b will be TRUE if the event was successfully posted.

CAUTION   *As with all other return values, don't be in the habit of assuming that a system call will succeed. The handset is a constrained device, and there's a real chance that a system call will fail for lack of memory or other resources. Neglecting to test return values for success or failure can lead to subtle failures that are difficult to find and reproduce in your application.*

Handling User Interface Events

Many of the events your application must process are user interface events that indicate keystrokes and menu selections. These events are at the heart of your application because the shell uses events to signal all user input.

The simplest form of user input is a keystroke—when you press and release a single key on the handset. In response to a keystroke, the system sends your application three events in succession. First, the system sends an EVT_KEY_PRESS event, indicating that you pressed a key. Next, when you release the key, the system sends an EVT_KEY event, followed by an EVT_KEY_RELEASE event. Typically, your application needs to respond only to the EVT_KEY event, rather than looking for individual press and release events. The system can also send the EVT_KEY_HELD event to signal that you're pressing and holding a key; this event is handy when implementing special controls such as game buttons.

With each keystroke event, the system indicates the key you pressed in the 16-bit parameter that accompanies the event (traditionally named wParam). This parameter encodes the key as a key code, matching one of the manifest constants in AEEVCodes.h, the include file that specifies event codes for keystrokes, display, and indicator interaction. Table 4-1 describes common keys and their corresponding key codes.

Table 4-1. Common Keys and Their Corresponding Key Codes

KEY	KEY CODE
0	AVK_0
1	AVK_1
2	AVK_2
3	AVK_3
4	AVK_4
5	AVK_5
6	AVK_6
7	AVK_7
8	AVK_8
9	AVK_9
*	AVK_STAR
#	AVK_POUND
Clear (the Back key)	AVK_CLR
Up arrow	AVK_UP
Down arrow	AVK_DOWN
Left arrow	AVK_LEFT
Right arrow	AVK_RIGHT
Select	AVK_SELECT
Send	AVK_SEND
End Call	AVK_END

A close look at Table 4-1 shows that something is missing when you compare QUALCOMM BREW to other platforms: keys representing individual letters. Because QUALCOMM BREW handsets only offer numeric keys, text input occurs through the IText control. This control handles the mapping of individual keystrokes, letting the user select different input methods such as numeric only, multitap, and platform-specific entry mechanisms such as Tegic's T9 or Motorola's iTAP method. To do this—in fact, to work with any of the QUALCOMM BREW user interface controls—you need to also pass user interface events to the user interface controls. Other controls, notably the IMenu control, use additional events to indicate user interaction. These controls use the EVT_COMMAND event to signal control-specific interaction, such as the selection of a menu event. As with the IText control, you must share incoming events with the control for it to operate correctly; you do this using the control's HandleEvent method. (You'll see how to do this later in the section "Presenting a Prototype User Interface" when you see SlideShow, a user interface prototyping tool that displays bitmaps.)

One final event you must give special attention is when the user presses the Clear key—sending your application the EVT_KEY event with a wParam attribute of AVK_CLR. By convention, the Clear key has two purposes: to backspace in a text line, rubbing out a single character, and to return to the previous screen in a multi-screen application. Although the IText control handles the backspace facility, it's up to your application to manage navigation between screens and return to the previous screen when you press the Clear key.

Building an Application Framework

Because so many of the event handling requirements are similar between different applications, it makes sense to build an application framework that assumes this responsibility, which you can reuse as you write new applications. The section that follows sketches out a lightweight application framework that handles common events such as EVT_SUSPEND and EVT_RESUME, and it handles navigation between screens.

This framework is the basis for the applications throughout this book, starting in this chapter with SlideShow (a program that displays a succession of bitmap images) and continuing through RocketMileage.

Representing Application Flow with Application States

A good model for representing your application is to divide it into individual states, with each state capturing one screen of interaction with the user. Your application then becomes a succession of states—a *state machine*, in computer science parlance.

Structuring your application as a state machine has several advantages. First, it's easy to build your application in pieces, adding states as you need to add incremental features to your application. Moreover, most states are fairly small and have limited interaction with other states in the application. It's also easy to manage navigation within the application using a state machine.

By keeping successive states in a stack, your application can easily handle both forward and backward flow through the user interface. Using a stack, the current application state is the topmost state in a stack of states. As you progress forward through your application's interface—say, by entering a display of results after selecting a choice from a menu—the application can push new states on the stack. When you press Clear to return to a previous screen, the application simply pops the topmost state, presenting the previous state on the stack to the user. Figure 4-1 illustrates this concept.

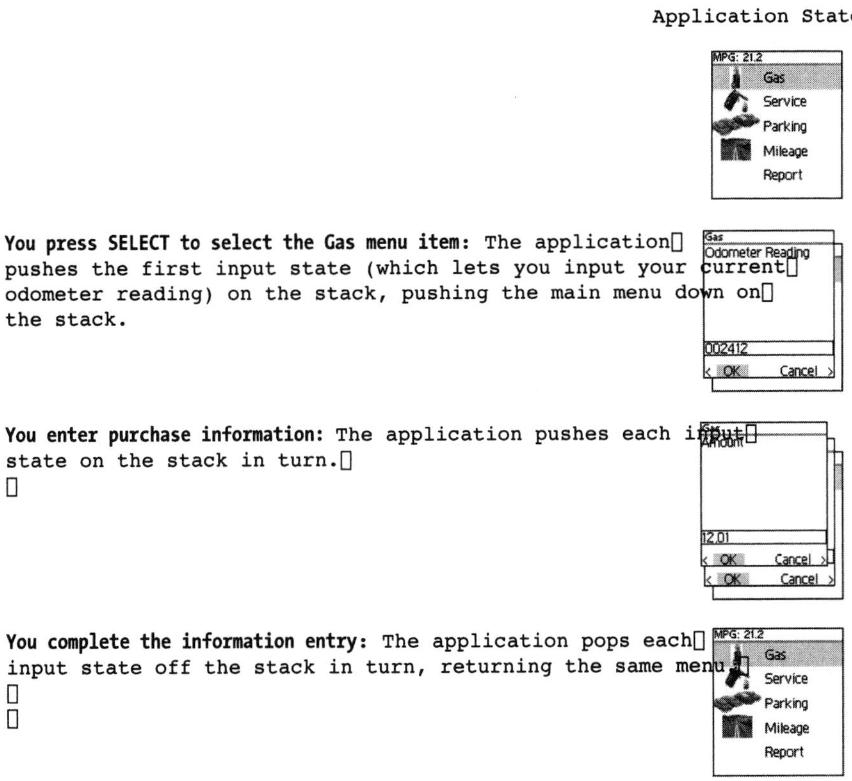

Application State St
MPG: 21.2
Gas
Service
Parking
Mileage
Report
You press SELECT to select the Gas menu item: The application pushes the first input state (which lets you input your current odometer reading) on the stack, pushing the main menu down on the stack.
Gas
Odometer Reading
002412
OK
Cancel
You enter purchase information: The application pushes each input state on the stack in turn.
Amount
12.01
OK
Cancel
OK
Cancel
You complete the information entry: The application pops each input state off the stack in turn, returning the same menu
MPG: 21.2
Gas
Service
Parking
Mileage
Report

Figure 4-1. Representing application interface flow with a stack of states

The framework's core responsibility is to maintain the stack of states, allocate new states when requested, and dispatch events from the event pump to the current state. As the framework operates, it manages suspend and resume events, treating them as exits and entries to the current state. A state itself is a simple structure representing a tuple of functions and an associated memory region the state can use to share data between each of the function invocations (see Listing 4-1).

Listing 4-1. The Application State Structure CState

```
 1: // State function type declarations
 2: typedef void (PFNSTATEENTRY)( void *pApp, EStateChange change );
 3: typedef void  (PFNSTATEEXIT)( void *pApp, EStateChange change );
 4: typedef boolean (PFNSTATEEVENT)( void *pApp,
 5:                     AEEEvent eCode,
 6:                     uint16 wParam, uint32 dwParam);
 7: typedef struct _CState
 8: {
 9:   struct _CState *m_pPrevState;
10:   PFNSTATEENTRY  *m_pfEntry;
11:   PFNSTATEEXIT   *m_pfExit;
12:   PFNSTATEEVENT  *m_pfEvent;
13:   void           *m_pData;
14: } CState, *CStatePtr;
```

The application framework maintains the stack as a singly linked list; the head of the list is the top state on the stack. The first member of the CState structure, m_pPrevState (on line 9), points to the previous state in the stack to maintain this list (thus, the head of the list is the current state, the last state is the state pointed to by the first m_pPrevState, and so on). The three functions m_pfEntry, m_pfExit, and m_pfEvent are the state's entry function, exit function, and event handler, respectively. The entry and exit functions each take a pointer to the application structure and the reason for the function's execution: an enumerated value indicating that the specific state is being pushed deeper on to the stack, that the specific state is being popped from the stack, or that the application has received a suspend or resume event. The event handler, by comparison, takes the same arguments as the application's event handler: a pointer to the application structure, the event code, and the word and long word arguments of the event. Hence, the three typedef statements on lines 2–4 define each of the state function interfaces. Finally, each state may allocate variables for its internal use, such as storing intermediate values between events. This information, a single pointer to a state-specific structure, is stored in the m_pData field of the CState structure.

Managing the Application's State Machine

To manage the application's state machine, the framework must provide several interfaces:

- An event handler, called each time your application receives an event. This handler is responsible for both dispatching events to the current state (the state at the top of the stack) and handling special events, such as a suspend or resume event or a Clear key press.

- The stack manipulation's push and pop, which pushes a new state and pops the current state from the stack, respectively. These interfaces are public, used by the various states of the application when moving from state to state.

- State manipulation functions representing the system suspend and resume events. These are separate interfaces apart from the push and pop interfaces because they're called only by the framework's event handler in response to system events.

- Accessor and mutator interfaces for a state's private data (the m_pData) pointer. Although not absolutely required, isolating this field from direct access makes it easy to change the implementation of the framework without changing the code that uses it.

- An interface to obtain the application's current state, used predominately by the application framework itself. As with the aforementioned m_pData accessor and mutator interfaces, this isn't required, but it's a good idea in case you want to change the framework's implementation later.

By convention—closely following QUALCOMM BREW's function naming convention—each of the application framework function names begins with a common keyword, State. Thus, you have the interfaces shown in Listing 4-2.

Listing 4-2. The State Management Interfaces

```
1: // Application Framework interfaces
2: #define State_GetState( p ) ( ((CStateAppPtr)(p))->m_pState )
3:
4: // Macros that could be functions...
5: #define State_GetStateData( s ) ( s->m_pData )
6: #define State_SetStateData( s, d ) ( s->m_pData = d );
7:
8 :// There is no SetCurrentState to keep the user from
```

```
 9: // corrupting the stack by mistake...
10: #define State_GetCurrentState( app ) \
11:    ( ((CStateAppPtr)(app))->m_pState )
12: #define State_GetCurrentStateData( app ) \
13:    ( (((CStateAppPtr)(app))->m_pState)->m_pData );
14: #define State_SetCurrentStateData( app, data ) \
15:    ( (((CStateAppPtr)(app))->m_pState)->m_pData = ( data ) );
16:
17: // Prototypes
18:
19: boolean State_Push( void *p,
20:                        PFNSTATEENTRY pfEntry,
21:                        PFNSTATEEXIT pfExit,
22:                        PFNSTATEEVENT pfEvent );
23: boolean State_Pop( void *p );
24: void State_Suspend( void *p );
25: void State_Resume( void *p );
26: boolean State_HandleEvent( void *pApp,
27:                        AEEEvent eCode,
28:                        uint16 wParam,
29:                        uint32 dwParam );
```

In the interests of efficiency, the simplest interfaces are implemented as macros.

You'll note that there's no initialization interface *per se*. In the interest of simplicity, the framework initializes the application framework on the first call to State_Push. Moreover, the implementation of the other functions contains guards against uninitialized framework data. This is a good idea not only because you might accidentally make a call to one of the interfaces before the framework is initialized, but also because an error in your program might overwrite part of the state stack, invalidating the *m_pPrevState field and corrupting the application and its behavior.

A key problem is where to store the base of the state stack. An obvious place is within the application structure; however, blithely placing it as a member within the application structure forces the implementation of the framework to know something about the rest of the application. Although not necessarily bad when constructing a single application, this is cumbersome when using the framework within multiple applications because each application's implementation of the framework needs to have knowledge of the application's state structure, and you need to revise the implementation to include this for each application.

Rather, you can use some of the same skullduggery that the QUALCOMM BREW system uses with the IApplet and AEEApplet structures: You can require that the beginning of the application structure follow a prescribed format. Just as the

AEEAppGen functions require that the first element of the application structure be an AEEApplet structure, the state machine framework requires that the second element of the application structure be a pointer to a structure that represents the application framework, which will contain the top of the state stack. Thus, any application that uses the framework must define its first members of the application structure:

```
1: typedef struct _CApp
2: {
3:   AEEApplet          a;
4:   CStateFrameworkPtr m_pFramework;
5:   // Other members here...
6: } CApp, *CAppPtr;
```

For now, CStateFrameworkPtr is simply a type definition equivalent to CStatePtr, pointing to the top of the state stack. (In later chapters, as you enhance the framework, CStateFrameworkPtr will point to an entire structure that contains other information about the application framework itself, including the state of the user interface controls.) In turn, the state machine views an application structure simply as a CStateApp structure:

```
1: typedef struct _CStateApp
2: {
3:   EEApplet          a;  // Must always be first
4:   CStatePtr          m_pState; // The current state
5: } CStateApp, *CStateAppPtr;
```

Because currently the CStateFrameworkPtr is simply a CStatePtr, you treat the second element as a CStatePtr in this type definition and throughout the following discussion.

So, how does all of this work in practice? Let's take a close look at each of the functions that implement the application framework's interface.

The State_Push and State_Pop interfaces are integral to the application framework because they provide the means by which user navigation in the interface controls the succession of application states. The operation of these is straightforward. Listing 4-3 shows State_Push.

Listing 4-3. The State_Push *Function*

```
1: /**
2: * Pushes indicated state on stack;
3: * Transitions to that state.
4: * @param void *p: pointer to app
```

```
 5: * @param PFNSTATEENTRY pfnEntry: call on function entry
 6: * @param PFNSTATEEXIT pfnExit: call on function exit
 7: * @param PFNSTATEEVENT pfnEvent: call on each event
 8: * return TRUE if transition succeeds, FALSE if not
 9: */
10: boolean State_Push( void *p,
11:                     PFNSTATEENTRY pfEntry,
12:                     PFNSTATEEXIT pfExit,
13:                     PFNSTATEEVENT pfEvent )
14: {
15:   CStateAppPtr pThis = ( CStateAppPtr )p;
16:   CStatePtr pCurState, pNewState;
17:
18:   ASSERT( pfEntry || pfExit || pfEvent );
19:
20:   pCurState = State_GetCurrentState( pThis );
21:   pNewState = State_Create( p, pfEntry, pfExit, pfEvent );
22:
23:   ASSERT( pNewState );
24:   if ( !pNewState ) return FALSE;
25:
26:   // Call the present state's exit function
27:   if ( pCurState && pCurState->m_pfExit )
28:     pCurState->m_pfExit( p,
29:                          StateChange_push );
30:
31:   // Push this state on to the stack.
32:   pNewState->m_pPrevState = pCurState;
33:   pThis->m_pState = pNewState;
34:
35:   // Call new state's entry function
36:   if ( pNewState->m_pfEntry )
37:     pNewState->m_pfEntry( p,
38:                           StateChange_push );
39:
40:   // No errors!
41:   return TRUE;
42: }
```

State_Push begins with a bit of debug housekeeping, ensuring that it's called with valid arguments (line 18). Assuming it is, it creates a new state using the function State_Create (which you can see later in this section), specifying a state's members as arguments (line 21). Assuming a valid state is created (lines 23–24), it notifies the current state that it's being exited because the application is pushing a new state on the stack (lines 27–29). The initial comparison on line 27 ensures that the current state's exit function will be called *only* if there's both a current state— that is, if the framework is already initialized—and if the state has an exit function.

> **NOTE** *The* ASSERT *macro actually isn't available in QUALCOMM BREW; but I define it in the include file utils.h. It does the same thing as the standard C* assert *macro: It tests its argument and, if the argument is false, prints an error and terminates execution. The* _DEBUG *compile-time constant ensures that the* ASSERT *macro occurs only in preproduction code; by building production releases with no* _DEBUG *flag set, you can be sure these assertions don't appear in shipping applications.*

Next, State_Push pushes the new state on the stack by linking it to the current state and then setting the application's notion of the current state to the new state. Note here you're using the application structure, referring to it as a CStateApp rather than the application's native application structure, so that any application following this convention can use the framework without modification (lines 15 and 31).

Finally, the function calls the new state's entry function, giving it a chance to allocate its state variables, manipulate the user interface, or do whatever it needs to do when it's entered (lines 36–38). As with the previous state's exit function, this tests the current state's entry function to be sure it exists (line 36), in case a particular state doesn't need an entry function. This small performance penalty reduces the need for empty handler functions, which lowers the application's overall memory footprint.

State_Pop operates in an analogous fashion, first calling the state's exit function, popping the state from the state stack and freeing its contents, and then calling the previous state's entry function (see Listing 4-4).

Listing 4-4. Manipulating the State Stack

```
1: /**
2: * Pushes indicated state on stack;
3: * Transitions to that state.
4: * @param void *p: pointer to app
5: * @param PFNSTATEENTRY pfnEntry: call on function entry
6: * @param PFNSTATEEXIT pfnExit: call on function exit
7: * @param PFNSTATEEVENT pfnEvent: call on each event
8: * return TRUE if transition succeeds, FALSE if not
9: */
```

```
10: boolean State_Pop( void *p )
11: {
12:   CStateAppPtr pThis = ( CStateAppPtr )p;
13:   CStatePtr pCurState, pOldState;
14:
15:   pCurState = State_GetCurrentState( pThis );
16:   pOldState = pCurState->m_pPrevState;
17:
18:   ASSERT( pCurState );
19:   if ( !pCurState ) return FALSE;
20:
21:   // Call the present state's exit function
22:   if ( pCurState->m_pfExit )
23:     pCurState->m_pfExit( p,
24:                           StateChange_pop );
25:
26:   // Pop the old state off of the stack.
27:   pThis->m_pState = pOldState;
28:   pCurState->m_pPrevState = NULL;
29:
30:   // Call new state's entry function
31:   if ( pOldState && pOldState->m_pfEntry )
32:     pOldState->m_pfEntry( p,
33:                           StateChange_pop );
34:
35: // Release the popped state
36: State_Release( p, pCurState );
37:
38: // No errors!
39: return TRUE;
40: }
```

As you can see, the logic is essentially the same but in reverse; after obtaining the current state and previous state (lines 15–16), the function calls the current state's exit function, if any (lines 22–24). Then, the function calls the previous state's entry function if there's a previous state that has an entry function (lines 31–33). Finally, the function releases the memory associated with the state that was popped (line 36).

Suspending and resuming the current state is a special case of popping and pushing states from the stack. In many cases, what an application must do when it's suspended is essentially the same as what it must do when it exits: Save its state and free any allocated resources. In the case of application suspension, of course, there's a tradeoff between what can be freed and what should persist because the user expects the application to resume in the same state it was in after being suspended, such as when a phone call occurs. Consequently, State_Suspend and State_Resume simply call the appropriate state's exit or entry function, respectively (see Listing 4-5).

Listing 4-5. Suspending the Current State

```
1: /**
2: * Issues suspend to current state.
3: * @param void *p: pointer to app
4: * @return nothing
5: */
6: void State_Suspend( void *p )
7: {
8:   CStateAppPtr pThis = ( CStateAppPtr )p;
9:   CStatePtr pCurState;
10:
11:  pCurState = State_GetCurrentState( pThis );
12:
13:  if ( pCurState && pCurState->m_pfExit )
14:    pCurState->m_pfExit( p,
15:                         StateChange_suspend );
16: }
17:
18: /**
19: * Issues resume to current state.
20: * @param void *p: pointer to app
21: * @return nothing
22: */
23: void State_Resume( void *p )
24: {
25:   CStateAppPtr pThis = ( CStateAppPtr )p;
26:   CStatePtr pCurState;
27:
28:   pCurState = State_GetCurrentState( pThis );
29:
30:   if ( pCurState && pCurState->m_pfEntry )
31:     pCurState->m_pfEntry( p,
32:                           StateChange_resume );
33: }
```

These functions are both pretty simple; they call the current state's appropriate function with the special flag indicating whether the state is being suspended or resumed.

The event handler performs most of the work on behalf of the framework, handling several application-wide events, including when the user presses the Clear key, when the event sends a suspend or resume, and application termination when the state stack has been emptied. All of this is done by the function State_HandleEvent, which the application's event handler must call for each event (see Listing 4-6).

Listing 4-6. Handling Events Within the State Framework

```
 1: /**
 2: * Handles incoming events.
 3: * Dispatches suspend and resume to current state.
 4: * Pops state on AVK_CLR
 5: * Pops all states on EVT_APP_STOP
 6: * @param void *p: pointer to app
 7: * @param AEEEvent eCode: event code
 8: * @param uint16 wParam: event parameter
 9: * @param uint32 dwParan: event parameter
10: * @return boolean FALSE if app framework should continue handling event
11: */
12: boolean State_HandleEvent( void *p,
13:                               AEEEvent eCode,
14:                               uint16 wParam,
15:                               uint32 dwParam )
16: {
17:   boolean result = FALSE;
18:   CStatePtr pCurState;
19:   CStateAppPtr pThis = ( CStateAppPtr )p;
20:
21:   ASSERT( pThis );
22:   pCurState = State_GetCurrentState( pThis );
23:
24:   if ( !pCurState ) return FALSE;
25:
26:   // We always give the state first dibs.
27:   if ( pCurState->m_pfEvent )
28:     result = pCurState->m_pfEvent( p, eCode, wParam, dwParam );
29:
30:   // If the state didn't do anything with it, we will.
31:   if ( !result ) switch( eCode )
32:   {
33:     // Tell the current state to suspend operations
34:     case EVT_APP_SUSPEND:
35:       State_Suspend( p );
```

```
36:        result = TRUE;
37:        break;
38:
39:      // Tell the current state to resume operations
40:      case EVT_APP_RESUME:
41:        State_Resume( p );
42:        result = TRUE;
43:        break;
44:
45:      // Pop ALL states from the stack -- we're exiting
46:      case EVT_APP_STOP:
47:        while( State_GetCurrentState( pThis ) )
48:          State_Pop( p );
49:        result = TRUE;
50:        break;
51:
52:      // If the user hits Clr, pop
53:      case EVT_KEY:
54:      if ( wParam == AVK_CLR &&
55:          State_GetCurrentState( pThis ) )
56:      {
57:        State_Pop( p );
58:        // If there are no more states, we exit by saying the event
59:        // isn't completely handled. The shell will send us an
60:        // EVT_APP_STOP after this.
61:        result = State_GetCurrentState( pThis ) ? TRUE : FALSE;
62:        break;
63:      }
64:    }
65:
66:    return result;
67: }
```

This is a long function, but its operation is quite straightforward. After first ensuring there's a state on the stack that might want to handle the function (if there isn't one, there's no work for the framework to do!), the function offers the event to the current state's event handler (lines 22–28). Then, if the state didn't handle the event, the framework examines the event (lines 31–64). By giving the current state first crack at the event and having the framework's event handler ignore events already handled by specific states, a particular state can override the default behavior of the application framework, such as when a state must handle the Clear key differently (say, during user input).

Handling the EVT_APP_SUSPEND and EVT_APP_RESUME events is quite simple (lines 34–43), merely calling either State_Suspend or State_Resume, respectively. The other cases—application termination and the Clear key—are a little more complex.

When the shell wants to terminate the application, it sends the EVT_APP_STOP event. The application framework must then perform an orderly shutdown of each state, popping it from the stack to ensure that each state has the opportunity to release any system resources it has consumed. The while loop on lines 47–48 of the EVT_APP_STOP case (lines 46–50) accomplishes this, popping each state from the stack in turn until none are left.

Handling a Clear key press is a little simpler although the logic is more complex because the system uses an EVT_KEY event with a value of AVK_CLR to indicate that you have pressed the Clear key and the application should return to the previous screen. Consequently, the event handler first tests the wParam of the event (line 54) and then checks to ensure that there's a valid state (line 55) before popping the current state (line 57). Unlike other events that use TRUE to signal that they've been completely handled by the system, this case returns TRUE *only* if the application should continue to run because the shell will send an EVT_STOP event to the application if it doesn't fully handle a Clear key press. By returning FALSE when the last state has been popped from the stack and the stack is now empty, the framework ensures that the system will request that the application terminate, rather than the framework forcibly needing to close the application.

The implementation of the State_Create and State_Release functions are straightforward, performing the minimum initialization and destruction required by a specific state. If you like, you can examine them in the State.c file that accompanies this chapter's examples (available in the Downloads section of the Apress Web site at http://www.apress.com/).

Presenting a Prototype User Interface

Previous chapters discussed the importance of prototyping in user interface design. Prototyping is often overlooked, especially on nascent platforms such as QUALCOMM BREW because there's a paucity of rapid development tools available. Unlike a desktop environment where tools including PowerPoint, Visual Basic, and Flash can create compelling prototypes, it seems difficult at best to develop a prototype for a cell phone.

It need not be that way, however. In practice, something as simple as a succession of bitmaps presented to potential users can often communicate far more about how an application might operate than dozens of use cases and flow diagrams. Consequently, a slide show renderer—a simple "bitmap flipper," if you will—becomes a powerful tool in any developer's arsenal. With a few hours in a simple program such as Microsoft Paint, you can create dozens of user scenarios to present to your potential customers and other shareholders. When you're through, you can keep a stack of family photos to show your friends.

The SlideShow application does just that, letting you assemble a sequence of bitmap images in a QUALCOMM BREW Application Resource (BAR) file (see Figure 4-2). You can place multiple BAR files in SlideShow's main directory using the QUALCOMM BREW Application Loader and then choose a specific file's bitmaps to display.

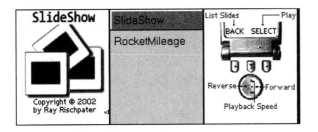

Figure 4-2. The SlideShow application

Once you choose a BAR file, you can flip backward and forward through each image using the left and right keys of the directional pad, or you can play them as an animated movie using the Select key and using the up and down arrows to control the playback speed.

In addition to leveraging the application framework presented earlier in this chapter, the application demonstrates several key instances of the QUALCOMM BREW interfaces, including loading dynamic resources, interacting with the handset's flash file system, and even accepting user input through the IMenuCtl interface (covered in the next chapter).

Using the Application Framework

On the surface, using the application framework is simple: You merely need to create state entry, exit, and event handling functions for each of your application's states. Then, during application startup, simply push your first state on the framework's stack and then let each state's event handler manage transitions to subsequent states.

In the case of SlideShow, little more needs to be done. The application consists of two states: one to show a list of BAR files—slide shows—so you can pick a specific show and another state that shows the bitmaps in the BAR file you select.

To keep things simple, the SlideShow application has three separate implementation files and associated header files that define the public interfaces to each implementation file. The application framework, which you've already seen, is in State.c and State.h. SlideShow's application-specific startup code and application structure are in SlideShow.c and SlideShow.h, and SlideShow's application states are defined in AppStates.c and AppStates.h. To keep from creating a rat's nest of includes, you can create a single file, inc.h, which includes both the application includes and the QUALCOMM BREW interface declarations. Every file (including State.c) includes this global include file.

Examining the SlideShow Startup Code

Broadly speaking, you can divide SlideShow's implementation into two parts: the first being application startup and data management and the second being state machine flow.

The SlideShow application structure contains not just the application's AEEApplet instance and application framework data but a bevy of other information (see Listing 4-7).

Listing 4-7. The Application Structure

```
 1: typedef struct _CApp
 2: {
 3:    AEEApplet a;
 4:    CStatePtr m_state;
 5:
 6:    // screen and font dimensions
 7:    int     m_cx;
 8:    int     m_cy;
 9:    int     m_nFontHeight;
10:    boolean m_bColor;
11:    boolean m_bCopyright;
12:    AEERect m_rc;
13:
14:    // BREW controls
15:    IMenuCtl *m_pIMenu;
16:
17:    // Application globals
18:    char    m_szFile[ MAX_FILE_NAME + 1 ];
19:    int     m_frameDelay;
20: } CApp, *CAppPtr;
```

SlideShow uses only some of these variables, such as the `m_rc` rectangle that denotes the screen size; because applications later in the book will need more of this information, you're learning how to fetch the data here as the application starts up.

SlideShow's application startup code is similar to what you've seen in previous chapters. The system starts the application by calling its `AEEClsCreateInstance` function, which tests the class ID against the class ID used by SlideShow and invokes the QUALCOMM Application Execution Environment (AEE) helper function `AEEApplet_New` if the class ID the system seeks matches the SlideShow application ID. (Because you've seen previous examples of this in Chapters 1 and 3, the listing of `AEEClsCreateInstance` has been omitted here.) In turn, `AEEClsCreateInstance` calls the function `SlideShow_Init`, where SlideShow has its opportunity to initialize its application structure (see Listing 4-8).

Listing 4-8. Initalizing the SlideShow Application

```
 1: /**
 2: * Initializes application structure, creating
 3: * necessary UI components.
 4: * @param CAppPtr pThis: pointer to application structure
 5: * @return AEE_SUCCESS on success, or else EFAILED
 6: */
 7: static int  SlideShow_Init( CAppPtr pThis )
 8: {
 9:   int result = AEE_SUCCESS;
10:   AEEDeviceInfo  dm;
11:
12:   if (pThis->a.m_pIDisplay && pThis->a.m_pIShell)
13:   {
14:     ISHELL_GetDeviceInfo( pThis->a.m_pIShell, &dm );
15:     pThis->m_cx = dm.cxScreen;
16:    pThis->m_cy = dm.cyScreen;
17:
18:     pThis->m_bColor = dm.nColorDepth > 2;
19:     pThis->m_rc.x = 0;
20:     pThis->m_rc.y = 0;
21:     pThis->m_rc.dx = (short)(dm.cxScreen);
22:     pThis->m_rc.dy = (short)(dm.cyScreen);
23:
24:     pThis->m_nFontHeight =
25:       IDISPLAY_GetFontMetrics( pThis->a.m_pIDisplay,
26:                             AEE_FONT_BOLD, NULL, NULL);
27:   }
```

```
28:   else
29:   {
30:     result = EFAILED;
31:   }
32:
33:   if ( result == AEE_SUCCESS )
34:     result = ISHELL_CreateInstance( pThis->a.m_pIShell,
35:                                     AEECLSID_MENUCTL,
36:                                     (void **)&pThis->m_pIMenu );
37:   return result;
38: }
```

Always the optimist, I seed SlideShow_Init's return value with AEE_SUCCESS on line 9. Then, assuming that the application has both a pointer to the IDisplay and IShell instances (line 12), the function interrogates the display to find both its dimensions and color depth (lines 14–22). In the unlikely event that the application was launched without a shell or display, it's unable to continue, and it indicates this by setting its return value to EFAILED.

Given a pointer to a device information structure—an AEEDeviceInfo_IDISPLAY—GetDeviceInfo populates its members. The AEEDeviceInfo structure, defined in AEEShell.h, contains lots of information about the target handset, including its screen size, character set encoding, available random access memory, and availability of specific features such as position determination and Music Industry Digital Interface (MIDI) support. SlideShow_Init simply copies the most commonly used fields of this structure—the screen's bit depth and dimensions—so that the application can use them later when sizing the menu control without needing to call AEEDeviceInfo again. For the sake of convenience, I store the screen size as both a rectangle using the AEERect structure, which stores rectangles as (top, left, height, width) tuples, and the maximum *x* and *y* offsets. Although this wastes 4 bytes of space, it's convenient in many applications because you don't have to constantly reference the individual members of the AEERect m_rc.

Once the function caches the device information, it needs only create an instance of the IMenuCtl that the menu state will use when presenting the list of BAR files. Although it's certainly reasonable in theory to allocate this control in the menu display state itself, it's a good idea in most applications to instantiate all of your user interface elements during application startup because your application won't run correctly if it can't allocate a user interface element. Consequently, by allocating these elements and caching them at application startup, you can be sure they're around when you need them. Moreover, if they're not, you can terminate your application gracefully, at launch, rather than being forced to include code to handle abnormal operation in the event that a control creation fails during a specific state.

Handling Application Events

The event handler takes care of the remainder of the application startup, so let's take a look to see what's there (see Listing 4-9).

Listing 4-9. The SlideShow Application Main Event Handler

```
 1: /**
 2:  * Handles all events for the application
 3:  * @param IApplet *p: pointer to application structure
 4:  * @param AEEEvent eCode: event code
 5:  * @param uint16 wParam: event parameter
 6:  * @param uint32 dwParam: event parameter
 7:  * @return TRUE if application handled event
 8:  */
 9:  static boolean SlideShow_HandleEvent( IApplet *p,
10:                                         AEEEvent eCode,
11:                                         uint16 wParam,
12:                                         uint32 dwParam )
13: {
14:    boolean result = FALSE;
15:    CAppPtr pThis = (CAppPtr)p;
16:
17:    // App Startup --- dismiss the copyright screen on
18:    // any keystroke
19:    if ( pThis->m_bCopyright && eCode == EVT_KEY )
20:    {
21:      HideCopyright( pThis );
22:      pThis->m_bCopyright = FALSE;
23:    }
24:
25:    result = State_HandleEvent( (void *)p, eCode, wParam, dwParam );
26:
27:    if ( !result ) switch (eCode)
28:      {
29:      case EVT_APP_START:
30:        // Show the splash screen
31:        ShowCopyright( pThis );
32:        result = TRUE;
33:        break;
34:
35:      case EVT_COPYRIGHT_END:
36:        // Enter the menu state as the first state
37:        result = State_Push( p,
```

```
38:                              AS_MenuEntry,
39:                              AS_MenuExit,
40:                              AS_MenuHandleEvent );
41:      break;
42:
 43:     default:
44:      break;
45:  }
46:  return result;
57:  }
```

After checking to see if the splash screen is still showing (lines 17–23), the event handler begins by offering application events—once the application is initialized—to the framework on line 25.

Showing the Application Splash Screen

The application-level event handler must handle events that occur before the application framework is initialized and after it's torn down just before the application exits. On lines 17–23 and again on lines 29–40, SlideShow_HandleEvent does just this, managing keystroke and startup events and displaying the application's splash screen.

When the application first launches, it shows its splash screen that describes the application name, purpose, and vendor. By convention, *all* QUALCOMM BREW applications must show an application-specific splash screen for 10 seconds or until any key is pressed to dismiss the splash screen. Although QUALCOMM BREW provides an interface to do this—ISHELL_ShowCopyright—the interface doesn't give the flexibility of showing a graphical splash screen. Instead, you can use the ShowCopyright function to do this (line 31) when the application first receives the EVT_APP_START event. Then, if the user presses any key while the splash screen is visible (recorded by the application member variable m_bCopyright), the event handler hides the splash screen (lines 19–23) using the function HideCopyright.

Regardless of how users dismiss the copyright screen—either via a key press or the splash screen timer—the application receives an EVT_COPYRIGHT_END event, indicating that it should show its first screen. (The ISHELL_ShowCopyright interface sends the EVT_COPYRIGHT_END event, so mimicking this behavior in this function makes it easier to substitute one for the other). The event handler manages this event on lines 35–41, where it pushes the application's first state on the stack.

Subsequent events will be managed by the current state, which receives events through the application framework via the call to State_HandleEvent on line 25.

Note that the application doesn't need to explicitly handle the EVT_APP_STOP event because the current state will handle its own cleanup, and the system will call the application destructor (registered by the original call to AEEApplet_New) when the application terminates. The application destructor, SlideShow_Free, simply frees the previously created menu control using a call to IMENUCTL_Release (see Listing 4-10).

Listing 4-10. Freeing Resources Used by the SlideShow Application

```
 1: /**
 2:  * Frees application structure, releasing
 3:  * necessary UI components.
 4:  * @param IApplet *p: pointer to application structure
 5:  * @return nothing
 6:  */
 7: static void SlideShow_Free( IApplet *p )
 8: {
 9:   CAppPtr pThis = (CAppPtr)p;
10:
11:   if ( pThis->m_pIMenu ) IMENUCTL_Release( pThis->m_pIMenu );
12: }
```

At the first glance, it may seem odd that the splash screen display is handled by the application directly, rather than being an application state. The reason for this is simple: When running the application, you should only see the splash screen *once*, when the application first starts. (You certainly don't want to see the splash screen again when the user exits the application by pressing Clear from the main screen!) Although it's possible to craft clever entry and exit functions for a splash screen state to make sure the splash screen isn't displayed as a result of a pop operation on the state stack, in practice things need not be so complicated.

Displaying the splash screen requires several steps. First, it must load the bitmap for the splash screen. Next, it must draw the bitmap on the display. Then, it must set a timer, indicating when the application should dismiss the splash screen if no key is pressed while it's showing. Finally, it must set the application structure member m_bCopyright to TRUE to indicate that the splash screen is showing. ShowCopyright does all of this (see Listing 4-11).

Listing 4-11. ShowCopyright

```
1: /**
2:  * Shows the copyright screen.
3:  * @param IApplet *p: pointer to application structure
4:  */
5: static void ShowCopyright(CAppPtr pThis )
6: {
7:   IImage *pImage;
8:
9:   // Fetch the copyright image
10:   pImage = ISHELL_LoadResImage( pThis->a.m_pIShell,
11:                                 APP_RES_FILE,
12:                                 IDI_COPYRIGHT );
13:   if (pImage)
14:   {
15:     IIMAGE_Draw( pImage, 0, 0 ) ;
16:
17:     // Free the image
18:     IIMAGE_Release( pImage );
19:     pImage = NULL;
20:   }
21:
22:   // Update the display
23:   IDISPLAY_Update( pThis->a.m_pIDisplay );
24:
25:   // Dismiss the splash screen automatically after a while
26:   ISHELL_SetTimer( pThis->a.m_pIShell,
27:                    APP_COPYRIGHT_CLOSE,
28:                    (PFNNOTIFY)HideCopyright,
29:                    pThis );
30:
31:   // Let everybody know we're showing this.
32:   pThis->m_bCopyright = TRUE;
33: }
```

ShowCopyright contains the largest number of QUALCOMM BREW interface invocations in a function that you've seen so far, so let's look at it line by line. To begin, the function uses the ISHELL_LoadImage interface on lines 10–12 to load the splash screen from the application's resource. ISHELL_LoadImage is one of a family of functions that loads resource data. Others include ISHELL_LoadResString, which you use to load strings from a resource file, and ISHELL_LoadResData, which loads opaque binary data from the resource file. These functions take a reference to the application shell as well as the resource filename and the desired resource identifier—typically a compile-time constant generated by the QUALCOMM BREW Resource Editor when building a resource file. The compile-time constant `APP_RES_FILE` is defined by the QUALCOMM BREW Resource Editor, along with all of the resource identifiers in the resource file, and placed in the file ending in `_res.h` when you build the application resource.

Assuming the splash screen exists—which it should, unless it's not in the resource file or there's not enough memory to load the image—the function draws the image and then frees the memory used by the image on lines 13–20. Because `ISHELL_LoadImage` returns a pointer to an `IImage` instance containing the bitmap to draw, drawing the image itself is as easy as invoking the `IIMAGE_Draw` method on the image and specifying the position of the upper-left corner of the drawing rect-angle. Similarly, to release the resources used by the image, you need only call `IIMAGE_Release`.

NOTE *Releasing the image doesn't clear it from the screen, as you can see from this example. Once the image is drawn to the screen, the bits in the image are effectively copied to the screen memory, so releasing the image doesn't clear the drawn image.*

The function then ensures that the drawn image appears on the screen by calling `IDISPLAY_Update` on the application's screen instance (line 23). Your applica-tions should do this *anytime* they've updated the screen and they want to be sure that the screen is redrawn, such as after a series of drawing instructions or when clearing the screen. Whether the display update occurs immediately when your application invokes `IDISPLAY_Update` or slightly later—say, before the system delivers the next event to your application—depends on the vendor's handset implementation, so you shouldn't make assumptions about precisely when the redraw occurs.

Next, the function uses a system timer to ensure that the splash screen disap-pears after 10 seconds using the `ISHELL_SetTimer` interface on lines 26–29. The system calls a timer's callback function when the timer elapses, passing it the pre-scribed argument. The `ISHELL_SetTimer` function takes four arguments: an instance of the shell, the duration before the timer elapses in milliseconds, the function to invoke when the timer elapses, and a pointer to pass to the function when it's called. Thus, this call tells the system to call the function `HideCopyright` after `APP_COPYRIGHT_CLOSE` milliseconds, passing it a pointer to the application structure `pThis`. `APP_COPYRIGHT_CLOSE` is defined in SlideShow.h to be 10 seconds on the handset (and a significantly shorter time on the emulator to help the patience impaired when debugging).

Finally, the function sets the flag m_bCopyright so the event handler knows that the splash screen is showing.

HideCopyright is simpler because it needs to only clear m_bCopyright, cancel the timer if the user pressed a key, and post an event to the application saying that the splash screen has been dismissed (see Listing 4-12).

Listing 4-12. Hiding the Copyright Screen

```
 1: /**
 2:  * Hides the copyright screen.
 3:  * @param IApplet *p: pointer to application structure
 4:  */
 5: static void HideCopyright(CAppPtr pThis)
 6: {
 7:   // We're done with the copyright screen.
 8:   pThis->m_bCopyright = FALSE;
 9:
10:   // Cancel the timer, in case we got here on a keypress.
11:   ISHELL_CancelTimer( pThis->a.m_pIShell,
12:                       (PFNNOTIFY)HideCopyright,
13:                       pThis );
14:
15:   // Tell the app that the copyright screen was over.
16:   ISHELL_PostEvent( pThis->a.m_pIShell,
17:                     AEECLSID_SLIDESHOW,
18:                     EVT_COPYRIGHT_END, 0, 0 );
19: }
```

Clearing the m_bCopyright flag occurs on line 8. On lines 11–13, the function clears the timer set by ShowCopyright. The system keeps a list of timers indexed by the timer function and timer argument pointer, so canceling a timer is simply a matter of specifying these to the ISHELL_CancelTimer function. It's okay to cancel a timer that has already elapsed: The system simply ignores the request because there's no timer to cancel.

TIP   *When your application exits and is released, all of your application's timers and callbacks will be cancelled.*

Finally, the function needs to let the application's event handler know that the splash screen has been dismissed; it does this on lines 16–18 by sending an EVT_COPYRIGHT_END event to the application. Posting an event is an asynchronous operation: The event is posted to the system's event queue, and the system will call the application's event handler at the next time it deems appropriate. (This is in contrast to ISHELL_SendEvent, which invokes the application's event handler *immediately*, returning control to the calling function only after the event has been handled by the application and the system.) When posting—or sending—an event, you must specify the application class ID to receive the event, as well as the event code and event arguments.

Examining the Menu State in SlideShow

The first state the application enters is the menu state, presenting you with the list of files from which to choose. The application enters this state when it first launches or after it receives a resume event when being suspended in the menu state. In each case, the setup is the same because when the state is exited or suspended, the menu is torn down to release as much of the phone's resources as possible.

Entering the Menu State

As the application enters the menu state, it invokes the AS_MenuEntry function to initialize and show the menu of resource files (see Listing 4-13).

Listing 4-13. Presenting the Menu of Slide Shows

```
 1: /**
 2:  * Prepares user interface for menu state.
 3:  * Initializes menu, sets menu rectangle to screen,
 4:  * @param void *p: this applicaton
 5:  * @param EStateChange change: why we entered this state
 6:  * @return nothing
 7:  */
 8: void AS_MenuEntry( void *p,
 9:                    EStateChange change )
10: {
11:   CAppPtr pThis = (CAppPtr)p;
12:
13:   UNUSED( change );
14:   ASSERT( pThis && pThis->m_pIMenu );
```

```
15:
16:    // Clear the display
17:    IDISPLAY_ClearScreen( pThis->a.m_pIDisplay );
18:
19:    // Reset the menu
20:    IMENUCTL_Reset( pThis->m_pIMenu );
21:
22:    // Set the menu's bounds
23:    IMENUCTL_SetRect( pThis->m_pIMenu, &pThis->m_rc );
24:
25:    // Populate the menu
26:    FillMenu( pThis );
27:
28:    // Activate the menu & update screen
29:    IMENUCTL_SetActive( pThis->m_pIMenu, TRUE );
30:    IDISPLAY_Update( pThis->a.m_pIDisplay );
31: }
```

Line 13 simply dismisses compiler warnings regarding unused variables with the UNUSED macro defined in utils.h. This macro works with both the Microsoft Visual Studio C compiler and the ARM C compiler, unlike more conventional #pragma instructions that are less portable. In a similar vein, line 14 tests the incoming variables in debug builds to ensure that both the application structure and the menu control are available.

Line 15 clears the display, which until now was showing the application splash screen.

Line 20 resets the menu control, ensuring that it contains no elements and default parameters at the outset. Resetting interface controls before using them is a good idea because otherwise they may contain values from their last invocation, especially if your application shares one control among multiple states. After resetting the menu, line 23 sets the menu's bounds to match the screen's bounds using IMENUCTL_SetRect and the screen dimensions obtained in SlideShow_Init so that the menu fills the entire display.

Next, the application populates the menu with the list of available files by calling the function FillMenu, which you'll learn about shortly (line 26). Finally, the function activates the menu control, so it knows it should process system events, and then updates the display to show the menu on lines 29–30.

The FillMenu function demonstrates one of QUALCOMM BREW's great strengths: Objects familiar to software developers from other platforms have familiar interfaces. In this case, the object in question is the file system because FillMenu must walk the list of file entries in the application's directory to find any resource files. Not surprisingly, QUALCOMM BREW provides you with both a file manager interface (IFileMgr) and a corresponding enumeration method for doing this (see Listing 4-14).

Listing 4-14. Obtaining a List of Files in a Directory

```
 1: /**
 2:  * Populates the menu with the list of slide shows.
 3:  * @param CAppPtr pThis: the application
 4:  * @return nothing
 5:  */
 6: static void FillMenu( CAppPtr pThis )
 7: {
 8:   IFileMgr *pIFileMgr;
 9:   FileInfo info;
10:   AECHAR wszBuff[ MAX_FILE_NAME + 1 ];
11:   uint16 nItem = 1;
12:   int result;
13:
14:   // Setup the file manager instance
15:   result = ISHELL_CreateInstance( pThis->a.m_pIShell,
16:                                   AEECLSID_FILEMGR,
17:                                   (void **)&pIFileMgr );
18:
19:   // Enumerate the list of .bar files
20:   if ( pIFileMgr )
21:   {
22:     // Begin enumeration
23:     if ( SUCCESS == IFILEMGR_EnumInit( pIFileMgr, "", FALSE ) )
24:     {
25:       while ( IFILEMGR_EnumNext( pIFileMgr, &info ) )
26:       {
27:         // We're interested in files that end in .bar
28:         if ( STRENDS( ".bar", info.szName ) )
29:         {
30:           // None was loaded, so create our own
31:           // Drop the .bar --- it looks hokey.
32:           info.szName[ STRLEN( info.szName ) - 4 ] = '\000';
33:
34:           // convert to a wide string
35:           STRTOWSTR( info.szName, wszBuff, MAX_FILE_NAME + 1 );
36:
37:           // Add it to the menu
38:           IMENUCTL_AddItem( pThis->m_pIMenu,
39:                             NULL, // Resource file for item
40:                             0,    // Don't use the resource file
41:                             nItem++,
42:                             wszBuff,
```

```
43:                              (uint32)0 );  // Item data
44:          } // add file name to menu
45:        } // file name enumeration
46:      } // enumeration guard
47:
48:      // Clean up
49:      IFILEMGR_Release( pIFileMgr );
50:    } // pIFileMgr guard
51:
52:  if ( nItem == 1 )
53:  {
54:      // Menu addition failed.
55:      // But we always have our .bar, so add it manually.
56:      // convert to a wide string
57:      STRTOWSTR( "SlideShow", wszBuff, MAX_FILE_NAME + 1 );
58:
59:      // Add it to the menu
60:      IMENUCTL_AddItem( pThis->m_pIMenu,
61:                        NULL, // Resource file for item
62:                        0,    // Don't use the resource file
63:                        nItem++,
64:                        wszBuff,
65:                        (uint32)0 );  // Item data
66:
67:    } // Add what is always there
68: }
```

Because you'll see more than you probably ever wanted to know about IMenuCtl in the following chapter, let's look closely only at the other functions in FillMenu. FillMenu begins by creating an instance of IFileMgr (line 20), which it uses to iterate over the directory entries in the application directory. It's okay if this creation fails, however, because you can be confident that if the application reaches this point, there's at least one resource file available: the application's (lines 52–67).

Assuming the shell can provide a file manager instance, line 23 initializes the file system enumerator. IFILEMGR_EnumInit takes three arguments: the IFileMgr to use, the directory over which to enumerate, and whether it should include directory names in its iteration. Thus, line 23 instructs pIFileMgr to iterate over the application's home directory, ignoring any subdirectories that might exist.

Assuming this is successful—which it should always be, unless your application's Module Information File (MIF) file is incorrect—the function enters the while loop spanning lines 25–45. For each filename the enumerator returns, the function tests it to see if it ends in the string *.bar*, and if it does, adds the filename to the menu. Each pass through the loop, the call to IFILEMGR_EnumNext fills the FileInfo structure info with a copy of the information about the next file in the directory, returning TRUE as long as a file is found.

Testing the filename is easy; the function simply uses the STRENDS helper function to test the filename, found in the szName member of the FileInfo structure (line 28). If the filename ends in *.bar*, line 32 pretties up the filename, removing the filename suffix.

Next, the function converts the string to a multibyte character using STRTOWSTR on line 35 because all of the interface controls require text in multibyte character strings (AEECHAR) to provide support for multiple languages. Finally, the function adds the filename in multibyte format to the menu on lines 38–43, specifying the item's text and numeric identifier.

The function invokes the failure case—lines 52–67—if the IFileMgr can't be created or if the application directory can't be enumerated. The application logic is the same as within the confines of the while loop on lines 25–45, first converting the filename (the application's resource file) to a wide string and then adding it to the menu.

Handling Events in the Menu State

The menu state's event handler must do two things: share incoming events with the IMenuCtl and transition to the slide state to show the bitmaps in the selected resource file when you select a specific menu item (see Listing 4-15).

Listing 4-15. Handling Events for the Menu State

```
 1: /**
 2:  * Handles events for the menu state
 3:  * @param void *p: this applicaton
 4:  * @param AEEEvent eCode: event code
 5:  * @param uint16 wParam: event parameter
 6:  * @param uint32 dwParam: event parameter
 7:  * @return TRUE if application handled event
 8:  */
 9: boolean AS_MenuHandleEvent( void *p,
10:                            AEEEvent eCode,
11:                            uint16 wParam, uint32 dwParam)
12: {
13:   CAppPtr pThis = (CAppPtr)p;
14:   boolean result = FALSE;
15:   CtlAddItem menuItem;
16:
```

```
17:    ASSERT( pThis && pThis->m_pIMenu );
18:
19:    // Give the control the first crack at it
20:    result = IMENUCTL_HandleEvent( pThis->m_pIMenu,
21:                                    eCode,
22:                                    wParam,
23:                                    dwParam );
24:
25:    if ( !result ) switch ( eCode )
26:    {
27:      case EVT_COMMAND:
28:        // Find the filename of the selected resource
29:        IMENUCTL_GetItem( pThis->m_pIMenu,
30:                          wParam,
31:                          &menuItem );
32:        WSTRTOSTR( menuItem.pText, pThis->m_szFile, MAX_FILE_NAME + 1);
33:        STRCAT( pThis->m_szFile, ".bar" );
34:
35:        // Start the slide show
36:        result = State_Push( p,
37:                             AS_SlideEntry,
38:                             AS_SlideExit,
39:                             AS_SlideHandleEvent );
40:        break;
41:
42:    }
43:
44:    return result;
45: }
```

Lines 20–23 share incoming events with the menu event, calling
IMENUCTL_HandleEvent to pass the event to the menu control. If the menu control
handles the event, the following switch statement is ignored, and the event
handler simply returns.

The switch statement, on lines 25–42, is admittedly overkill because it tests
only a single case, EVT_COMMAND. The menu control generates this event when you
press the Select key on a menu item. Line 29 extracts the contents of the selected
menu item—corresponding to a specific resource file's name—from the menu.
Line 32 then converts this string from a multibyte string to a conventional C string,
stashing the results in the application structure's m_szFile member so that the
slide state will know which resource file you chose when it started. Finally, on
lines 36–39, the event handler uses the application framework to transition to the
slide state.

Exiting the Menu State

Once you select an item on the menu and the menu state's event handler has pro-
cessed the EVT_COMMAND event and called State_Push to transition to the slide state,
the menu state's exit function AS_MenuExit is invoked. This function simply
clears the menu and disables it, releasing memory for the next state (see
Listing 4-16).

Listing 4-16. Exiting the Menu State

```
 1: /**
 2:  * Exits the user interface for menu state.
 3:  * Removes all menu entries and deactivates the menu
 4:  * @param void *p: this applicaton
 5:  * @param EStateChange change: why we exited this state
 6:  * @return nothing
 7:  */
 8: void AS_MenuExit( void *p,
 9:                   EStateChange change )
10: {
11:   CAppPtr pThis = (CAppPtr)p;
12:
13:   UNUSED( change );
14:
15:   ASSERT( pThis && pThis->m_pIMenu );
16:
17:   // Reset the menu
18:   IMENUCTL_Reset( pThis->m_pIMenu );
19:
20:   // Deactivate this menu
21:   IMENUCTL_SetActive( pThis->m_pIMenu, FALSE );
22: }
```

The only interesting work this function does is on lines 18 and 21, where the
function first resets the menu control and then deactivates it.

Examining the Slide State in SlideShow

The slide state is slightly more complex than the menu state because it must keep
information about the next slide to show and the status of animation between
calls to the state's event handler. Although QUALCOMM BREW provides image
animation features that you'll encounter in later chapters, SlideShow won't use
these features because the animation support assumes that an animated image is

a series of animation frames residing as adjacent rectangles on a long bitmap, much like a roll of film (but turned on its side). Consequently, SlideShow uses the memory reserved for state variables and timers to provide animation.

Central to the slide state is the CSlideShow structure:

```
1: typedef struct _CSlideShow
2: {
3:    char    *m_szFile;
4:    uint16  m_next;
5:    uint16  m_timer;
6:    int8    m_dir;
7:    boolean m_bAnimate;
8: } CSlideShow, *CSlideShowPtr;
```

This structure keeps a copy of the pointer to the slide show's resource file, an integer indicating the next slide that should be shown, the animation delay, the direction of animation, and whether the slide show is animating, respectively.

The ShowNextSlide function extensively uses this structure because it determines what needs to be done as the animation timer elapses or a key is pressed. This function is invoked both during entry into the slide state and by the slide state's event handler (see Listing 4-17).

Listing 4-17. Showing the Next Slide

```
 1: /**
 2:  * Shows the next slide.
 3:  * Sets a timer for animation if necessary.
 4:  * @param void *p: this applicaton
 5:  * @return nothing
 6:  */
 7: static void ShowNextSlide( void *p )
 8: {
 9:    CAppPtr pThis = (CAppPtr)p;
10:    CStatePtr pState;
11:    CSlideShowPtr pInfo;
12:
13:    ASSERT( pThis );
14:    pState = State_GetCurrentState( pThis );
15:    ASSERT( pState );
16:
17:    // Clear the display
18:    IDISPLAY_ClearScreen( pThis->a.m_pIDisplay );
19:
```

```
20:    if ( ( pinfo = State_GetStateData( pState ) ) != NULL  )
21:    {
22:      IImage *pImage;
23:
24:      // Point to the current image
25:      pInfo->m_next += pInfo->m_dir;
26:      if ( pInfo->m_next == 0 )
27:      {
28:        pInfo->m_next = 1;
29:        pInfo->m_dir = 1;
30:      }
31:
32:      // Load the bitmap
33:      pImage = ISHELL_LoadResImage( pThis->a.m_pIShell,
34:                                    pInfo->m_szFile,
35:                                    pInfo->m_next );
36:
37:      // Wrap back around to first image if nothing is shown
38:      if ( !pImage )
39:      {
40:        pInfo->m_next = 1;
41:        pImage = ISHELL_LoadResImage( pThis->a.m_pIShell,
42:                                      pInfo->m_szFile,
43:                                      pInfo->m_next );
44:      } // Do we have an image? no? then wrap around
45:
46:      // Display the bitmap
47:      if (pImage)
48:      {
49:        IIMAGE_Draw( pImage, 0, 0 ) ;
50:
51:        // Free the image
52:        IIMAGE_Release( pImage );
53:        pImage = NULL;
54:      } // Do we have an image
55:
56:    // Update the screen
57:    IDISPLAY_Update( pThis->a.m_pIDisplay );
58:
59:    // Set the timer to do it again if necessary
60:    if ( pInfo->m_bAnimate != 0 )
61:      ISHELL_SetTimer( pThis->a.m_pIShell,
62:                       pInfo->m_timer,
63:                       (PFNNOTIFY) ShowNextSlide,
```

```
64:                          pThis );
65:     } // Do we have valid slide info?
66:   } // Do we have valid state data?
67: }
```

This function gets interesting on line 20, where it obtains a pointer to the state's `CSlideShow` information in `pInfo`. It then calculates the resource ID of the next bitmap to load by incrementing or decrementing `pInfo->m_next` based on the value of `pInfo->m_dir`. Lines 26–30 guard against trying to wrap below the first bitmap in the resource by switching playback to the forward direction when the first slide is reached (`pInfo->m_next` is equal to zero). Lines 33–35 try to load the image—this time from the specified resource file, not the application resource—using the current image's ID. If this fails, the function assumes it has reached the end of the bitmaps to show, resets the image counter, and loads the first image on lines 38–44.

With the image to draw now in `pImage`, the function draws the image (line 48) and releases the resources used by the image (lines 52–53). It then updates the screen (line 57) and sets a timer to draw the next image if the animation flag `pInfo->m_bAnimate` is `TRUE`.

As with the menu state before it, the slide state doesn't differentiate between entry and exit operations because of the manipulation of the state stack or between suspend and resume events. State operation is identical in either state, reflecting the fact that on exiting the state for any reason, the slide state frees all resources and cancels the animation timer, waiting for the next state entry to begin showing slides again.

NOTE   *This behavior works well for an application such as this for viewing developer prototypes, but it might not be what an end user expects when viewing an animation of, say, personal slides when she receives a phone call. After the phone call, she might well expect her slide show to pick up where it left off before the call. This is precisely the kind of question you can answer with prototypes, where you can gauge your user's response.*

Entering the Slide State

When the menu state pushes the slide state onto the application framework's stack, the framework calls `AS_SlideEntry`, which allocates space for the `CSlideShow` structure (see Listing 4-18).

Listing 4-18. Entering the Slide Show State

```
 1: /**
 2:  * Prepares user interface for slide show state
 3:  * Shows the first slide.
 4:  * @param void *p: this applicaton
 5:  * @param EStateChange change: why we entered this state
 6:  * @return nothing
 7:  */
 8: void AS_SlideEntry( void *p,
 9:                     EStateChange change )
10: {
11:   CAppPtr pThis = (CAppPtr)p;
12:   CStatePtr pState;
13:   CSlideShowPtr pInfo;
13:   UNUSED( change );
14:
15:   pState = State_GetCurrentState( pThis );
16:   ASSERT( pThis && pState);
17:
18:   // Allocate memory for the state info
19:   pInfo = MALLOC( sizeof( CSlideShow ) );
20:   if ( pInfo )
21:   {
22:     SetStateData( pState, pInfo );
23:     pInfo->m_szFile = pThis->m_szFile;
24:     pInfo->m_next = 0;
25:     pInfo->m_timer = pThis->m_frameDelay ?
26:     pThis->m_frameDelay : TIMER_DEFAULT;
27:     pInfo->m_dir = 1;
28:     pInfo->m_bAnimate = FALSE;
29:     // Show this slide
30:     ShowNextSlide( p );
31:   }
32: }
```

This function is primarily bookkeeping. First, it uses MALLOC to allocate space for the CSlideShow structure on line 19 and then (assuming the memory allocation succeeds) initializes the state's data member and the fields of the CSlideShow structure to reasonable defaults on lines 22–28. Note especially that the m_szFile member of the state's CSlideShow structure is a copy of the *pointer* to the application's storage for the resource filename—not a copy of the filename itself. Because the state doesn't need to change the filename at any point, doing this is memory efficient while also ensuring readability in ShowNextSlide when it must access the resource file. Finally, the function updates the screen by drawing the first slide in the sequence by calling ShowNextSlide.

Handling Events in the Slide State

The slide state's event handler must handle keystroke events for the Select key to start and stop animation, as well as the directional pad to select the previous or next slide and control the animation speed. AS_HandleEvent is one of the longer functions in AppStates.c, but it really doesn't do much besides manipulate the contents of the state variables (see Listing 4-19).

Listing 4-19. Handling Events in the Slide Show State

```
 1: /**
 2:  * Handles events for the menu state
 3:  * @param void *p: this applicaton
 4:  * @param AEEEvent eCode: event code
 5:  * @param uint16 wParam: event parameter
 6:  * @param uint32 dwParam: event parameter
 7:  * @return TRUE if application handled event
 8:  */
 9:  boolean AS_SlideHandleEvent( void *p,
10:                                 AEEEvent eCode,
11:                                 uint16 wParam, uint32 dwParam)
12: {
13:    CAppPtr pThis = (CAppPtr)p;
14:    CStatePtr pState;
15:    CSlideShowPtr pInfo;
16:    boolean result = FALSE;
17:
18:    ASSERT( pThis );
19:
20:    pState = State_GetCurrentState( pThis );
21:    ASSERT( pState );
22:
23:    pInfo = GetStateData( pState );
24:
25:    if ( pInfo ) switch ( eCode )
26:    {
27:      case EVT_KEY:
28:        switch( wParam )
29:        {
```

```
30:        case AVK_SELECT:
31:          pInfo->m_bAnimate = !pInfo->m_bAnimate;
32:          ShowNextSlide( p );
33:          result = TRUE;
34:          break;
35:
36:        case AVK_UP:
37:          if ( pInfo->m_timer > TIMER_MINIMUM )
38:          {
39:            pInfo->m_timer /= 2;
40:            ISHELL_CancelTimer( pThis->a.m_pIShell,
41:                              (PFNNOTIFY) ShowNextSlide,
42:                              pThis );
43:            ShowNextSlide( p );
44:            result = TRUE;
45:          }
46:          break;
47:
48:        case AVK_DOWN:
49:          if ( pInfo->m_timer && pInfo->m_timer < TIMER_DEFAULT )
50:          {
51:            pInfo->m_timer *= 2;
52:            ISHELL_CancelTimer( pThis->a.m_pIShell,
53:                              (PFNNOTIFY) ShowNextSlide,
54:                              pThis );
55:            ShowNextSlide( p );
56:            result = TRUE;
57:          }
58:          break;
59:
60:        case AVK_LEFT:
61:          ISHELL_CancelTimer( pThis->a.m_pIShell,
62:                            (PFNNOTIFY) ShowNextSlide,
63:                            pThis );
64:          // Point to the currently displayed frame
65:          pInfo->m_dir = -1;
66:          ShowNextSlide( p );
67:          result = TRUE;
68:          break;
69:
70:        case AVK_RIGHT:
71:          ISHELL_CancelTimer( pThis->a.m_pIShell,
72:                            (PFNNOTIFY) ShowNextSlide,
73:                            pThis );
```

```
74:            pInfo->m_dir = 1;
75:            ShowNextSlide( p );
76:            result = TRUE;
77:            break;
78:        }
79:        break;
80:    }
81:    return result;
82: }
```

Rather than examine this function on a case-by-case basis, this section hits the highlights because by now you have the general idea of how it works. For a given keystroke, the handler must mutate the pInfo structure to represent the behavior desired by the user. The Select key (lines 30–34) toggles the m_bAnimate flag in pInfo, letting the timer expire of its own accord after displaying an additional frame. The up and down keys (lines 36–58) adjust the delay between successive frames by factors of 2, pinning the resulting values between the compile-time constants TIMER_MINIMUM and TIMER_DEFAULT (one-eighth of a second and a trifle more than two seconds, respectively). After adjusting the frame rate, these cases cancel the timer and immediately display the next frame, ensuring that you receive prompt feedback regarding the animation speed change you requested. Finally, the left and right keys (lines 60–77) cancel the animation timer and toggle the value of m_dir in pInfo, selecting between reverse and forward play (or the previous or next slide if no animation is taking place).

One thing the event handler doesn't have to do is handle navigation back to the menu state: It gets that for free from the application framework's event handler, State_HandleEvent, described previously.

Exiting the Slide State

Exiting the slide state is an exercise in resource reclamation, as you can see in AS_SlideExit (see Listing 4-20).

Listing 4-20. AS_SlideExit

```
1: /**
2:  * Tears down the UI for the slide show.
3:  * Cancels the animation timer.
4:  * @param void *p: this applicaton
5:  * @param EStateChange change: why we exited this state
6:  * @return nothing
7:  */
```

```
 8:  void AS_SlideExit( void *p,
 9:                         EStateChange change )
10: {
11:    CAppPtr pThis = (CAppPtr)p;
12:    CStatePtr pState;
13:    CSlideShowPtr pInfo;
14:
15:    UNUSED( change );
16:
17:    pState = State_GetCurrentState( pThis );
18:    ASSERT( pThis && pState);
19:    pInfo = GetStateData( pState );
20:
21:    // Free the state data
22:    if ( pInfo )
23:    {
24:      // Save the current playback frame rate
25:      pThis->m_frameDelay = pInfo->m_timer;
26:
27:      FREE( pInfo );
28:      SetStateData( pState, NULL );
29:    }
30:
31:    // Cancel the animation timer
32:    ISHELL_CancelTimer( pThis->a.m_pIShell,
33:                          (PFNNOTIFY) ShowNextSlide,
34:                          pThis );
35: }
```

The function begins by getting a pointer to the current state (line 17) and its state variables (line 19). Assuming the state has a state variable—it should, but it never hurts to be sure, and it definitely hurts to dereference a null pointer!—it stashes the currently selected animation speed in the application's structure on line 25 and then frees the state's variable space on line 27. Line 28 nulls out the state's variable pointer, ensuring that the debugging scaffolding in State.c doesn't complain about potential memory leaks. Finally, on lines 32–34, the function cancels the animation timer.

Summary

This chapter covered the following key points:

- Your application must provide an event handler to respond to events that the system delivers from the event pump.

- Because the QUALCOMM BREW environment is single-threaded, all of your application's operation (save initialization and termination) centers on managing the events your application receives.

- System events consist of an event code and two arguments, one a single word and one a double word.

- Your application must be able to handle the EVT_APP_START, EVT_APP_STOP, EVT_SUSPEND, and EVT_RESUME events.

- Representing your application as a sequence of states, with one state for each application screen, gives you a good structure in which to develop your application and provide predictable application flow to your users.

- Using an application framework that encapsulates the state machine encourages reuse and raises the likelihood that subsequent applications using the same state machine will pass external verification because you use a minimum of new code in each application.

Interacting with the User

INTERACTING WITH THE user is a primary responsibility for any application. QUALCOMM BREW provides the usual gamut of user input/output controls, including static and mutable text controls, a versatile menu control, custom controls for entering the time and date, and even a simple Hypertext Markup Language (HTML) viewer you can use to present documents formatted in simple HTML. This chapter shows you the most common controls you'll encounter in QUALCOMM BREW, as well as how to extend the previous chapter's framework to simplify handling your application's controls.

Understanding Modes of User Interaction

Applications running under QUALCOMM BREW can interact with the user in three primary means: visually, aurally, and tactilely. Each has specific strengths and weaknesses. More important, users expect certain kinds of interaction from their phone to have specific meanings—for example, a vibration may be appropriate to notify the user of an incoming message or to add excitement to a game but isn't appropriate in other settings, such as when reporting the successful completion of a network transaction.

Using the Display and Keyboard to Interact with the User

The handset display and keypad are the primary mediums by which your application will interact with the user. Your application will display text and graphics, and it will accept user input via the keys and direction pad.

When designing applications for wireless handsets, you need to keep several things in mind. First, wireless handsets are *small*. A handset's display isn't suited to presenting a great deal of information at once, and the keypad constrains your ability to enter a great deal of text information. Consequently, it's best to set up the interface of your application to use icons rather than text, wherever possible, and rely on menus and canned text to speed text input.

NOTE *Even with today's rapid-entry systems such as Motorola's iTap and Tegic's T9, text input can still be a frustrating and time-consuming experience, especially for applications that rely on text, such as messaging and chat applications. Applications requiring a great deal of text input should provide menus with customizable quick-text entries for common phrases.*

There are few user interface conventions for QUALCOMM BREW applications, but those that exist are largely immutable:

- All applications should begin with a full-screen splash screen that identifies the application. This splash screen should appear for 10 seconds or until the user presses a key.

- From any screen, the Clear key should bring the user to the logical previous screen. If you're viewing the application's main screen, Clear should exit the application.

- In virtually all applications, there should be only one input control (such as an input line or full-screen menu) on the display at once. (Notable exceptions include the text control with a soft key menu discussed in the section "Using the ITextCtl Control" and applications with a browser-like interface that can show more than one selectable hyperlink at once.)

- From any screen, the Select key should accept a current action, such as selecting a menu choice or completing text input, and it should bring the user to the next logical screen.

In a sense, the Clear and Select keys are analogous to the Back and Next buttons on a Web browser: The Clear key brings you *back* to the item you've just seen, and the Select key brings you to the next screen, as if you selected a link in a browser.

A notable exception to this user flow that you must keep in mind is how network activity and other status dialog boxes change application flow. For example, consider a stock quote application, where you enter a stock ticker symbol and then the application makes a network request to obtain the current value of the stock. When viewing the results of a query, pressing Clear should show you the stock ticker input screen, *not* the network status display. This is generally true for any application that includes status annunciators or screens; pressing Clear should bring you to the step prior to the action that requires a status display.

You have two choices for generating text and images for the display: using the QUALCOMM BREW display controls (discussed in this chapter) or using the raw graphics interfaces, which are implemented in classes such as IDisplay and IGraphics and are covered in Chapter 8, "Drawing Graphics."

Some controls, such as the IStatic control, only display text and don't accept user input. Most, however, such as the IMenuCtl control, both display things on the screen and accept input from the user. When using these controls, your application's event handler shares incoming events with the control and looks for EVT_COMMAND events that signal events from the control that your application must process, such as a menu selection or the completion of text input.

In addition to these controls, the IShell interface provides the ISHELL_Message and ISHELL_MessageBox functions to display a simple text dialog box with a title and text message on the screen. In practice, these functions are good when writing test programs or when debugging.

Using Audio to Interact with the User

QUALCOMM BREW provides support for rich audio, including playing files in MP3, MIDI, and QCP formats, as well as playing individual tones, including the Dual-Tone Multi-Frequency (DTMF) tones you hear when dialing a touch-tone phone.

NOTE *MP3 stands for Moving Pictures Expert Group Audio Layer 3, and MIDI stands for Music Industry Digital Interface.*

Most users expect sound support for specific purposes, including providing additional feedback for an alert or alarm (perhaps for an appointment or an incoming message), setting the mood in a game, and providing status in a game. Using QUALCOMM BREW's support for WAV, MP3, and QCP, you can provide sampled sounds, such as those you hear on a computer, including the ability to play back voice samples for simple vocal feedback. The MIDI format, on the other hand, is best used to play simple songs or to provide additional ring tones to handsets. Of course, you can also use simple tones to provide audio feedback when selecting menu items and the like.

Because wireless handsets are often used in public settings, it's important your application provides users with the ability to quickly silence sounds when using your application. Not all handsets map a user's sound settings in the Original Equipment Manufacturer's (OEM) settings panels to applications running under QUALCOMM BREW, so it's important you let users silence your application when using it in some situations, such as while in a meeting or in a movie theater.

QUALCOMM BREW provides two interfaces to the handset to support sound, aptly named the ISound and ISoundPlayer interfaces. You use the ISound interface to perform system management functions such as setting the sound volume and playing single or DTMF tones, and you use the ISoundPlayer interface to play more complex sounds asynchronously, such as MP3 or MIDI sound files. Because OEMs make the decision as to which sound formats a specific handset can support, it's important you architect your application to support sound files of the appropriate format for specific handsets. Chapter 9, "Playing with Sounds," discusses the ISound and ISoundPlayer controls in detail.

Using Tactile Feedback to Interact with the User

QUALCOMM BREW provides two tactile (touch) interfaces. The first is immediately obvious: the keypad. Your application can use the keypad in conjunction with the input controls to accept input, or you can look for specific key presses in your application's event handler by waiting for and intercepting EVT_KEY events, as you saw in the SlideShow program in the previous chapter. Input controls are best used for specific kinds of user input, and managing raw keyboard events is best when writing custom input controls or in a game, where a single key press maps to a distinct change in application flow.

In addition to being able to accept these tactile events, QUALCOMM BREW also provides the ability to activate the built-in vibration device found in most wireless handsets today. Using the ISOUND_Vibrate method, you can have the handset vibrate for a specific amount of time; using the ISOUND_StopVibrate method, you can cancel a current vibration. Vibration alerts can provide extra feedback in games or provide notification of exceptional events (such as a message receipt) when the user has silenced audio from your application.

Using the QUALCOMM BREW Controls

Within the QUALCOMM BREW inheritance hierarchy, all of the QUALCOMM BREW user interface controls inherit from the IControl interface. The IControl interface is abstract; that is, you can't instantiate an IControl interface for your own use. Instead, you use the IControl interfaces to invoke methods on an arbitrary control, such as when you have an array containing different kinds of controls.

The `IControl` interface provides the following methods, which all controls implement:

You use the `ICONTROL_HandleEvent` method to send an event to the control. You should use this method to forward all incoming events to controls before you handle them and only handle events that aren't handled by the control. `ICONTROL_HandleEvent` returns `TRUE` if the control handled the event and `FALSE` if the application or another control should handle the event.

You use the `ICONTROL_Redraw` method to force a control to redraw itself on the display, such as after setting its contents.

You use the `ICONTROL_SetActive` method to give focus to a control. Only the active control will process the events you pass it when calling `ICONTROL_HandleEvent`.

You use the `ICONTROL_IsActive` method to determine whether the specified control is active—that is, whether it will process the events handed to it by calling `ICONTROL_HandleEvent`.

You use the `ICONTROL_SetRect` method to set the display rectangle for the specified control.

You use the `ICONTROL_GetRect` method to get the display rectangle for the specified control.

You use the `ICONTROL_SetProperties` method to set a control's properties. Every control has up to 32 control-specific properties, each represented by a bit in a 4-byte bitfield. When you first create a control using `ISHELL_CreateInstance`, all of its properties are set to 0. Properties indicate specific attributes of a control, such as whether a text control is single-line or multiline.

You use the `ICONTROL_GetProperties` method to determine the settings of the properties for the indicated control.

You use the `ICONTROL_Reset` method to instruct a control to free its under-lying resources and clear its active flag so that it will no longer process any events it receives.

Of course, if you know the type of a specific control, you may invoke that control's method directly. For example, if you're working with the `IMenuCtl` instance pIMenu, the following two lines of code are equivalent:

```
1:  ICONTROL_Reset( pIMenu );
2:  IMENUCTL_Reset( pIMenu );
```

A common use for the `IControl` interface is when managing an array of controls, any one of which may be active, without your application needing to track the currently active control.

The following discussion uses snippets of code, rather than entire applications, to demonstrate the use of each control. For the purposes of the discussion, this chapter continues to use the application structure introduced in the previous chapter to contain an application's global data, with a single modification:

```
 1: typedef struct _CApp
 2: {
 3:   AEEApplet    a;
 4:   CStatePtr    m_state;
 5:   boolean      m_bSplashing;
 6:
 7:   // screen and font dimensions
 8:   int          m_cx;
 9:   int          m_cy;
10:   int          m_colorDepth;
11:   int          m_nFontHeight;
12:   Boolean      m_bInit;
13:   Boolean      m_bColor;
14:   AEERect      m_rc;
15:   // Application controls
16:   IControl     *m_apControl[ MAX_NUM_CONTROLS ];
17: } CApp, *CAppPtr;
```

The field `m_apControl` provides a central repository for the application's controls. The slots in this array are initialized as the application starts and accessed throughout the application, such as during the application's event handler.

To create a control, you simply use `ISHELL_CreateInstance`, passing it the class ID of the desired control. For example, to create an `IStatic` control, use the following code:

```
1: /*
2:  *  In your application's initialization routine
3:  */
4:
5: // Create an instance of an IStatic text control
6: if ( ISHELL_CreateInstance( pThis->a.m_piShell,
7:                                 AEECLSID_STATIC,
8:      (void **)&(pThis->m_apControl[0])) != SUCCESS)
9:    return;
```

When creating a control, it's best to do so when the application launches to ensure that there's enough memory for the application to execute correctly. Once created, your control can remain inactive and invisible, and you need only set its contents and properties when you use the control.

TIP *Preallocation is a good defensive programming strategy. By preallocating objects and memory that your application simply can't do without while it starts, you minimize the likelihood of failure due to out-of-memory errors during execution because you simply can't start if you can't obtain the necessary resources. This makes your application easier to implement, test, and debug.*

Because each control tracks for itself whether it needs to process events (based on its active flag, which you can set and examine using ICONTROL_IsActive and ICONTROL_SetActive), it's easy to pass events to the currently active control in your application's event handler:

```
1:
2: /*
3:  * in your HandleEvent()
4:  */
5: boolean result = FALSE;
6: int i;
7:
8: // The controls always get first dibs
9: for ( i = 0; i < MAX_NUM_CONTROLS; i++ )
10: {
11:   if ( pThis->m_apControl[i] &&
12:      ICONTROL_IsActive( pThis->m_apControl[i] ) )
13:      result = ICONTROL_HandleEvent( pThis->m_apControl[i],
14:                                   eCode, wParam, dwParam );
15:    if ( result ) break;
16: }
17: if ( !result ) switch( eCode )
18: {
19:   // handle other events here...
20: }
21: return result;
```

The loop on lines 9–16 simply walks each slot in the list of controls pThis->m_apControl. If a given slot contains a pointer to a control and the control is active (lines 11–12), the event passes to the control (line 13). If the control handles the event and no further processing is necessary, ICONTROL_HandleEvent returns TRUE, and the loop exits on line 15. Otherwise, the loop continues until it has exhausted all controls in the list, and your code will get a chance to process the event starting on line 17.

 CAUTION *As you'll see in subsequent sections of this chapter, this can be a little tricky when you're mixing a lot of different controls in the* m_apControl *array, such as text input and soft key menu controls. For an example of a full general-purpose* HandleEvent *function that you'd want to use in your application, see the "Integrating Controls with Your Application Framework" section.*

Finally, as with any other QUALCOMM BREW interface, you must release objects to prevent memory leaks when you're finished with the object. In general, it's best to free the objects created at application launch when the application terminates. Releasing the application's controls is a simple loop:

```
 1: /*
 2:  * When the application exits
 3:  */
 4: // Free the control
 5:
 6: for ( i = 0; i < MAX_NUM_CONTROLS; i++ )
 7: {
 8:   if ( pThis->m_apControl[i] )
 9:     ICONTROL_Release( pThis->m_apControl[ 0 ] );
10: }
```

This loop is straightforward; it simply calls ICONTROL_Release on any allocated controls.

Using the IStatic Control

The IStatic control is the simplest to understand and use. This control simply presents a title and scrollable text message, just like the one you see in Figure 5-1.

```
Welcome!
Hello world!
```

Figure 5-1. The IStatic *control in action*

Using the IStatic control is easy: Simply create it by passing the class ID
AEECLASSID_STATIC, set its options and content, and then redraw it to have it draw
on the display. Periodically—every pass through your event loop—you should
pass incoming events to the IStatic instance using IStatic_HandleEvent (or its
superclass method, IControl_HandleEvent). Listing 5-1 shows how you can use an
IStatic control in your application, assuming that the first entry (at index 0) of the
application's m_apControl is set to a valid IStatic instance.

Listing 5-1. Using IStatic

```
 1: /*
 2:  * Populating and showing a text control
 3:  */
 4: AECHAR pszTitle[ 64 ];
 5: AECHAR pszText[ 256 ];
 6:
 7: // Read in the title and text string from the resource file
 8: nCharCount = ISHELL_LoadResString( pThis->a.m_pIShell,
 9:                                    APP_RES_FILE,
10:                                    IDS_CENTERTEXT_TITLE,
11:                                    pszTitle,
12:                                    sizeof(pszTitle));
13: nCharCount = ISHELL_LoadResString( pThis->a.m_pIShell,
14:                                    APP_RES_FILE,
15:                                    IDS_CENTERTEXT_TEXT,
16:                                    pszText,
17:                                    sizeof( pszText ) );
18:
19: // Set the dimensions of the control to fill the screen.
20: ISTATIC_SetRect( pThis->m_apControl[0],
21:          &pThis->m_rc );
22:
23: // Set the properties that specify
```

```
24: // centering of control text lines and title
25: ISTATIC_SetProperties( pThis->m_apControl[0],
26:                         ST_CENTERTEXT | ST_CENTERTITLE );
27:
28: // Set the values of the title and
29: // text strings for this control
30: ISTATIC_SetText( pThis->m_apControl[0],
31:                  pszTitle,
32:                  pszText,
33:                  AEE_FONT_BOLD, AEE_FONT_NORMAL );
34:
35: // Make the text control active
36: ISTATIC_SetActive( pThis->m_apControl[0], TRUE );
37: // Display the text control
38: ISTATIC_Redraw( pThis->m_apControl[0] );
```

This code is straightforward and representative of how you'll use almost any control in QUALCOMM BREW. The first lines—from line 1 until line 18—are housekeeping, loading some preset text from a resource. (You could just as easily use programmatically generated text—say, from SPRINTF—and convert the resulting text to BREW multibyte strings using STR_TO_WSTR for dynamic content. When using STR_TO_WSTR, it's important to remember that you must provide a destination buffer large enough to hold the resulting string.)

TIP *As with other platforms, it's best to put as many of your strings in the resource file rather than scattering strings around your code. By doing so, you make it easier when you find you need to localize your code or change text contents to meet requirements for specific customers or handsets.*

Next, set the control's bounds using the ISTATIC_SetRect Application Programming Interface (API) on lines 20–21. This call takes an AEERect structure, which has four slots: x, y, dx, and dy. These specify the corners of a rectangle: x and y are the coordinates of the rectangle's upper-left corner, and dx and dy are the rectangle's width and height, respectively. QUALCOMM BREW follows the popular convention of numbering pixels from left to right along the *x* axis and from top to bottom along the *y* axis. Line 20 simply sets the control's bounds to the full extent of the screen, previously calculated in the application initialization routine described in the previous chapter. You should always set your control's bounds before drawing it because there are no preset defaults for a control's bounds.

The IStatic control has several options, two of which are on lines 25–26. The ST_CENTERTEXT option tells the control that the text should be centered within the control, and the ST_CENTERTITLE option tells the control that the title should be centered within the title bounds. Table 5-1 describes the other properties of the IStatic control.

Table 5-1. IStatic *Options*

OPTION	PURPOSE
ST_CENTERTEXT	Centers text along the x axis of the bounding rectangle.
ST_CENTERTITLE	Centers title along the x axis of the bounding rectangle.
ST_NOSCROLL	Does not scroll text.
ST_TEXTALLOC	Text string was allocated on heap; caller must take responsibility for freeing it.
ST_TITLEALLOC	Title string was allocated on heap; caller must take responsibility of freeing it.
ST_MIDDLETEXT	Centers title along the y axis of the bounding rectangle.
ST_UNDERLINE	Underlines the title.
ST_ASCII	Text is a single-byte string.
ST_ENABLETAB	Generates EVT_CTL_TAB when scrolling reaches the top or bottom.
ST_ENABLE_HLGHT	Highlights the control if it has focus (ISTATIC_IsActive is TRUE).

Most of the IStatic properties pertain to a text control's appearance—whether the title should be underlined or centered; whether the contents should be centered horizontally, vertically, or both in the bounding rectangle; and so forth.

Most of the time, you simply pass the IStatic instance pointers to the content it should display, and the control makes copies of the contents so that you don't have to worry about the memory used by the control's contents. At times, however, you may want to avoid the additional memory overhead, especially when displaying a large amount of information or when you want your control to provide a view of dynamically changing data. To do this, you assert either the ST_TEXTALLOC or ST_TITLEALLOC properties to indicate that your application is responsible for freeing the content's text or title (or both, if you assert both properties) buffers.

By default, the IStatic control will scroll its contents marquee-style down the display if the contents are larger than the bounding rectangle. You can prevent this behavior by setting the ST_NOSCROLL property; however, if you do so, you won't be able to see the control's entire contents if the contents don't fit in the bounding box. (At present, QUALCOMM BREW doesn't provide user or programmatic control of the IStatic control's scrolling behavior.) You can also assert the ST_ENABLE_TAB property so that the text control sends your application the EVT_CTL_TAB event when scrolling has reached the top or bottom of the control contents.

NOTE *In current implementations of QUALCOMM BREW, the* IStatic *control doesn't use events in its operation. However, to ensure full compatibility with later releases of QUALCOMM BREW, your application should use one of the two* _HandleEvent *methods to pass events to your application's active* IStatic *controls.*

Using the IMenuCtl Control

The IMenuCtl is actually the interface to four separate classes:

- The *menu control* provides an array of menu elements organized with one menu item per each row of the control and lets you choose and select another item using the directional pad (see Figure 5-2).

- The *list control* shows the currently selected menu item on the display and lets you choose and select another item using the directional pad (see Figure 5-3).

- The *soft key menu control* shows menu items side by side along the bottom line of the screen and lets you choose an item using the left and right keys on the directional pad (see Figure 5-4).

- The *icon view menu control* shows an array of bitmaps singularly or in a grid and lets you choose one using the directional pad (see Figure 5-5).

Table 5-2 provides the class ID for each kind of control.

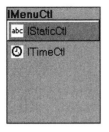

Figure 5-2. The standard menu control

Figure 5-3. The list control

Figure 5-4. The soft key menu control

Figure 5-5. The icon view menu control

Table 5-2. Class IDs for Menu Controls

MENU CONTROL	CLASS ID
Standard menu control	AEECLSID_MENUCTL
List menu control	AEECLSID_LISTCTL
Soft key menu control	AEECLSID_SOFTKEYCTL
Icon view menu control	AEECLSID_ICONVIEWCTL

When using any kind of menu, the general sequence of operations your application must perform is as follows:

1. Create the appropriate kind of menu control using ISHELL_CreateInstance.

2. Set the bounds of the menu control using IMENUCTL_SetRect.

3. Set any desired menu options using IMENUCTL_SetOpt.

4. Construct the menu's contents using the IMENUCTL_AddItem, IMENUCTL_AddItemEx, and IMENUCTL_DeleteItem methods.

5. Mark the currently selected item (if any) using the IMENUCTL_SetSel method.

6. Set the menu to process events using the IMENUCTL_SetActive method.

7. Redraw the menu using IMENUCTL_Redraw.

8. Send events to the menu control using IMENUCTL_HandleEvent.

9. When you're done with the menu, release it using IMENUCTL_Release or ICONTROL_Release.

You first saw a menu control in action in the previous chapter in the SlideShow application. Let's take another look at it now. The application creates the menu when the application first launches in the application's SlideShow_Init function, called within AEEClsCreateInstance (see Listing 5-2).

Listing 5-2. Application Initialization

```
 1: /**
 2:  * Initializes application structure, creating
 3:  * necessary UI components.
 4:  * @param CAppPtr pThis: pointer to application structure
 5:  * @return AEE_SUCCESS on success, or else EFAILED
 6:  */
 7: static int  SlideShow_Init( CAppPtr pThis )
 8: {
 9:   int result = AEE_SUCCESS;
10:   AEEDeviceInfo  dm;
11:
12:   if (pThis->a.m_pIDisplay && pThis->a.m_pIShell)
13:   {
14:     // Get the screen's bounds, color support
15:     // and font info here...
16:     // ...
17:   }
18:   else
19:   {
20:     result = EFAILED;
21:   }
22:
23:   if ( result == AEE_SUCCESS )
24:     result =
25:       ISHELL_CreateInstance( pThis->a.m_pIShell,
26:                              AEECLSID_MENUCTL,
27:                              (void **)&pThis->m_pIMenu );
28:   return result;
29: }
```

For brevity, I've removed the statements that were in lines 13–16 to determine the device's display capabilities. Lines 25–27 create a menu, storing it in the SlideShow application's application pointer slot m_pIMenu.

Once you create the menu, you initialize it by clearing the display, setting its bounds, and adding its menu items:

```
1: // Clear the display
2: IDISPLAY_ClearScreen( pThis->a.m_pIDisplay );
3: // Reset the menu
4: IMENUCTL_Reset( pThis->m_pIMenu );
5: // Set the menu's bounds
6: IMENUCTL_SetRect( pThis->m_pIMenu, &pThis->m_rc );
7: // Populate the menu
8: FillMenu( pThis );
```

FillMenu builds the menu using the names of BREW Archive (BAR) files in the application's directory, as shown in Listing 5-3.

Listing 5-3. Building the Menu

```
 1: /*
 2:  * Populates the menu with the list of slide shows.
 3:  * @param CAppPtr pThis: the application
 4:  * @return nothing
 5:  */
 6: static void FillMenu( CAppPtr pThis )
 7: {
 8:   IFileMgr *pIFileMgr;
 9:   FileInfo info;
10:   AECHAR wszBuff[ MAX_FILE_NAME + 1 ];
11:   uint16 nItem = 1;
12:   int result;
13:
14:   // Setup the file manager instance
15:   result = ISHELL_CreateInstance( pThis->a.m_pIShell,
16:                                   AEECLSID_FILEMGR,
17:                                   (void **)&pIFileMgr );
18:
19:   // Enumerate the list of .bar files
20:   if ( pIFileMgr )
21:   {
22:     // Begin enumeration
23:     if ( SUCCESS == IFILEMGR_EnumInit( pIFileMgr, "", FALSE ) )
24:     {
25:       while ( IFILEMGR_EnumNext( pIFileMgr, &info ) )
26:       {
27:         // We're interested in files that end in .bar
```

```
28:          if ( STRENDS( ".bar", info.szName ) )
29:          {
30:            // Create our own name for the menu item
31:            info.szName[ STRLEN( info.szName ) - 4 ] = '\000';
32:
33:            // convert to a wide string
34:            STR_TO_WSTR( info.szName, wszBuff, 2 * MAX_FILE_NAME + 2 );
35:
36:            // Add it to the menu
37:            IMENUCTL_AddItem( pThis->m_pIMenu,
38:                                NULL, // Resource file for item
39:                                0,    // Don't use the resource file
40:                                nItem++,
41:                                wszBuff,
42:                                (uint32)0 );  // Item data
43:          } // add file name to menu
44:        } // file name enumeration
45:      } // enumeration guard
46:
47:      // Clean up
48:      IFILEMGR_Release( pIFileMgr );
49:    } // pIFileMgr guard
50:
51:    if ( nItem == 1 )
52:    {
53:      // Menu addition failed.
54:      // But we always have our .bar, so add it manually.
55:      STRTOWSTR( "SlideShow", wszBuff, MAX_FILE_NAME + 1 );
56:
57:      // Add it to the menu
58:      IMENUCTL_AddItem( pThis->m_pIMenu,
59:                          NULL, // Resource file for item
60:                          0,    // Don't use the resource file
61:                          nItem++,
62:                          wszBuff,
63:                          (uint32)0 );  // Item data
64:
65:    } // Add what is always there
66: }
```

Although a lengthy routine, the logic behind FillMenu is simple: For each file (lines 1–25) ending in the characters *.bar*, line 28 uses the name of the file. As with most other QUALCOMM BREW interfaces, the IMENUCTL interface looks for character strings in multibyte format. Thus, line 34 converts the name of the menu item to add from a C-style null-terminated character string to a QUALCOMM BREW multibyte null-terminated AECHAR string using STR_TO_WSTR. Lines 37–42 add the menu item to the menu using IMENUCTL_AddItem.

IMENUCTL_AddItem lets you add menu items to a menu either as multibyte strings from the heap or as resource strings from a resource file, such as the application's resource file. In either case, the menu control *copies* the strings, taking responsibility for deleting the contents when the application releases menu control structures using IMENUCTL_Reset or releases them using IMENUCTL_Release. This method takes a reference to the menu control to accept the new item along with the item number and takes information about the item to add. When adding a resource item to a menu, the second and third arguments should be the name of the resource file and the resource ID of the item, respectively. When adding a string, the second and third arguments are zero, and you pass a pointer to the multibyte string as the fifth argument. Regardless of which way you add an item, you also provide a unique integer that the event handler will receive as an argument to the EVT_COMMAND message when you select the event as the fourth argument, and you can pass a long integer or pointer to be kept with the menu item as the last argument.

The event handler for your menu control is straightforward, at least until it needs to determine what item you selected from the menu. Menu controls signal menu selections using the EVT_COMMAND event, passing the selected item's identifier (which you set when you called one of the AddItem APIs) as the wParam to your event handler (see Listing 5-4).

Listing 5-4. Handling a Menu Selection

```
 1: /*
 2:  * In HandleEvent()
 3:  */
 4:   result = IMENUCTL_HandleEvent( pThis->m_pIMenu,
 5:                                  eCode,
 6:                                  wParam,
 7:                                  dwParam );
 8:   if ( !result ) switch ( eCode )
 9:   {
10:     case EVT_COMMAND:
11:       // Find the filename of the selected resource
12:       IMENUCTL_GetItem( pThis->m_pIMenu,
13:                         wParam,
14:                         &menuItem );
15:       WSTR_TO_STR( menuItem.pText, pThis->m_szFile, MAX_FILE_NAME + 1);
16:       STRCAT( pThis->m_szFile, ".bar" );
17: ... // HandleEvent continues...
```

The HandleEvent function first shares incoming events with the menu control so that it can process key events from the navigation pad and the Select key.

Because menu controls can also have images—in fact, even ordinary textual menus can include images as icons—there's also an IMENUCTL_AddItemEx function. Unlike IMENUCTL_AddItem, which takes a veritable horde of arguments, IMENUCTL_AddItemEx takes a pointer to a structure describing what you want to add to the menu. This structure, a CtlAddItem structure, looks like this:

```
1: typedef struct _CtlAddItem
2: {
3:    const AECHAR *pText;
4:    IImage      *pImage;
5:    const char  *pszResImage;
6:    const char  *pszResText;
7:    uint16      wText;
8:    uint16      wFont;
9:    uint16      wImage;
10:   uint16      wItemID;
11:   uint32      dwData;
12: } CtlAddItem;
```

When calling IMENUCTL_AddItemEx, you can fill any or some of the fields in this structure. If the pText slot is valid, the contents are added to the menu's text label. If not, the method uses the resource indicated by wText in the resource file you specify in pszResText. If pImage is valid, the control will increment the image's reference count (so you can release your reference to the image using IIMAGE_Release) and add the image to the menu item. If you'd rather use an image from a resource file, that's okay, too—simply place the ID of the image in the wImage slot and the name of the resource file in pszResImage. For example, the following snippet initializes a menu item with an icon and a string from the application's resource file:

```
1:    CAppPtr pThis = (CAppPtr)p;
2:    CtlAddItem addItemInfo = { 0 };
3:    int itemID = 0;
4:
5:    ...
6:    // Build a menu of choices for controls.
7:    addItemInfo.wItemID = itemID++;
8:    addItemInfo.dwData = (uint32)AS_StaticHandleEvent;
9:    addItemInfo.pszResText = APP_RES_FILE;
10:   addItemInfo.pszResImage = APP_RES_FILE;
11:   addItemInfo.wText = IDS_STATIC;
12:   addItemInfo.wImage = IDI_STATIC;
```

```
13:    IMENUCTL_AddItemEx( (IMenuCtl *)
14:      pThis->m_app.m_apControl[ Ctl_NavMenu ],
15:      &addItemInfo );
```

As you might imagine, using IMENU_AddItemEx is really just a matter of initial-izing a CtlAddItem structure with the description of the item and then making the API call. Here, line 7 sets the menu item's specific ID, and then the code uses the menu item's double-word storage to hold a pointer to the next state's event handler. The icon and text data are both in the application's resource file, so lines 9–10 set the pszResText and pszResImage slots to the pointer containing the application resource filename (defined by the QUALCOMM BREW Resource Builder in the _res.h file). Lines 11 and 12 set the wText and wImage slots to contain the resource ID of the text and image for the item, respectively. Finally, lines 13–15 add the menu item to the menu control. (Note that because the m_apControl array is an array of IControl pointers, you must cast the pointer to an IMenuCtl pointer to avoid compile-time warnings on line 13.)

A special kind of menu is the soft key menu, discussed in the next section.

Using the ITextCtl Control

Your application accepts input using the ITextCtl control, which lets you enter text using multitap or OEM-provided text input methods, such as Motorola's iTap or Tegic's T9. You have control over the text control being single-line or multiline, the title of the control, and the input method the control provides to the user. Figure 5-6 shows two ITextCtl instances: one spanning the entire screen and another with an accompanying soft key menu.

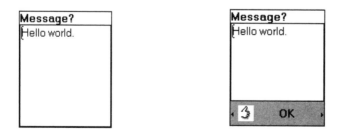

Figure 5-6. A plain-text control (left) and a text control with a soft key menu (right)

Using a text control is just like using any of the other controls: You create it, set the options, set its size, and show it. Of course, you'll also want to set its title and the text it should contain when it's first shown (see Listing 5-5).

Listing 5-5. Using ITextCtl

```
1:    CAppPtr pThis = (CAppPtr)p;
2:    AECHAR pszTitle[32];
3:    AECHAR pszText[256];
4:    ITextCtl *pITextCtl =
5:      (ITextCtl *)pThis->m_app.m_apControl[ Ctl_TextInput ];
6:
7:    // Clear the display
8:    IDISPLAY_ClearScreen( GetDisplay( pThis ) );
9:
10:   // Set the control's options
11:   ITEXT_SetProperties( pITextCtl,
12:       TP_MULTILINE | TP_FRAME | TP_T9_MODE );
13:
14:   // Set the control's contents
15:   STR_TO_WSTR( "Message?", pszTitle, sizeof( pszTitle ) );
16:   STR_TO_WSTR( "Hello world.", pszText, sizeof( pszText ) );
17:
18:   ITEXTCTL_SetTitle( pITextCtl, NULL, 0, pszTitle );
19:   ITEXTCTL_SetText( pITextCtl, pszText, -1 );
20:
21:   // Size the control.
22:   ITEXT_SetRect( pITextCtl, &pThis->m_rc );
23:   ITEXT_SetActive( pITextCtl, TRUE );
24:   ITEXT_Redraw( pITextCtl );
25:
26:   // Update the display
27:   IDISPLAY_Update( GetDisplay( pThis ) );
28:
29:   return TRUE;
```

By now, this should look familiar to the point of boring. Assuming that the text control instance has been stored in the Ctl_TextInput slot of the control array (lines 4–5), the code begins by clearing the display (line 8) and selecting a framed multiline input line that will use the OEM text input method by default (lines 11–12).

Lines 14–19 set the text control's title and default input text using compile-time strings. Although not portable, this serves to show how you can convert a standard C string to a multibyte string (line 15) for use with the text control's title. You also have the choice of using a resource file entry by passing the name of the file as the second argument to ITEXTCTL_SetTitle. If you do this, be sure to pass the ID of the desired text resource as the third item and pass NULL instead of a multibyte zero-terminated string buffer.

Unlike the title, you must provide default text using ITEXTCTL_SetText in its own buffer, but the control will copy the contents of the buffer rather than keep a reference to it. The final argument to ITEXTCTL_SetText is simply the number of characters in the string you provide that should be used to seed the text control's default input text. If you want to use all of the text in the buffer, simply pass –1 (or use the WSTRLEN function to compute the length of the string in the buffer, which is what ITEXTCTL_SetText probably does anyway).

Lines 21–24 perform the usual control initialization: They set the size of the control, activate the control so it'll accept events, and redraw the control on the display. There's nothing special about using the ITextCtl methods here instead of the more generic IControl interfaces. Because you need explicit ITextCtl pointers to set the title and text, it's easier to use the ITextCtl interfaces every-where and save time and space casting.

When using ITextCtl, your event handler must pass all incoming events to the control using ITEXTCTL_HandleEvent before processing any events. When you finish entering text, you press the Select key, so your application will receive an EVT_KEY with a key code of AVK_SELECT to indicate that text input is complete (see Listing 5-6).

Listing 5-6. Handling Events with ITextCtl

```
1:    boolean result = FALSE;
2:    char pszText[512];
3:    AECHAR *psz;
4:    ITextCtl *pITextCtl =
5:      (ITextCtl *)pThis->m_apControl[ Ctl_TextInput ];
6:
7:    result = ITEXTCTL_HandleEvent( pITextCtl,
8:      eCode, wParam, dwParam );
9:
10:
11:   if ( !result &&
12:        eCode == EVT_KEY &&
13:        ITEXTCTL_IsActive( pITextCtl )
14:   {
15:     if ( wParam == AVK_SELECT )
16:     {
17:       psz = ITEXTCTL_GetTextPtr( pITextCtl );
18:       if ( psz )
19:       {
20:         WSTR_TO_STR( psz, pszText, sizeof( pszText ) );
```

```
21:        DBGPRINTF("entered %s", pszText );
22:        result = TRUE;
23:      }
24:    }
25:    else if ( wParam == AVK_CLR )
26:    {
27:      // The user cancelled text input by pressing CLR
28:      DBGPRINTF("hit CLR" );
29:      result = TRUE;
30:    }
31:     // Handle other events...
```

Lines 7–8 share all incoming events with the text control. The text control consumes keystroke events (including when you press Clear to rub out the last letter you typed). You'll want to watch for two specific keystrokes that the text control doesn't handle on your behalf: AVK_SELECT, indicating that text input is complete, and AVK_CLR, indicating that you pressed Clear in the text field when there's no text to rub out, which your application should treat as a request to navigate to the previous screen.

CAUTION   *Some handsets may handle* AVK_CLR *in a text control differently, so this is an area where you should be sure to test your application on the actual hardware as you develop.*

Lines 11–30 do exactly this, first confirming that the text control did nothing with the event (line 11), that the event code is a keystroke (EVT_KEY, line 12), and that the text control is active (line 13).

CAUTION   *Don't mistake the* EVT_KEY *event for the* EVT_KEY_PRESS, EVT_KEY_RELEASE, *or* EVT_KEY_HELD *events, which correspond to the key moving downward, the key moving upward, and the user holding their key down, respectively.*

Next, the code simply checks to see if the unhandled keystroke is from the Select key (line 15) or the Clear key (line 25), and it prints either the input text or a diagnostic message indicating that you cancelled text input. In a real application, these would be cues to update an application's state variables and transition to a new state.

Things are a little more complex—but a lot more interesting—when you combine a soft key menu with an input text line. By doing so, you can create all kinds of custom user interfaces, including simply spicing up the look of text entry, adding menu items to select specific input methods, using quick-text to save typing, and so forth. The general steps for combining a text control with an input line are as follows:

1. Create an instance of ITextCtl using its ID AEECLSID_TEXTCTL and an instance of a soft key IMenuCtl using the ID AEECLSID_SOFTKEYCTL.

2. Set the text control's title and default text.

3. Set the text control's properties.

4. Add menu items to the soft key menu using IMENUCTL_AddItem or IMENUCTL_AddItemEx.

5. Size the text control to fill the screen, leaving room for the menu control, which will appear directly under the text control at the bottom of the screen.

6. Attach the soft key menu control to the text control using ITEXTCTL_SetSoftKeyMenu.

7. Activate and redraw the text control.

By doing this, your text control will be adorned with an accompanying soft key menu, and the soft key menu will include both the items you add and the OEM-specific menu items to control the input method (such as picking multitap or Tegic's T9 text input). Listing 5-7 shows the code.

Listing 5-7. Adorning an ITextCtl *Control with a Soft Key Menu*

```
1:   CAppPtr pThis = (CAppPtr)p;
2:   AECHAR pszTitle[32];
3:   AECHAR pszText[256];
4:   AEERect rc;
5:   CtlAddItem addItemInfo = { 0 };
6:   ITextCtl *pITextCtl =
7:     (ITextCtl *)pThis->m_app.m_apControl[ Ctl_TextInput ];
8:   IMenuCtl *pIMenuCtl =
```

```
 9:     (IMenuCtl *)pThis->m_app.m_apControl[ Ctl_SoftKeyMenu ];
10:
11:     // Clear the display
12:     IDISPLAY_ClearScreen( GetDisplay( pThis ) );
13:
14:     // Set the text control's options
15:     ITEXTCTL_SetProperties( pITextCtl,
16:       TP_MULTILINE | TP_FRAME | TP_T9_MODE);
17:
18:     // Set the text control's contents
19:     STR_TO_WSTR( "Message?", pszTitle, sizeof( pszTitle ) );
20:     STR_TO_WSTR( "Hello world.", pszText, sizeof( pszText ) );
21:
22:     ITEXTCTL_SetTitle( pITextCtl, NULL, 0, pszTitle );
23:     ITEXTCTL_SetText( pITextCtl, pszText, -1 );
24:
25:     // Set the menu control's contents
26:     addItemInfo.wItemID = 0;
27:     addItemInfo.dwData = 0;
28:     addItemInfo.pszResText = APP_RES_FILE;
29:     addItemInfo.pszResImage = APP_RES_FILE;
30:     addItemInfo.wText = IDS_OK;
31:     addItemInfo.wImage = IDI_OK;
32:     IMENUCTL_AddItemEx( pIMenuCtl, &addItemInfo );
33:
34:     addItemInfo.wItemID = 1;
35:     addItemInfo.dwData = 0;
36:     addItemInfo.pszResText = APP_RES_FILE;
37:     addItemInfo.pszResImage = NULL;
38:     addItemInfo.wText = IDS_CANCEL;
39:     addItemInfo.wImage = IDI_CANCEL;
40:     IMENUCTL_AddItemEx( pIMenuCtl, &addItemInfo );
41:
42:     // Size the control.
43:     IMENUCTL_GetRect( pIMenuCtl, &rc );
44:     SETAEERECT( &rc, 0, 0, pThis->m_cx, pThis->m_cy - rc.dy );
45:     ITEXTCTL_SetRect( pITextCtl, &rc );
46:
47:     // Attach the soft key menu to the control
48:     ITEXTCTL_SetSoftKeyMenu( pITextCtl,  pIMenuCtl );
49:
50:     ITEXTCTL_SetActive( pITextCtl, TRUE );
51:
52:     ITEXTCTL_Redraw( pITextCtl );
```

```
53:
54:    // Update the display
55:    IDISPLAY_Update( GetDisplay( pThis ) );
```

Things progress as you'd expect until lines 26–40, which use the IMENUCTL_AddItemEx method to initialize two menu items: one to confirm text input and one to cancel text input. Each of these includes an icon and a text label.

 TIP   *Always be sure that a soft key menu accompanying an input line includes a way to accept the text you enter because the Select key moves focus from the text control to the soft key menu. Without a choice on the menu to accept input, you can't move to the next screen in your application because the Select key moves between the input line and the soft key menu.*

Lines 42–45 resize the text control to leave room for the soft key menu. Finally, line 48 ties the soft key menu to the text control, and line 50 activates the text control.

When using a soft key menu with a text control, you need to share events with both controls, as in Listing 5-8.

Listing 5-8. Sharing Events with an IMenuCtl *Soft Key Menu and an* ITextCtl

```
1:    ITextCtl *pITextCtl =
2:      (ITextCtl *)pThis->m_app.m_apControl[ Ctl_TextInput ];
3:    IMenuCtl *pIMenuCtl =
4:      (IMenuCtl *)pThis->m_app.m_apControl[ Ctl_SoftKeyMenu ];
5:
6:    result = ITEXTCTL_HandleEvent( pITextCtl,
7:      eCode, wParam, dwParam );
8:    if (!result) IMENUCTL_HandleEvent( pIMenuCtl,
9:      eCode, wParam, dwParam );
10:
11:   // Key up in text control with soft key menu
12:   // activates text control
13:   if ( !result &&
14:        eCode == EVT_KEY && wParam == AVK_UP &&
15:        !ITEXTCTL_IsActive( pITextCtl ) &&
16:        IMENUCTL_IsActive( pIMenuCtl ) )
17:   {
18:     IMENUCTL_SetActive( pIMenuCtl, FALSE );
```

```
19:      ITEXTCTL_SetActive( pITextCtl, TRUE );
20:      result = TRUE;
21:    }
22:
23:    // Key up in text control with soft key menu
24:    // activates text control
25:    if ( !result &&
26:        eCode == EVT_KEY && wParam == AVK_DOWN &&
27:        ITEXTCTL_IsActive( pITextCtl ) &&
28:        !IMENUCTL_IsActive( pIMenuCtl ) )
29:    {
30:      IMENUCTL_SetActive( pIMenuCtl, TRUE );
31:      ITEXTCTL_SetActive( pITextCtl, FALSE );
32:      result = TRUE;
33:    }
34:
35:    // Menu selection navigates to new state
36:    if ( !result && eCode == EVT_COMMAND )
37:    {
38:      switch( wParam )
39:      {
40:        // wParam contains the id of the item selected
41:      }
42:    }
43:
44:    // Handle other events...
```

The event handler is pretty simple, but handling the up and down keystrokes between the text control and the menu is a little tricky, so let's take a closer look. After giving both controls an opportunity to handle the event (lines 6–9), the event handler checks the incoming event to see if it's a keystroke and, if so, checks which item has focus. Then it changes focus accordingly (lines 11–33). For example, lines 13–16 test the incoming event to see if it hasn't already been handled (line 13), if it's an up arrow keystroke (line 14), and if the menu currently has focus (lines 15–16). It assigns focus to the text control alone and marks the event as handled (lines 18–20).

CAUTION *QUALCOMM BREW doesn't support the notion of exclusive focus. That is, you can include multiple calls to* ICONTROL_SetActive *to activate several controls. In almost all cases, this works but can result in user interface bugs in your application. Consequently, it's best to clear the active flags of other controls when activating a specific control.*

Using Other Controls

Most of the time, you'll work with the menu control, soft key menu control, static control, and text control. But there are several other controls, as shown in Table 5-3.

Table 5-3. QUALCOMM BREW Control Interface and Class ID Summary

CONTROL PURPOSE	INTERFACE NAME	CLASS ID	NOTES
Static item display	IStatic	AEECLASSID_STATIC	Displays static text or image
Clock	ITimeCtl	AEECLSID_CLOCKCTL	Displays time with A.M./P.M. indication
Countdown timer	ITimeCtl	AEECLSID_COUNTDOWNCTL	Displays countdown clock in hours, minutes, and seconds
Stopwatch timer	ITimeCtl	AEECLSID_STOPWATCHCTL	Displays incrementing clock in hours, minutes, and seconds
Date entry	IDateCtl	AEECLSID_DATECTL	Permits input of month, day, and year
Day of month entry	IDateCtl	AEECLSID_DATEPICKCTL	Permits input of day of month or selection of month on monthly calendar

Table 5-3. QUALCOMM BREW Control Interface and Class ID Summary (Continued)

CONTROL PURPOSE	INTERFACE NAME	CLASS ID	NOTES
Image viewer	IImageCtl	AEECLSID_IMAGECTL	Lets user scroll around an image larger than the viewable rectangle
Menu	IMenuCtl	AEECLSID_MENUCTL	Displays one menu item per screen row and permits selection and scrolling
List	IMenuCtl	AEECLSID_LISTCTL	Displays current selection of the menu item on a single line and permits selection and scrolling
Soft key menu	IMenuCtl	AEECLSID_SOFTKEYCTL	Displays soft key menu items along the bottom of the screen and permits selection and left/right scrolling
Icon menu	IMenuCtl	AEECLSID_ICONVIEWCTL	Displays a table of bitmap icons and permits selection of an item with accompanying name display
Text input	ITextCtl	AEECLSID_TEXTCTL	Permits single-line or multiline text input
HTML display	IHTMLViewer	AEECLSID_HTML	Permits display of simple HTML

Most of these controls use the EVT_COMMAND event to notify your application when you finish entering data. Some controls—notably those that implement the ITimeCtl or the IMenuCtl interface—also send your application an EVT_CTL_TAB event when the user changes from one part of the control (such as a menu item) to another part of the same control.

One control, the IHTMLViewer control, also uses a notification function that it invokes in response to specific actions, such as when you select a link. This function takes a pointer to a structure that describes the reason for the call, along with a pointer you can use to pass additional data to the function. Chapter 6, "Streaming Data," shows you how to use the IHTMLViewer control.

Integrating Controls with Your Application Framework

Although managing a group of controls isn't hard, doing so in a uniform way across a larger application requires you to be organized because it's easy to create controls and forget to free them or to construct event handlers that don't pass events to controls in the right sequence.

If you're coding an application from scratch, you can do the following to make your life a little easier:

Preallocate all of your controls and free them only when your application exits. Limiting where you allocate and free items makes it easier to find sources of leaks and simplifies your error handling code when your application can't allocate a resource.

Consolidate your event handling by control. If needed, break your event handler into multiple functions. In a large application, your event handler is likely to be one of the most complex sections of code (outside of proprietary algorithms such as image manipulation or game artificial intelligence), and by keeping it simple, it's easier to debug.

Keep your user interface simple. Keeping, at most, one input item active at a time (two in the case of a text control with a soft key menu) makes it easy for you to track which control should receive events at different points in your application. Not only that, but it'll make your application easier to use for your customers!

A better idea, as discussed in general terms in the previous chapter, is to build a framework that does the bookkeeping for your application behind the scenes so you can worry about getting the rest of your program done. Because QUALCOMM BREW applications generally have several points in common—such as tracking state, managing preferences, and handling events—if you can encapsulate these features in modules of tried-and-true code, you won't have to reinvent the wheel each time you start to write a new application.

Let's take a closer look at how you can add support for controls to the framework presented in the previous chapter.

Simplifying the State Machine Structure

The previous chapter's framework defined a state as the following structure:

```
1: // State function type declarations
2: typedef void (PFNSTATEENTRY)( void *pApp, EStateChange change );
3: typedef void  (PFNSTATEEXIT)( void *pApp, EStateChange change );
4: typedef boolean (PFNSTATEEVENT)( void *pApp,
5:                 AEEEvent eCode,
6:                 uint16 wParam, uint32 dwParam);
7: typedef struct _CState
8: {
9:   struct _CState *m_pPrevState;
10:   PFNSTATEENTRY  *m_pfEntry;
11:   PFNSTATEEXIT   *m_pfExit;
12:   PFNSTATEEVENT  *m_pfEvent;
13:   void           *m_pData;
14: } CState, *CStatePtr;
```

The CState structure is simple, dividing a state into three functions: one responsible for entry, one responsible for exit, and one responsible for handling events while the state is active. This is simple and easy to maintain, but it has the detraction that to refer to a state, you need to refer to it as a tuple of function pointers: pfnEntry, pfnExit, and pfnEvent. If you're constructing applications with many states, it can be tedious to keep track of all the pointers.

It would be better to use only *one* state function to uniquely identify a state. Fortunately, there's an easy way to do this: You can use some of the QUALCOMM BREW events that are pertinent only to the application to capture the purpose of the entry and exit functions. Recall that the framework calls a state's entry function when a state is entered or the application is resumed, and recall that the framework calls the state's exit function when the state is exited or the application is suspended. You can do the same by using events to indicate these conditions to the state's event handler.

You could either define new event codes or use existing QUALCOMM BREW events and overload them so that the events have their QUALCOMM BREW meaning when the system delivers them to the framework application handler. You can then use them for another purpose for each state's event handler because the state event handler doesn't normally see them. Intuitively, it makes sense to use existing events. Thus, I have four to use for this purpose:

- The EVT_APP_START event, indicating that the application—or a state—is being started.

- The EVT_APP_STOP event, indicating that the application—or a state—is being exited.

- The EVT_APP_RESUME event, indicating that the system has resumed your application's execution.

- The EVT_APP_SUSPEND event, indicating that the system has suspended your application's execution.

By extending the state machine's event handler to handle these four events (calling separate functions if needed), you can simplify the notion of a state to a simple linked list containing two pointers: one to a region holding the state's state variable and the other to the state's function pointer (see Listing 5-9).

Listing 5-9. Managing the List of States

```
1: /**
2:  * @name _Node
3:  * @memo Singly linked list.
4:  * @doc Provides the implementation for a simple
5:  * singly-linked list with weak typing.
6:  * The head of the list is denoted with the
7:  * data fields set to NULL.
8:  */
9: typedef struct _Node
10: {
11:   /// Next node
12:   struct _Node *m_pNext;
13:   /// Pointer to data for this node
14:   void *m_pData;
15:   /// Pointer to any additional data for this node.
16:   void *m_pMetaData;
17: };
18:
19: /**
20:  * @name NodeLinkNext
21:  * @memo Inserts one node after another.
22:  * @doc  Inserts new node n2 after existing
```

```
23:   * node n1.
24:   * Returns the second node.
25:   */
26:  #define NodeLinkNext( n1, n2 ) \
27:    { n2->m_pNext = n1->m_pNext; n1->m_pNext = n2; }
28:
29:  /**
30:   * @name NodeUnlinkNext
31:   * @memo Unlinks the next node from the list.
32:   * @doc  Unlinks the next node after the indicated node.
33:   * Frees the unlinked node.
34:   */
35:  #define NodeUnlinkNext( n1 ) \
36:    { struct _Node *_p; _p = n1->m_pNext; \
37:        n1->m_pNext = _p->m_pNext; FREE( _p ); }
38:
39:  /**
40:   * @name NodeNext
41:   * @memo Returns the next node after the current node.
42:   * @doc  Returns the next node after the current node.
43:   */
44:  #define NodeNext( n ) \
45:    ( n->m_pNext )
46:
47:  // Returning true indicates event was handled.
48:  typedef boolean (PFNSTATEEVENT)( void *pApp,
49:                  AEEEvent eCode,
50:                  uint16 wParam, uint32 dwParam);
51:  typedef struct _Node CState;
52:  typedef struct _Node *CStatePtr;
53:
54:  /**
55:   * @name State_GetStateData
56:   * @memo Returns the indicated state's data.
57:   * @doc Returns the state data for the indicated state.
58:   */
59:  #define State_GetStateData( s ) ( s->m_pData )
60:
61:  /**
62:   * @name State_SetStateData
63:   * @memo Sets the indicated state's data.
64:   * @doc Assigns the state data for the indicated state
65:   * to the given pointer.
66:   */
```

```
67: #define State_SetStateData( s, d ) ( (s)->m_pData = ( d ) )
68:
69: /**
70:  * @name State_GetStateEventHandler
71:  * @memo Returns the indicated state's event handler.
72:  * @doc Returns the state event handler
73:  * for the indicated state.
74:  */
75: #define State_GetStateEventHandler( s ) \
76:   ( (PFNSTATEEVENT *)((s)->m_pMetaData) )
77:
78: /**
79:  * @name State_SetStateEventHandler
80:  * @memo Sets the indicated state's event handler
81:  * @doc Assigns the state event handler for the
82:  * indicated state to the given pointer.
83:  */
84: #define State_SetStateEventHandler( s, d ) \
85:   ( (s)->m_pMetaData = d )
```

Most of this code is bookkeeping for the link list, and the remaining lines are macros to implement the state machine interface on top of the linked list implementation. Lines 1–17 define the linked list node; each node has a pointer to the next node (line 12), along with two slots for data: one pointing to the node's data and the other pointing to metadata about the node. This approach simplifies memory management pertaining to states, rather than allocating a structure that contains a state's data and event handler, and links that to a single slot in the node.

Lines 19–45 provide simple macros to link an element into the list (lines 20–27), unlink the last node of a list (lines 29–37), and return the next node of a list given a specific node (lines 39–45). All of these rely on the notion that the head of a list is a placeholder and that subsequent nodes are linked using only the m_pNext slot of the _Node structure. There's no special reason for making these macros other than simplicity: It's easier to fix a logic error in how the linked list is managed by fixing one macro instead of fumbling through an entire module. For a newcomer to the code, it's also easier to understand a line like this:

```
pNewNode = NodeNext( pCurrentNode );
```

instead of the equally functional but slightly more cryptic line:

```
pNewNode = pCurrentNode->m_pNext;
```

In a similar vein, the framework has macros that wrap the notion of the _Node structure as a CState structure, beginning with the type definitions on lines 47–52. After defining the state event handler function type on lines 48–50, the code defines a CState and a CStatePtr to be a struct _Node and a struct _Node pointer, respectively. Doing this hides the implementation of a state from its users, as do the definitions in the remainder of the listing, which simply provide accessors and mutators for a state's data (lines 54–67) and state event handling (lines 69–85).

With these changes to the notion of a state structure, there are small changes to the implementation of State_Push and State_Pop. The key change is for state changes to invoke the state's single function rather than calling different functions depending on whether the state change is an entry or an exit. Because a state function might want to know the reason for the state change, the state change functions include a cause code as the wParam to the event handler.

The old implementation had an additional weakness. There was no way for a state to indicate that it couldn't be entered. For simple Graphical User Interface (GUI)–only applications, this isn't a major flaw, but for applications that involve data communication, this makes error handling difficult because if a state has an internal error, it must manage the error and shift to another state after it has been entered. To remedy this problem, the altered framework can now refuse a state transition and either force the application to remain in the same state or offer a state that it should enter instead.

For example, consider a simple Web-based application that downloads financial data. The application might have four states: one to prompt for a ticker symbol, one to perform the network transaction and receive the ticker's fundamentals, one to display the results, and one to display an error if the handset doesn't have wireless service. Using the new framework, the network state can attempt to start the network transition as it's entered. If it fails, instead of entering, the network state can direct the framework to transition instead to the error display state. Moreover, from the error state, pressing Clear would bring you back to the ticker prompt state because the network state was never kept on the application's state stack.

To do this, a state function needs a way to communicate a state change failure and a desired new state to the framework. You can do this using the event handler's return code and the dwParam argument to the state handler, which points to a region that can contain a reference to a new state handler. If the state function returns TRUE to an EVT_APP_START event (indicating that the application should enter that state), the state is placed on the state stack. Otherwise, the application's behavior depends on the following:

- If *dwParam is NULL, don't push or pop. Stay in the same state and return FALSE.

- If *dwParam is !NULL and a state is being pushed, push the state indicated by *dwParam instead.

- If *dwParam == State_RewindState, pop the current state instead of pushing anything.

- If *dwParam is !NULL and a state is being popped, pop the state and push *dwParam instead.

- If *dwParam == State_RewindState and a state was being popped, pop both the current state and the previous state.

The constant State_RewindState is merely defined as (uint32)(-1), and it lets the application indicate that a state should be popped rather than providing a new state.

Although somewhat more complicated to implement in State_Push and State_Pop, the results are far more flexible because now a state can decide if the handset and application is in a position to perform a state's actions and can suggest another course of action in the event of an error. Because the changes are fairly simple—spanning only logic changes and order of operation within State_Push and State_Pop—refer to the sample code that accompanies this chapter if you're interested in the details.

Initializing Controls and States

All of the changes discussed so far make managing states easier and more flexible, but they don't directly pertain to managing controls. For the framework to provide a good basis for managing controls, it should do at least the following:

- Provide controls for the most common operations: menu selection and text entry.

- Give the application states an opportunity to initialize their controls when the application launches.

- Track the application's use of controls through all states.

- Automatically free controls on application exit.

- Dispatch events to controls on behalf of each state.

The changes to do all of this are far simpler than the refactoring of the state management itself. You've already seen the first change: modifications to the CApp structure that represents an application, as shown in Listing 5-10.

Listing 5-10. Framework Extensions to Support Controls

```
 1: /**
 2:  * @name MAX_NUM_CONTROLS
 3:  * @memo number of controls.
 4:  * @doc This tells the framework how many controls
 5:  * it must manage when handling events.
 6:  */
 7: #define MAX_NUM_CONTROLS ( 10 )
 8:
 9: typedef struct _CStateApp
10: {
11:     /// The application context.
12:     /// This must always be the first field.
13:   AEEApplet a;
14:
15:   /// The state stack
16:   CStatePtr     m_pState;
17:
18:   /// The application preferences
19:   void    *m_pAppPrefs;
20:
21:   /// The application global data
22:   void    *m_pAppData;
23:
24:   /// The pool of controls that the framework will manage.
25:   IControl      *m_apControl[ MAX_NUM_CONTROLS ];
26:   uint8         m_nControl;
27: } CStateApp, *CStateAppPtr;
28:
29: /**
30:  * @name CApp
31:  * @memo Application context.
32:  * @doc This stores the application's current
33:  * context and state information.
34:  */
```

```
35: typedef struct _CApp
36: {
37:    /// Stores the application framework information.
38:    CStateApp    m_app;
39:
40:    /// Screen width
41:    int      m_cx;
42:    /// Screen height
43:    int      m_cy;
44:    /// Color depth
45:    int      m_colorDepth;
46:    /// Font height in pixels
47:    int      m_nFontHeight;
48:    /// Does the screen support color?
49:    boolean     m_bColor;
50:    /// A rectangle with the drawable bounds
51:    AEERect     m_rc;
52:    /// True if the splash screen is showing.
53:    boolean    m_bSplashing;
54: } CApp, *CAppPtr;
```

In addition to tracking the current state and the state stack, the framework now maintains a pool of controls, stored in the m_apControl array of the CStateApp structure, and an associated count of initialized controls, m_nControl, declared on lines 25–26. (You can disregard the m_pAppPrefs and m_pAppData slots in this structure for now; you'll see what they're for in the next chapter.) The application structure, CApp, no longer needs to store controls, as it did in the previous chapter's SlideShow application (lines 35–54).

This uses a static array of controls—the m_apControl slot of CStateApp—to store the application's controls rather than using a linked list, as for states, because unlike the depth of the state stack in the application, it's easy to predict how many controls a particular application will preallocate. If, for a specific application, it's better to let states create and destroy their own controls, then it's fairly simple to replace m_apControl with a list of _Node structures or simply size the array to be the upper bound on the number of controls.

The framework must allocate common controls on launch and provide access to these common controls. It does this using an enumeration of defined controls and the application's initialization function, as shown in Listing 5-11.

Listing 5-11. Allocating Common Controls in the Control Pool

```
 1: /**
 2:  * @name EStateControl
 3:  * @memo Delineates framework controls.
 4:  */
 5: typedef enum
 6: {
 7:    /// Navigation menu.
 8:    Ctl_NavMenu = 0,
 9:    /// Soft Key menu.
10:    Ctl_SoftKeyMenu,
11:    /// Text input control.
12:    Ctl_TextInput,
13:
14:    // End of the list... don't mess with this one!
15:    Ctl_LastFrameworkControl
16: } EStateControl;
17:
18:
19: /*
20:  * In the application's initialization function
21:  * invoked by AEEClsCreateInstance
22:  */
23:
24: // Create the UI elements for the framework.
25: pThis->m_app.m_nControl = MAX_NUM_CONTROLS;
26: for ( i = 0; i < MAX_NUM_CONTROLS; i++ )
27:   pThis->m_app.m_apControl[ i ] = NULL;
28:
29: ISHELL_CreateInstance( GetShell( pThis ),
30:   AEECLSID_MENUCTL,
31:   (void **)&pThis->m_app.m_apControl[ Ctl_NavMenu ]);
32:
33: ISHELL_CreateInstance( GetShell( pThis ),
34:     AEECLSID_SOFTKEYCTL,
35:     (void **)&pThis->m_app.m_apControl[ Ctl_SoftKeyMenu ]);
36: ISHELL_CreateInstance( GetShell( pThis ),
37:     AEECLSID_TEXTCTL,
38:     (void **)&pThis->m_app.m_apControl[ Ctl_TextInput ]);
39:
40: result = pThis->m_app.m_apControl[ Ctl_NavMenu ] &&
41:     pThis->m_app.m_apControl[ Ctl_SoftKeyMenu ] &&
42:     pThis->m_app.m_apControl[ Ctl_TextInput ] ?
```

```
43:        SUCCESS : EFAILED;
44:
45: if ( result == EFAILED )
46: {
47:   for ( i = 0; i < MAX_NUM_CONTROLS; i++ )
48:   {
49:     if ( pThis->m_app.m_apControl[ i ] )
50:     {
51:       ICONTROL_Release( pThis->m_app.m_apControl[ i ] );
52:       pThis->m_app.m_apControl[ i ] = NULL;
53:     }
54:   }
55:   return result;
56: }
57:
58: /*
59:  * Reset all framework controls to begin with.
60:  */
61: for ( i = 0; i < Ctl_LastFrameworkControl; i++ )
62:   ICONTROL_Reset( pThis->m_app.m_apControl[ i ] );
63:
64: result = AS_Init( pThis );
65:
66: /*
67:  * In the application's termination function
68:  *  invoked when the application exits
69:  */
70: // Release all controls
71: for ( i = 0; i < MAX_NUM_CONTROLS; i++ )
72: {
73:   if ( pThis->m_app.m_apControl[ i ] )
74:   {
75:     ICONTROL_Release( pThis->m_app.m_apControl[ i ] );
76:     pThis->m_app.m_apControl[ i ] = NULL;
77:   }
78: }
79:
80: // Release any application state stuff
81: AS_Free( pThis );
```

The EStateControl enumeration on lines 1–16 provides you with an easy way to access a specific control in the application's m_apControl array. (By the way, you could have just as easily used the C preprocessor to define macros to do the same thing.)

The application's entry function—invoked by AEEClsCreateInstance when the application launches—should preallocate each of these controls, just as the application's termination function should destroy them when the application exits. Lines 24–62, taken from the application's entry function, does just that. First, for housekeeping, on lines 26–27 all of the control instances are set to NULL so that the array will point to either valid controls or NULL. Next, lines 29–31 create the main menu control, and lines 33–38 create the soft key menu control and the associated text control. The conditional expression on lines 40–43 simply assures the application that the three controls were created; it's a critical error if the application can't obtain the controls it needs to function. Thus, lines 45–56 clean up by destroying any allocated controls in the event of an error and return the error to AEEClsCreateInstance. Assuming success, lines 61–62 reset all controls, ensuring that none of them will have focus or occupy screen space once they're created. (Although not required, this is a good idea, just like initializing newly created stack variables before you use them!) Finally, line 64 gives you an opportunity to create other controls or do any one-time initialization during application launch. Just as you create state functions, you define the function AS_Init in your code, which can create controls, allocate memory, and so on.

Application termination is the inverse of application initialization: The destructor must release all allocated controls and then invoke your termination function to let you do any final cleanup. The loop on lines 71–78 simply walks the list of controls, releasing any control in the array and setting its slot to NULL to keep the remainder of the application from attempting to release it again, which would result in an application failure. Finally, on line 81, the framework calls your AS_Free function, which can undo any initialization it performed in AS_Init.

Handling Events

The last thing the framework must do is share incoming events with active controls before sending them to application states. You've already seen bits and pieces of this code scattered around this chapter. The framework now has two event handlers: one to pass events either to controls or the current state and the other to handle events sent to the framework controls. The event handler for the state framework itself is unchanged, save that it now invokes a separate function for passing events to each of the controls. Let's see how the controls receive their events (see Listing 5-12).

Listing 5-12. Dispatching Events to Controls

```
 1: /**
 2:  * Handles incoming events sent to framework controls.
 3:  * @param void *p: pointer to app
 4:  * @param AEEEvent eCode: event code
 5:  * @param uint16 wParam: event parameter
 6:  * @param uint32 dwParan: event parameter
 7:  * @return boolean FALSE if app framework should
 8:  * continue handling event
 9:  */
10: static boolean
11: _controlHandleEvent( CStateAppPtr pThis,
12:                      AEEEvent eCode,
13:                      uint16 wParam,
14:                      uint32 dwParam )
15: {
16:   boolean result = FALSE;
17:   boolean bTextControlOnscreen =
18:     ITEXTCTL_GetTextPtr( (ITextCtl *)
19:           pThis->m_apControl[ Ctl_TextInput ] )
20:             != NULL ? TRUE : FALSE;
21:   boolean bSoftMenuOnscreen =
22:     IMENUCTL_GetItemCount( (IMenuCtl *)
23:           pThis->m_apControl[ Ctl_SoftKeyMenu ] )
24:             != 0 ? TRUE : FALSE;
25:   int wCurrCtl;
26:
27:   // Dispatch the event to any of the active controls
28:   for ( wCurrCtl = 0;
29:         wCurrCtl < pThis->m_nControl;
30:         wCurrCtl++ )
31:   {
32:    if ( pThis->m_apControl[ wCurrCtl ] &&
33:       ICONTROL_IsActive( pThis->m_apControl[ wCurrCtl ] ) )
34:     {
35:      result =
36:        ICONTROL_HandleEvent(
37:          pThis->m_apControl[ wCurrCtl ],
38:          eCode, wParam, dwParam );
39:      if ( result ) break;
40:     }
41:   }
42:
```

```
43:    // Select on a text field with no soft key pops state
44:    if ( eCode == EVT_KEY && wParam == AVK_SELECT &&
45:       ICONTROL_IsActive( pThis->m_apControl[ Ctl_TextInput ] ) &&
46:       !bSoftMenuOnscreen )
47:    {
48:      State_PopEx( pThis, StateChangeInfo_SELECT );
49:      result = TRUE;
50:    }
51:
52:    // Key up in text control with soft key menu
53:    // activates text control
54:    if ( bSoftMenuOnscreen && bTextControlOnscreen &&
55:       eCode == EVT_KEY && wParam == AVK_UP &&
56:       !ICONTROL_IsActive( pThis->m_apControl[ Ctl_TextInput ] ) &&
57:       ICONTROL_IsActive( pThis->m_apControl[ Ctl_SoftKeyMenu ] ) )
58:    {
59:      ICONTROL_SetActive(
60:        pThis->m_apControl[ Ctl_SoftKeyMenu ],
61:        FALSE );
62:      ICONTROL_SetActive(
63:        pThis->m_apControl[ Ctl_TextInput ],
64:        TRUE );
65:      result = TRUE;
66:    }
67:
68:    // Key down in text control with soft key menu
69:    // activates menu control
70:    if ( bSoftMenuOnscreen && bTextControlOnscreen &&
71:       eCode == EVT_KEY && wParam == AVK_DOWN &&
72:       ICONTROL_IsActive( pThis->m_apControl[ Ctl_TextInput ] ) &&
73:       !ICONTROL_IsActive( pThis->m_apControl[ Ctl_SoftKeyMenu ] ) )
74:    {
75:      ICONTROL_SetActive(
76:        pThis->m_apControl[ Ctl_SoftKeyMenu ],
77:        TRUE );
78:      ICONTROL_SetActive(
79:        pThis->m_apControl[ Ctl_TextInput ],
80:        FALSE );
81:      result = TRUE;
82:    }
83:    // Menu selection navigates to new state
84:    if ( !result && eCode == EVT_COMMAND )
85:    {
86:      if ( ICONTROL_IsActive( pThis->m_apControl[ Ctl_NavMenu ] ) ||
```

```
87:        ICONTROL_IsActive( pThis->m_apControl[ Ctl_SoftKeyMenu ] ) )
88:    {
89:      PFNSTATEEVENT *pState;
90:      IMenuCtl *pIMenu;
91:      pIMenu = ICONTROL_IsActive(
92:        pThis->m_apControl[ Ctl_NavMenu ] ) ?
93:          (IMenuCtl *)( pThis->m_apControl[ Ctl_NavMenu ] ) :
94:          (IMenuCtl *)( pThis->m_apControl[ Ctl_SoftKeyMenu ] );
95:
96:      IMENUCTL_GetItemData( pIMenu,
97:        wParam, (uint32 *)(&pState) );
98:
99:      if ( pState != NULL )
100:      {
101:        State_PushEx( pThis, pState,
102:          (unsigned char)(wParam & 0xFF));
103:        result = TRUE;
104:      }
105:      else
106:      {
107:        DBGPRINTF("Error? Menu state null");
108:      }
109:    }
110:  }
111:  return result;
112: }
```

Listing 5-12 is the longest function in the chapter, so let's take it one logical block at a time. Lines 16–25 define four variables: result, which indicates if a control consumed the event; bTextControlOnscreen, which determines if the text control is on-screen by seeing if it has a valid pointer to input text; bSoftMenuOnscreen, which determines if the soft key menu is on-screen; and wCurrCtl, which iterates through the list of controls.

You need to perform the skullduggery on lines 18–24 to determine whether these controls are actually on-screen and active because there's no method for either ITextCtl or IMenuCtl to determine whether they're on-screen and active. This is especially true of IMenuCtl, where a count of the number of menu items determines whether it's visible.

Lines 27–41 simply iterate across all of the controls in the framework, offering the event to each control using ICONTROL_HandleEvent (lines 36–38) and exiting the loop if a specific control consumes the event (line 39).

The remainder of the function handles specific activities common to all controls:

1. A Select keystroke in a text control with no soft key menu signifies the end of text input and pops the state from the state stack (lines 43–50).

2. An Up keystroke in a soft key menu with a text control gives the text control focus (lines 52–66).

3. A Down keystroke in a text control with a soft key menu gives the soft key menu focus (lines 68–82).

4. Selecting a menu—either a soft key menu item or a navigation menu item—causes a transition to a new state.

Lines 43–50 are straightforward. If the event is a Select keystroke (line 44), the text control is active (line 45), and the menu control isn't on-screen (line 46), pop the current state, which indicates to the state function that the user pressed the Select key to cause the state change (line 48).

The second two cases—where a text control is connected to a menu control—are a little more tricky because you want the framework to support a state using the text control or the soft key menu in isolation, and there's no good way to determine that from either of the control's settings. Instead, you can use the flags bTextControlOnscreen and bSoftMenuOnscreen to ensure that *both* controls are on-screen (even though only one can be active at a time) on lines 54 and 70 to handle Up and Down keystrokes. (In other cases, these keystrokes should be passed to the state.) If these are both on-screen and the event is the appropriate keystroke, the code on lines 52–66 and 68–82 swaps focus from one control to the other.

Finally, the framework automates changing to new states when a menu item is selected if the menu stores a reference to the new state function in its dwData pointer. Lines 84–87 tests to see if the event is a menu selection on an active menu, and if so, lines 91–94 determine which menu accepted the selection by seeing which currently is active. Lines 96–97 use IMENUCTL_GetItemData to find the dwData field of the current menu item, which may be a state function. If it is, lines 99–104 push the new state on the stack, passing the lower byte of the selected menu item so the state knows which menu item invoked the state change. Otherwise, a debugging message is generated indicating that there may be an error in using the framework, and the framework passes the menu event to the current state's event handler.

Tying It All Together

To create the illustrations in this chapter, I needed a quick way to programmatically create and display the controls. Rather than using a separate application for each control, I used the framework I've described to build an application with a menu that shows a list of controls to select and then enters a state for each control. The following sections show how to use the framework to accomplish this by looking at a couple of the states in the application. (You can see the source code for the entire application in the ControlSample application that accompanies this book).

Initializing the Framework

Begin by extending the list of controls to include the controls in the example:

```
1: typedef enum
2: {
3:    /// IStatic used for demonstrating IStatic.
4:    Ctl_Static = Ctl_LastFrameworkControl + 1,
5:    Ctl_Time,
6:
7:    /// Used to mark
8:    Ctl_LastControl
9: } EStateCtlPoolIdx;
```

You could just as easily use preprocessor definitions or even keep track of them in your head, but it's easier this way. Throughout each of the states, you can now refer to a specific control by looking at the appropriate slot in the m_apControl array, just as you can with the framework's controls.

Next, you need to add the code to initialize the IStatic and ITime controls. Rather than modifying the main startup code in Main.c, you simply do it in the AS_Init function (see Listing 5-13).

Listing 5-13. Initializing the Application's Variables

```
1: /**
2:  * Initialize the application-specific data.
3:  * @param void *pThis: application
4:  * @return: EFAILED or ESUCCESS
5:  */
6: int AS_Init( CAppPtr pThis )
7: {
```

```
 8:    int result = SUCCESS;
 9:
10:    ASSERT( pThis );
11:    // Create the application controls here.
12:    result = ISHELL_CreateInstance( GetShell( pThis ),
13:      AEECLSID_STATIC,
14:      (void **)&pThis->m_app.m_apControl[ Ctl_Static ]);
15:
16:    if ( result == SUCCESS )
17:      result = ISHELL_CreateInstance( GetShell( pThis ),
18:        AEECLSID_CLOCKCTL,
19:        (void **)&pThis->m_app.m_apControl[ Ctl_Time ]);
20:
21:    return result;
22: }
```

Pretty dull stuff here—just create two controls and return the result code of either SUCCESS or any failure ISHELL_CreateInstance returns.

While on the topic of startup and teardown, it's worthwhile to note that you don't have any specific teardown to do in AS_Free because the framework will destroy these controls on your behalf:

```
 1: /**
 2:  * Free allocated resources.
 3:  * We don't have to release the controls in the
 4:  * control pool --- the framework does this for
 5:  * us.
 6:  * @param void *pThis: application
 7:  * @return nothing
 8:  */
 9: void AS_Free( CAppPtr pThis )
10: {
11:   UNUSED( pThis );
12: }
```

With application startup and teardown complete, let's take a look at two states: the main menu state and a state that demonstrates a time control.

Managing the Main Menu State

The main menu state simply delegates state initialization and teardown to separate private functions (see Listing 5-14).

Listing 5-14. Starting Up and Tearing Down the Main State

```
 1: /**
 2:  * Handles events for the first state
 3:  * @param void *p: this applicaton
 4:  * @param AEEEvent eCode: event code
 5:  * @param uint16 wParam: event parameter
 6:  * @param uint32 dwParam: event parameter
 7:  * @return TRUE if application handled event
 8:  */
 9: boolean AS_MainHandleEvent( void *p,
10:                 AEEEvent eCode,
11:                 uint16 wParam, uint32 dwParam)
12: {
13:   CAppPtr pThis = (CAppPtr)p;
14:   boolean result = FALSE;
15:
16:   ASSERT( pThis );
17:
18:   if ( !result ) switch ( eCode )
19:   {
20:     case EVT_APP_START:
21:     case EVT_APP_RESUME:
22:       result = mainEntry( p, wParam );
23:       break;
24:
25:     case EVT_APP_STOP:
26:     case EVT_APP_SUSPEND:
27:       result = mainExit( p, wParam );
28:       break;
29:
30:     default:
31:       break;
32:   }
33:
34:   return result;
35: }
```

When this state is entered—either as a result of a state change or application resumption—it calls the function mainEnter to set up the main menu. Similarly, when the state exits, it calls mainExit to free the resources used by the menu. The mainEnter function is long but simple at heart (see Listing 5-15).

Listing 5-15. Entering the Main State

```
 1: /**
 2:  * Prepares user interface for the first state
 3:  * @param void *p: this applicaton
 4:  * @param EStateChangeCause change: why we entered this state
 5:  * @return nothing
 6:  */
 7: static boolean mainEntry( void *p,
 8:                               EStateChangeCause change )
 9: {
10:    CAppPtr pThis = (CAppPtr)p;
11:    CtlAddItem addItemInfo = { 0 };
12:    int itemID = 1;
13:    UNUSED( change );
14:
15:    ASSERT( pThis );
16:
17:    // Clear the display
18:    IDISPLAY_ClearScreen( GetDisplay( pThis ) );
19:
20:    IMENUCTL_SetTitle( (IMenuCtl *)
21:      pThis->m_app.m_apControl[ Ctl_NavMenu ],
22:      APP_RES_FILE,
23:      IDS_MAINMENUTITLE,
24:      NULL );
25:
26:    // Build a menu of choices for controls.
27:    addItemInfo.wItemID = itemID++;
28:    addItemInfo.dwData = (uint32)AS_StaticHandleEvent;
29:    addItemInfo.pszResText = APP_RES_FILE;
30:    addItemInfo.pszResImage = APP_RES_FILE;
31:    addItemInfo.wText = IDS_STATIC;
32:    addItemInfo.wImage = IDI_STATIC;
33:    IMENUCTL_AddItemEx( (IMenuCtl *)
34:      pThis->m_app.m_apControl[ Ctl_NavMenu ],
35:      &addItemInfo );
36:
37:    addItemInfo.wItemID = itemID++;
38:    addItemInfo.dwData = (uint32)AS_TextHandleEvent;
39:    addItemInfo.pszResText = APP_RES_FILE;
40:    addItemInfo.pszResImage = APP_RES_FILE;
41:    addItemInfo.wText = IDS_TEXT;
42:    addItemInfo.wImage = IDI_TEXT;
```

```
43:    IMENUCTL_AddItemEx( (IMenuCtl *)
44:      pThis->m_app.m_apControl[ Ctl_NavMenu ],
45:      &addItemInfo );
46:
47:    addItemInfo.wItemID = itemID++;
48:    addItemInfo.dwData = (uint32)AS_TextWithMenuHandleEvent;
49:    addItemInfo.pszResText = APP_RES_FILE;
50:    addItemInfo.pszResImage = APP_RES_FILE;
51:    addItemInfo.wText = IDS_TEXTWITHMENU;
52:    addItemInfo.wImage = IDI_OK;
53:    IMENUCTL_AddItemEx( (IMenuCtl *)
54:      pThis->m_app.m_apControl[ Ctl_NavMenu ],
55:      &addItemInfo );
56:
57:    addItemInfo.wItemID = itemID++;
58:    addItemInfo.dwData = (uint32)AS_TimeHandleEvent;
59:    addItemInfo.pszResText = APP_RES_FILE;
60:    addItemInfo.pszResImage = APP_RES_FILE;
61:    addItemInfo.wText = IDS_TIME;
62:    addItemInfo.wImage = IDI_TIME;
63:    IMENUCTL_AddItemEx( (IMenuCtl *)
64:      pThis->m_app.m_apControl[ Ctl_NavMenu ],
65:      &addItemInfo );
66:
67:    addItemInfo.wItemID = itemID++;
68:    addItemInfo.dwData = (uint32)AS_MenuHandleEvent;
69:    addItemInfo.pszResText = APP_RES_FILE;
70:    addItemInfo.pszResImage = APP_RES_FILE;
71:    addItemInfo.wText = IDS_MENU;
72:    addItemInfo.wImage = IDI_MENU;
73:    IMENUCTL_AddItemEx( (IMenuCtl *)
74:      pThis->m_app.m_apControl[ Ctl_NavMenu ],
75:      &addItemInfo );
76:
77:    ICONTROL_SetProperties(
78:      pThis->m_app.m_apControl[ Ctl_NavMenu ],
79:      MP_UNDERLINE_TITLE );
80:
81:    // Size the menu.
82:    ICONTROL_SetRect( pThis->m_app.m_apControl[ Ctl_NavMenu ],
83:      &pThis->m_rc );
84:    ICONTROL_SetActive( pThis->m_app.m_apControl[ Ctl_NavMenu ],
85:      TRUE );
86:    ICONTROL_Redraw( pThis->m_app.m_apControl[ Ctl_NavMenu ] );
```

```
87:
88:    IDISPLAY_Update( GetDisplay( pThis ) );
89:
90:    return TRUE;
91: }
```

This function is a straightforward application of the interface to IMenuCtl. It begins by clearing the display (line 18) and then setting the title of the menu to a string defined in the resource file (lines 20–24). (Recall that when using a resource entry to set a menu title, you provide the name of the resource file and the ID of the resource, and don't pass a buffer as the last argument.) Next, on lines 26–75, the function adds each item to the menu using IMENUCTL_AddItemEx. The only clever bits of code here are the first two lines of each item addition, such as lines 27–28. Here, the variable itemID stores a unique ID for each menu item, incrementing it after each assignment. On the following line, the menu's dwData pointer stores the state function for the state corresponding to the menu choice so that the framework will automatically push that state when you select a menu item.

The remainder of the function completes the menu initialization by selecting an underlined title (lines 77–79), sizing the menu to fill the display (lines 82–83), activating the menu (lines 84–85), and redrawing the menu (line 86). Finally, the function updates the display (line 88) and exits.

By contrast, mainExit is a simple function (see Listing 5-16).

Listing 5-16. Exiting the Main State

```
 1: /**
 2:  * Exits the user interface for the first state.
 3:  * @param void *p: this application
 4:  * @param EStateChangeCause change: why we exited this state
 5:  * @return nothing
 6:  */
 7: static boolean mainExit( void *p,
 8:                 EStateChangeCause change )
 9: {
10:   CAppPtr pThis = (CAppPtr)p;
11:
12:   UNUSED( change );
13:
14:   ASSERT( pThis );
15:
16:   ICONTROL_Reset( pThis->m_app.m_apControl[ Ctl_NavMenu ] );
17:
18:   return TRUE;
19: }
```

The mainExit function needs only to reset the navigation menu so that it's ready for use the next time it's needed.

How the application handles the entry and exit of other states is the same.

Summary

This chapter covered the following key points:

- The IControl interface is the base interface from which all user interface controls are derived.

- QUALCOMM BREW provides user interfaces for static text and image display, text input, time display (clock, countdown, and count up timers), calendars, menus, and a simple HTML viewer.

- You create control instances as you would instances of other interfaces, using ISHELL_CreateInstance, passing the desired class ID for the class instance you want.

- When using a control, the sequence of events is to set its properties, set its rectangles, activate it, and update the display. While the control is active, you must share application events with the control for it to function correctly. When you're finished, you must reset the control and release it when you're done using it.

- It's best to preallocate resources crucial to your application's execution such as controls when the application starts so that you don't need to deal with failures associated with not having them when you need them.

CHAPTER 6

Streaming Data

DEVICES RUNNING QUALCOMM BREW have stringent memory, embedded file system, and processor constraints. At the same time, users demand increasing functionality, including access to rich multimedia streams such as polyphonic MIDI or sophisticated animations. This kind of content often occupies a great deal of memory. To mitigate memory constraints, QUALCOMM BREW provides *stream* interfaces to access content from network sockets and the file system, as well as a memory buffer. With the stream interface, your application uses a fraction of the total memory required by content when passing data from its source to your application. Moreover, the stream interface is *asynchronous*; in other words, your application can continue executing while waiting for data from the file system or a network resource.

This chapter introduces you to the abstract stream interface IAStream as well as the interfaces that implement it: IFile, ISocket, IMemAStream, and IUnzipAStream. After reading this chapter, you'll understand how to use streams, as well as how to convert a stream interface to its cousin, an ISource, which you can use to process data in chunks such as lines. Because RocketMileage doesn't use streams, this chapter shows how to use streams with a simple application that plays multimedia data from files.

Understanding the Stream Interface

If you've ever used the low-level socket file Application Programming Interfaces (APIs) under Unix, Windows, Mac OS X, or another operating system, you're already familiar with the notion of a stream of data. Put simply, a stream of data is one where you can read each datum in turn as it's available, starting with the beginning of a stream.

To use a stream, you need to open it, call its read method to read data, set a callback if the read doesn't have data, and continue doing this until you've read all the data you need. The process is quite simple:

1. Begin by obtaining an instance of the concrete interface of a stream, such as IFile or ISocket.

2. Call the interface's Read method (such as IFILE_Read to read from a file) to begin reading data from the stream.

3. If the Read method returns the error AEE_STREAM_WOULDBLOCK, you'll need to defer reading until more data is available. In this case, you should register a callback function using the Readable function (such as IFILE_Readable).

4. The stream will invoke your callback function when more data is available. At that point, you can call the interface's Read method again, scheduling a callback if necessary using Readable.

5. If Read ever returns fewer bytes than you request, simply call it again (scheduling a callback if necessary).

6. When you're done, release the interface using its Release method.

From an application design perspective, it's generally best to place all of your reading activities within callback functions so that your application can proceed normally while the stream operations take place. By doing this, it makes it easy for your application to report progress during the stream activities as well as to transition to an error state in the event of an error.

Understanding the Implementations of IAStream

The IFile, ISocket, IMemAStream, and IUnzipAStream interfaces all inherit the IAStream interface (see Figure 6-1). Moreover, other interfaces, such as the IWeb interface (explained in detail in Chapter 10, "Networking Your Data"), provide an ISource object, which you can convert to a stream and then read from as you would any other stream.

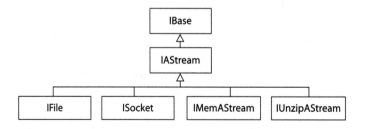

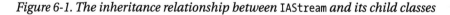

Figure 6-1. The inheritance relationship between IAStream *and its child classes*

Understanding the IFile Interface

All QUALCOMM BREW–enabled handsets include a flash memory resident file system that you can access using the IFile interface. Most handsets have a megabyte or more of flash memory, which all installed applications on the handset share. You can use the file system to store persistent data in text or binary files or to store database information created with the QUALCOMM BREW database interfaces discussed in the next chapter.

The file system is divided into directories, with one directory for each installed application and a shared directory that all applications can access. However, you must assert the appropriate privileges in your application's Module Information File (MIF) before you can access either your own directory or the shared directory (see Chapter 2, "Designing for the QUALCOMM BREW Platform").

You can't just create an instance of the IFile interface using ISHELL_CreateInstance. Instead, you need to use the IFileMgr interface, which provides the base functionality for manipulating items on the file system, including getting the names of files in a current directory, removing files, making new directories, removing directories, and opening files for reading and writing. (You'll recall that Chapter 4, "Handling Events," used the IFileMgr interface when enumerating the available slide show resource files for the SlideShow application.)

To create an IFile instance, then, you must first create an IFileMgr instance and use its IFILE_OpenFile method to open a named file with the desired read/write attributes. This, in turn, returns an IFile interface, which you can read from using the IAStream interfaces. If you've opened your file for writing, you can also write to the file using the IFILE_Write command, which lets you specify a buffer containing data and the size of the buffer to write to the file. The IFile interface closely parallels the POSIX style file system APIs, so you can also seek to an arbitrary location in a file or truncate a file at a specific length.

Understanding the ISocket Interface

The ISocket interface provides a low-level network socket interface similar in appearance to the Berkeley socket interface found in most flavors of Unix, the Winsock interfaces found on Microsoft Windows, and the socket implementation on the Palm Powered platform.

Chapter 10, "Networking Your Data," discusses the ISocket interface in more detail.

Understanding the IMemAStream Interface

The IMemAStream interface provides a streaming interface to a memory buffer. At first, this seems counterintuitive. After all, why would you want to load a potentially memory-hungry item into Random-Access Memory (RAM) just to turn it into a stream so you can save memory by reading it?

In practice, that's actually *not* why you'd use the IMemAStream interface. Instead, if you have something in RAM for another purpose already—say, as part of its normal operation, your application caches an item in RAM—you can use the interfaces in media viewers such as IImage to read data directly from the stream and display the image contained in the stream.

You do this using the IMEMASTREAM_Set interface, which sets the stream to begin reading from a specific memory region. The actual call looks like this:

```
1: void IMEMASTREAM_Set(
2:                     IMemAStream *pIMemAStream,
3:                     byte *pBuff,
4:                     uint32 dwSize,
5:                     uint32 dwOffset,
6:                     boolean bSysMem
7:                     );
```

The IMEMASTREAM_Set call takes the stream to initialize and the beginning of the memory region from which to read. Because the stream will release the memory region when it's released, you must pass not only the beginning of the allocated region (in pBuff) but also where the stream should actually start reading (as dwOffset, the number of bytes after pBuff). You must also specify the region's size (dwSize) and whether the stream should free the region using FREE—the usual case, where you've created the memory region using MALLOC—or SYSFREE. (SYSFREE is an API that lets you free memory allocated by the handset's underlying real-time operating system from the system heap rather than the application heap.)

Thus, the purpose of the IMemAStream interface isn't so much to preserve memory as it is to make it easy to render content from data already in memory.

Understanding the IUnzipAStream Interface

The IUnzipAStream interface gives you a slick way to preserve memory with your data—by compressing it first. Rather than devising your own compression scheme and then implementing a decompression algorithm on QUALCOMM BREW, you can simply use the IUnzipAStream interface to decompress Lempel-Ziv 77 (LZ77) compressed data as a stream while you read from the stream.

In practice, this is mind-numbingly easy. First, establish a stream—either use a real stream such as an IFile or ISocket stream or use IMemAStream to decompress LZ77 data in memory. Next, create an instance of IUnzipAStream. Finally, point the IUnzipAStream instance at the target stream using the IUNZIPASTREAM_SetStream method. As you'll see shortly, this simply takes the IUnzipAStream instance and the stream from which the IUnzipAStream should read:

```
1: IUNZIPASTREAM_SetStream( pIUnzipAStream, pIAStream );
```

The easiest way to generate compressed data that the IUnzipAStream utility can manage is via the open-source gzip utility available under Unix, Linux, Mac OS, and Windows. In addition to being available as a command-line utility—handy when you're packaging specific resources for file system or Web distribution for your application—it's also available as a source code and library on most development platforms.

> **NOTE** *The* IUnzipAStream *interface is available in QUALCOMM BREW 1.1 and above. You can't instantiate an* IUnzipAStream *interface in QUALCOMM BREW 1.0.*

Using the Stream Interface

The StreamSample application accompanying this chapter shows how to use streams. Built using the example framework, it's a simple application that lets you select a BMP image or an LZ77-compressed bitmap image—which reduces an image size by up to a factor of four—from the file system and display it (see Figure 6-2).

Figure 6-2. The StreamSample application

To use the StreamSample application, simply place BMP files or LZ77-compressed BMP files (with suffixes *.bmp* and *.gz*, appropriately) in the StreamSample directory and run the application. Once the application is running, select the bitmap you want to see, and the application displays it on the screen. Obviously, seeing *how* the application works is more interesting than the application itself!

Using the Framework in StreamSample

The StreamSample application consists of two states. The first state, managed by AS_MainHandleEvent, is responsible for generating a list of BMP and LZ77 files (files ending in *.gz*) using code similar to the FillMenu function in Chapter 4, "Handling Events," for SlideShow. The second state, managed by AS_ShowBitmapHandleEvent, loads the selected item from the file system as a stream and uses the IImage interface to display the image.

Because only the second state uses streams, let's skip a discussion of the framework—which you can review in the previous two chapters—and instead see how the application actually uses streams.

Using Streams in StreamSample

In the show bitmap state—managed by AS_ShowBitmapHandleEvent—the state entry code does all of the work. Specifically, it must do the following:

1. Open the selected file.

2. Determine if the file is compressed and, if it is, create an IUnzipAStream interface to unzip the data.

3. Create an IImage instance to display the image.

4. Set the IImage instance to accept data from the stream.

5. Draw the image.

In addition, for the morbidly curious, the state entry code also prints memory usage at several points to the debugging console so you can see the difference in memory consumption between using LZ77-compressed streams. (In practice, LZ77-compressed streams generally cost around 2 kilobytes.)

The routine that does all of this is showBitmapEntry (see Listing 6-1).

Listing 6-1. Entering the Bitmap State

```
 1: /**
 2:  * Enters the ShowBitmap state.
 3:  * @param void *p: this applicaton
 4:  * @param EStateChange change: why we entered this state
 5:  * @return TRUE on success; FALSE if state should not be entered.
 6:  */
 7: static boolean showBitmapEntry( void *p,
 8:                        EStateChangeCause change )
 9: {
10:    CAppPtr pThis = (CAppPtr)p;
11:    IImage *pIImage = NULL;
12:    CAppDataPtr pAppData = NULL;
13:    IAStream *pIAStream = NULL;
14:    int result;
15:
16:    UNUSED( change );
17:    ASSERT( pThis );
18:
19:    pAppData = GetAppData(pThis);
20:
21:    // Clear the display
22:    IDISPLAY_ClearScreen( GetDisplay( pThis )  );
23:
24:    // Note how much heap we start with...
25:    DBGPRINT_HeapUsed( pThis );
26:
27:    // Get the stream for the file.
28:    pIAStream = GetStreamFromFile( pThis, pAppData->szName );
29:
30:    if ( pIAStream == NULL ) return NULL;
31:
32:    // If the steam is compressed,
33:    if ( STRENDS( ".gz", pAppData->szName ) )
34:    {
35:      // we need to get a stream to uncompress it
36:      pIAStream = GetUnzipStreamFromStream( pThis, pIAStream );
37:    }
38:
39:    // Create an IImage control to display the bitmap.
40:    result = ISHELL_CreateInstance( GetShell( pThis ),
41:      AEECLSID_WINBMP,
42:      (void **)&pIImage );
```

```
43:   pThis->m_app.m_apControl[ Ctl_Image ] = (IControl *)pIImage;
44:
45:   if ( result != SUCCESS || !pIImage )
46:   {
47:     IASTREAM_Release( pIAStream );
48:     return FALSE;
49:   }
50:
51:   // Set the image to the stream
52:   IIMAGE_SetStream( pIImage, pIAStream );
53:
54:   // Draw the image
55:   DrawCentered( pThis, pIImage );
56:
57:   DBGPRINT_HeapUsed( pThis );
58:
59:   // We no longer need this interface.
60:   if ( pIAStream ) IASTREAM_Release( pIAStream );
61:
62:   // Update the display
63:   IDISPLAY_Update( GetDisplay( pThis ) );
64:   return TRUE;
65: }
```

The state entry begins by validating its preconditions (line 17) and getting the application's global variables using the macro GetAppData, which fetches the application's globals from the state machine structure. (This is essentially the same as what you did in prior chapters—stashing application globals in the application's structure. However, by providing the GetAppData and SetAppData macros, it's easier to maintain applications apart from the state machine framework.) In StreamSample, there's only one global variable: szName, the filename of the image you selected in the previous state.

Next, it calls the macro DBGPRINT_HeapUsed, a little utility that uses BREW's IHeap interface to get the amount of heap currently in use (see Listing 6-2).

Listing 6-2. Showing the Amount of Heap Consumed by the Application

```
1: /**
2:  * @name DBGPRINT_HeapUsed
3:  * @memo Prints amount of heap used to log.
4:  * @doc Prints the amount of heap used to the debug console.
5:  */
6: #define DBGPRINT_HeapUsed( pThis ) \
```

```
 7: {\
 8:   IHeap *pIHeap;\
 9:   ISHELL_CreateInstance( GetShell( pThis ), \
10:             AEECLSID_HEAP, \
11:             (void **)&pIHeap);\
12:   if ( pIHeap )\
13:   {\
14:     uint32 nMemoryUsed = IHEAP_GetMemStats(pIHeap);\
15:     DBGPRINTF("%s(%d) : %d bytes used", \
16:             __FILE__, __LINE__, nMemoryUsed );\
17:     IHEAP_Release( pIHeap );\
18:   }\
19: }
```

This bit of code simply creates an instance of IHeap on lines 9–11 and then calls its IHEAP_GetMemStats method to determine how many bytes of the heap are being used. Of course, the actual value is slightly more than is actually used by the application because it doesn't take into account the amount of space being consumed by the IHeap instance if its implementation allocates memory on the heap. However, it suffices for this purpose.

By calling DBGPRINT_HeapUsed on line 25, you establish the baseline amount of the heap consumed by the application to this point. (In practice, this number is around 46 kilobytes.) Once you know this, the routine gets a stream for the selected file using GetStreamFromFile on line 28.

This function is a simple utility function that hides from the caller the need to use an IFileMgr instance to obtain a stream to a file (see Listing 6-3).

Listing 6-3. Getting a Stream from a Filename

```
 1: /**
 2:  * Gets a stream for a file.
 3:  * @param CAppPtr *p: this applicaton
 4:  * @param char *szName: file name
 5:  * @return pointer to IAStream instance or NULL on failure.
 6:  */
 7: static IAStream *GetStreamFromFile( CAppPtr pThis,
 8:                                     char *szName )
 9: {
10:   IFileMgr *pIFileMgr = NULL;
11:   IFile *pIFile = NULL;
12:   int result;
13:
14:   // Setup the file manager instance
```

```
15:   result = ISHELL_CreateInstance( GetShell( pThis ),
16:                                    AEECLSID_FILEMGR,
17:                                    (void **)&pIFileMgr );
18:
19:   if ( result != SUCCESS || !pIFileMgr ) return NULL;
20:
21:   // Open the specific file to get a stream to the image.
22:   pIFile = IFILEMGR_OpenFile( pIFileMgr,  szName, _OFM_READ );
23:   IFILEMGR_Release( pIFileMgr );
24:
25:   return (IAStream *)pIFile;
26: }
```

There's no reason to separate this code into a separate function other than that it makes the tediously long showBitmapEntry a little shorter. It creates an IFileMgr instance (on lines 15–17) and returns if it fails to obtain one (line 19). On line 22, the real magic happens: The routine obtains an IFile stream from the file by opening it. Next, the routine frees the previously allocated IFileMgr instance and returns the opened file—as an abstract stream—on line 25.

NOTE   *This routine can open files for reading only as streams for two reasons. First, call* IFILEMGR_OpenFile *with the flag* _OFM_READ, *which marks a file for read-only access. Second, the resulting file instance is explicitly recast to an* IAStream *instance. If you want to use the full gamut of* IFile *methods to read and write from a file, open it with* _OFM_READWRITE *instead and be sure to keep its type as an* IFile *instance.*

Next, if the stream is compressed—that is, if the filename indicates compression using the *.gz* suffix found on gzipped files—the routine creates an IUnzipAStream instance on line 36 using GetUnzipStreamFromStream. This function is simply another short helper function that you might find handy to keep around and use elsewhere (see Listing 6-4).

Listing 6-4. Replacing a Stream with an IUnzipAStream

```
1: /**
2:  * Replaces a stream with a IUnzipAStream to the same stream.
3:  * @param CAppPtr *pThis: this applicaton
4:  * @param IAStream *pStream
5:  * @return pointer to IAStream instance or NULL on failure.
6:  */
```

```
 7: static IAStream *GetUnzipStreamFromStream( CAppPtr pThis,
 8:                        IAStream *pIAStream )
 9: {
10:   IUnzipAStream *pIUnzipAStream = NULL;
11:   int result;
12:
13:   // Setup the file manager instance
14:   result = ISHELL_CreateInstance( GetShell( pThis ),
15:                         AEECLSID_UNZIPSTREAM,
16:                           (void **)&pIUnzipAStream );
17:   if ( result != SUCCESS || pIUnzipAStream == NULL )
18:   {
19:     return NULL;
20:   }
21:   // Set the zip's source stream
22:   IUNZIPASTREAM_SetStream( pIUnzipAStream, pIAStream );
23:
24:   // Release our reference to the original stream
25:   IASTREAM_Release( pIAStream );
26:
27:   return (IAStream *)pIUnzipAStream;
28: }
```

There aren't any real surprises here: It begins by creating an instance of
IUnzipAStream on lines 14–16 and, if it's successful, sets the new stream's source
as the indicated stream. Next, on line 25, it releases the application's reference to
the original stream because once linked to the IUnzipAStream instance, the
IUnzipAStream will increment its reference count and take responsibility for freeing
the source stream when it's released.

Macros, Functions, and You: Making the Choice

You may wonder, given how short this function is, why I chose to make this function a function and the DBGPRINT_HeapUsed macro a macro. The answer is one
largely based on style. For short routines such as this that I use only in debugging
code, I tend to make them macros to avoid the function call overhead at the cost
of making my compiled code size larger. In contrast, for routines such as this that
exist in production versions of an application, it's probably better to conserve
space. Really, there's little practical difference—I've simply established a habit
that makes sense with the way I work.

Returning to `showBitmapEntry`, the next thing it does is create the `IImage` interface it uses to show the loaded image on lines 39–42, saving the image in the `Ctl_Image` slot of the application's control pool on line 43. Assuming this operation succeeds—something tested for on lines 45–49—the stream is assigned to the image on line 52 using `IIMAGE_SetStream`. This is functionally equivalent to the more lengthy and memory-expensive approach of loading the image into RAM and drawing it using `IDISPLAY_BitBlt`, which is discussed in Chapter 8, "Drawing Graphics." Moreover, by using the `IImage` interface, you can select an appropriate `IImage` instance by the data's type so that if you had other image types (such as PNG, JIF, or JPEG) on handsets that support these image types you could select the appropriate image decoder and display the image.

The `DrawCentered` routine simply draws the image centered on the display. There's little difference between this routine and the `ShowNextSlide` routine discussed in Chapter 4, "Handling Events," so there's no need to show it in this chapter.

Finally, the routine shows the total heap consumed by the operation (line 47) and then releases the stream interface (line 60) because it is now owned by the `IImage` interface. After that, it updates the display (line 63) and exits (line 64).

It's important to remember when using QUALCOMM BREW, most of the media interfaces use a `SetStream` style interface to present their content. Although this isn't clearly delineated through a specific inheritance chain, quickly skimming the header files shows that many viewers use it, including the `IHTMLViewer` control (used to display simple HTML files), the `ISoundPlayer` interface (used to play sounds, including MIDI and MP3 streams, as well as QUALCOMM's PureVoice format used by the network protocols), and the `IMedia` interface, which encapsulates the management of arbitrary rich media types supported by specific handset vendors.

NOTE *MIDI stands for Music Industry Digital Interface, and MP3 stands for Moving Pictures Expert Group Audio Layer 3.*

Summary

This chapter covered the following key points:

- The stream interface in QUALCOMM BREW gives you a memory-efficient way of obtaining data from a large object in small segments.

- QUALCOMM BREW provides a stream interface to files on the handset's flash memory file system as well as network sockets, memory regions, and data compressed using the popular LZ77 algorithm.

- QUALCOMM BREW's media APIs—including those that display HTML, images, and play sounds—accept data from streams, rather than a fully allocated memory buffer containing all of the data, so it's easy to render multimedia content in a minimum of memory.

CHAPTER 7

Storing Data

ALTHOUGH A SMALL platform, QUALCOMM BREW often provides more than one way to accomplish a specific task such as storing data. In the previous chapter, you saw how you could use streams to your advantage to store data on a handset's file system or remote server. This chapter shows you another way to store your application's data: in a database.

QUALCOMM BREW provides a general-purpose database interface that lets you create databases—collections of records—stored in a file on the handset's file system. Using the database interfaces, you can easily create, store, and recall application-specific records without worrying about developing an underlying database implementation. As you read this chapter, you'll see how the QUALCOMM BREW database implementation works, learn when you should use a database instead of files to store your application's data, and see how to address some issues you may encounter when using databases. Finally, the chapter shows how you can use databases in the RocketMileage application to store vehicle events, such as purchasing gas or service.

Choosing to Use a Database

Because QUALCOMM BREW provides two ways to store persistent data—files and databases—it's important to understand how they're different so you can make the right architecture decision when designing your application. As you saw in the previous chapter, files allow you to store data for access in a stream. Databases, on the other hand, provide a record-oriented mechanism for storing data.

Understanding the Database Implementation

The database implementation on QUALCOMM BREW lets you create *records* consisting of one or more *fields*, each of which has a fundamental *data type* such as integer, string, or binary data. Unlike other mobile platforms such as the Palm Powered platform, there's no direct correspondence between a database record and a structure in C, so you're free to devise an arbitrarily simple (or complex) schema for your database.

You begin by creating or opening a database using the IDBMgr interface, which provides methods for opening a database, initializing a database with a specific number of records and reserved size, and removing a database. When you create a database, you give it a unique name, which the system uses when creating the underlying files to store your database records. After opening a database with IDBMgr, the system provides your application with an IDatabase instance, which you use to access records in your database.

With the IDatabase instance, you can access individual records in your database, create new records by defining a list of fields for the record, and iterate over all records in the database. Each of these operations provides your application with an IDBRecord instance, which you use to access fields within a specific record.

The IDBRecord interface provides methods for accessing each field in a database record. Like the IDatabase interface, the IDBRecord interface provides an enumerative interface to record fields. The record interface begins by providing information about the first field, and as you fetch data for the current field, it automatically steps forward and returns information about the next field of the record. Using the IDBRecord interface, you can access and change the fields in a record, as well as delete a record and get the specific database ID of the record being manipulated.

Under the hood, QUALCOMM BREW uses two files for each database you create. One file, the *index* file, has the name you provide when opening the database with the suffix *.idx* and contains a set of offsets to each record in your database. The other file bears only the name you use when opening the database and contains the records in a proprietary format bearing each field, the application-specific identification for each field, and the field data.

 TIP *You shouldn't rely on the format or names of database files because QUALCOMM has made no assurances that these won't change in the future. Instead, be sure to always use the methods provided by the* IDBMgr, IDatabase, *and* IDBRecord *interfaces when interacting with database files.*

Understanding Database Requirements

For your application to use the database interfaces, it must satisfy two simple requirements:

> It must have either the File privilege or the All privilege asserted in your application's Module Information File (MIF).

> It must be willing to allocate two files out of the total number of files the application will use (a carrier-dependent figure made to ensure that multiple applications can coexist on handsets) for each database. These files can exist in your application's directory or in the shared directory if the database contents will be shared with another application. (Note, however, that if you use the shared directory, you'll also need to assert the Write Access to Shared Directory privilege in your application's MIF.)

> Because databases use files, you must be able to read from and write to files to use databases. Moreover, if you're storing a database in a shared directory, you must be sure you can also access the shared directory. To do this, be sure you set the correct privileges in your application's MIF.

> To encourage cooperative resource sharing between installed applications, some carriers may require that applications use fewer than some set number of files to prevent one application from hoarding the lion's share of file system resources. Consequently, you should be aware that each database you use requires two files: one for the index and one for the records themselves. Depending on your application's design and purpose, you may need to limit the number of databases you use or apply for a waiver when submitting your application to a specific carrier and describe your need for files in excess of the number mandated by the carrier.

Interfacing with a Database

Given the power and flexibility of the QUALCOMM BREW database implementation, the interfaces are surprisingly simple. The interfaces to databases span three separate classes: the IDBMgr class, responsible for managing databases; the IDatabase class, responsible for interfacing to a specific database; and the IDBRecord class, responsible for managing a specific record within an already-open database.

Using the IDBMgr Interface

The IDBMgr interface is analogous to the IFileMgr interface you encountered in the previous chapter. Instead of managing files and directories, however, the IDBMgr interface manages databases.

Besides the obligatory IDBMGR_AddRef and IDBMGR_Release methods, which let you adjust the reference count for an instance of IDBMgr, this class has three other methods. Two, IDBMGR_OpenDatabase and IDBMGR_OpenDatabaseEx, let you open a specific database, returning an IDatabase interface for the database you specify. The third, IDBMGR_Remove, deletes the files that correspond to a specific database.

Normally, you'll open a database using IDBMGR_OpenDatabase, which takes as arguments a reference to an IDBMgr interface, the name of the database, and whether the database should be created if it doesn't already exist:

```
1:  IDBMgr *pIDBMgr;
2:  IDatabase *pIDatabase;
3:  if ( ISHELL_CreateInstance( GetShell( pThis ),
4:                             AEECLSID_DBMGR, (void **)&pIDBMgr
5:                             ) != SUCCESS ) return;
6:  pIDatabase = IDBMGR_OpenDatabase( pIDBMgr,
7:                             APP_DATABASE_NAME, TRUE );
8:  IDBMGR_Release( pIDBMgr );
9:  if ( !pIDatabase ) return;
```

Some applications—such as those written by Original Equipment Manufacturers (OEMs)—may need to reserve a specific amount of space for their databases. To do this, you can use the IDBMGR_OpenDatabaseEx function, which takes as additional arguments the minimum size of a database record and the minimum number of records the database will contain. In turn, when creating the database, QUALCOMM BREW will reserve that many records' worth of space on the file system for the database. Listing 7-1 shows how to open a database.

Listing 7-1. Opening a Database

```
1:  #define MIN_RECORD_COUNT ( 100 )
2:  #define MIN_RECORD_SIZE ( 8 * sizeof( uint32 ) )
3:  IDBMgr *pIDBMgr;
4:  IDatabase *pIDatabase;
5:  if ( ISHELL_CreateInstance( GetShell( pThis ),
6:                             AEECLSID_DBMGR, (void **)&pIDBMgr
7:                             ) != SUCCESS ) return;
```

```
 8:  pIDatabase = IDBMGR_OpenDatabaseEx( pIDBMgr,
 9:                                      APP_DATABASE_NAME, TRUE,
10:                                      MIN_RECORD_SIZE,
11:                                      MIN_RECORD_COUNT );
12:  IDBMGR_Release( pIDBMgr );
13:  if ( !pIDatabase ) return;
```

Generally, your application's success shouldn't be predicated on the use of
IDBMGR_OpenDatabaseEx. If all developers use this function to stake out the likely
resource needs for their applications in advance, it's quite possible that most
handsets won't have enough room to store application data because the handset is
a cooperative environment. Instead, it's generally better to use the minimum
amount of space when your application first runs and specifically handle the possibility that there will be no room to store additional records.

When your application needs to delete a database, it should use the
IDBMGR_Remove function to do this. This function removes both the data file and the
index file. This function takes the name of the database as well as an instance of
the IDBMgr class:

```
1:  IDBMgr *pIDBMgr;
2:  if ( ISHELL_CreateInstance( GetShell( pThis ),
3:                              AEECLSID_DBMGR, (void **)&pIDBMgr
4:                              ) != SUCCESS ) return;
5:  IDBMGR_Remove( pIDBMgr, APP_DATABASE_NAME );
6:  IDBMGR_Release( pIDBMgr );
```

With IDBMGR_Remove, there's no need to remove each record of the database.
Because the function removes the underlying data files, the data is destroyed and
space on the file system is reclaimed automatically.

Using the IDatabase Interface

Once you open a database using IDBMGR_OpenDatabase (or its counterpart
IDBMGR_OpenDatabaseEx), you can perform operations to create and obtain individual records in the database using the IDatabase interface for that database. This
interface provides two basic ways to access a database: by using a record's unique
ID and by using an iterative interface that lets you walk through every record in the
database.

The easiest way to obtain a specific record is using its unique ID, assigned
when a database record is first created. To fetch a record by ID, you use

IDATABASE_GetRecordByID, which returns the IDRecord interface to the record (or NULL if the record doesn't exist):

```
1: IDBRecord *pIDBRecord;
2: pIDBRecord = IDATABASE_GetRecordByID( pIDatabase, (uint16)nRecordID );
3: // Do something with pIDBRecord here
4: IDBRECORD_Release( pIDBRecord );
```

Many times, of course, you won't know the ID of the record you want to access. When this is the case, you use the functions IDATABASE_Reset and IDATABASE_GetNextRecord to iterate over all of the records in the database, like this:

```
1: IDBRecord *pIDBRecord;
2: IDATABASE_Reset( pIDatabase );
3: while ( pIDBRecord = IDATABASE_GetNextRecord( pIDatabase ) )
4: {
5:   // Do something with pIDBRecord here...
6:   IDBRECORD_Release( pIDBRecord );
7: }
8: // IDATABASE_Reset( pIDatabase ) before iterating again!
```

Because IDATABASE_GetNextRecord returns NULL, this loop visits each record exactly once. If you'd rather use a for loop, you can either use a similar termination case or use IDATABASE_GetRecordCount, which returns the number of records in the database, like this:

```
1: IDBRecord *pIDBRecord;
2: int i, nCount;
3: nCount = IDATABASE_GetRecordCount( pIDatabase );
4: IDATABASE_Reset( pIDatabase );
5: for ( i = 0; i < nCount; i++ )
6: {
7:   IDATABASE_GetNextRecord( pIDatabase );
8:   // Do something with pIDBRecord here...
9:   IDBRECORD_Release( pIDBRecord );
10: }
11: // IDATABASE_Reset( pIDatabase ) before iterating again!
```

As you'll see in the next section, you must release the database record interfaces returned by both IDATABASE_GetRecordByID and IDATABASE_GetNextRecord before you can close the database by releasing it using IDATABASE_Release.

CAUTION *There's no documented evidence that a record's ID is immutable across the lifespan of a database, so it's best not to treat this ID as a means to identify a unique database entry except when a database is open. As such, the record's ID is more of an index to the record in the database, rather than a record in the traditional sense.*

Of course, all of this does little good until after you've placed something into your database in the first place. To do this, you define an array of database fields of type AEEDBField for a single record and then create that record in the database using the IDATABASE_CreateRecord function. Each entry in the array of AEEDBFields defines the properties and contents of a specific field in your database.

The AEEDBField structure has four fields to describe a database record field:

- The fType field stores the database field's type as a specific value of the AEEDBFieldType enumeration. Table 7-1 describes the valid type fields supported by the interface.

- The fName field stores the database field's name as an integer. You can either use the AEEDBFieldName enumeration to name your database fields or create your own enumeration that assigns a unique integer to each record field.

- The wDataLen field stores the size of the current field's data.

- The pBuffer field stores a pointer to the data for the current field.

Table 7-1. AEEDBFieldType *Definitions*

AEEDBFieldType VALUE	FUNDAMENTAL DATA TYPE
AEEDB_FT_BYTE	byte
AEEDB_FT_WORD	int16 or uint16
AEEDB_FT_DWORD	int32 or uint32
AEEDB_FT_STRING	Null-terminated array of AECHAR
AEEDB_FT_BINARY	Binary blob of bytes
AEEDB_FT_BITMAP	Windows bitmap

Creating a record can be a time-consuming task because you need to fill out an AEEDBField structure for each field. This process—*serializing* a memory structure for database storage—looks something like the code in Listing 7-2.

Listing 7-2. Serializing a Memory Structure

```
 1: typedef enum
 2: {
 3:    Fld_EntryType = 1,
 4:    Fld_Time,
 5:    Fld_Miles,
 6:    Fld_Other,
 7:    Fld_Cost,
 8:    Fld_DueTime,
 9:    Fld_DueMiles,
10:    Fld_LastField
11: } EAppRecordFieldName;
12:
13: IDBRecord *StoreRecord( IDatabase *pIDatabase,
14:                         CAppRecordPtr pRecord )
15: {
16:    AEEDBField arFields[ Fld_LastField ];
17:    uint16 iFieldName = 1;
18:
19:    ASSERT( pIDatabase && pRecord );
20:
21:    arFields[iFieldName-1].fType = AEEDB_FT_WORD;
22:    arFields[iFieldName-1].fName = iFieldName;
23:    arFields[iFieldName-1].wDataLen = sizeof( uint16 );
24:    arFields[iFieldName-1].pBuffer = (void*)&(pRecord->m_type);
25:    iFieldName++;
26:
27:    arFields[iFieldName-1].fType = AEEDB_FT_DWORD;
28:    arFields[iFieldName-1].fName = iFieldName;
29:    arFields[iFieldName-1].wDataLen = sizeof( uint32 );
30:    arFields[iFieldName-1].pBuffer = (void*)&(pRecord->m_nTime);
31:    iFieldName++;
32:
33:    arFields[iFieldName-1].fType = AEEDB_FT_DWORD;
34:    arFields[iFieldName-1].fName = iFieldName;
35:    arFields[iFieldName-1].wDataLen = sizeof( uint32 );
36:    arFields[iFieldName-1].pBuffer = (void*)&(pRecord->m_nMiles);
37:    iFieldName++;
38:
```

```
39:     arFields[iFieldName-1].fType = AEEDB_FT_DWORD;
40:     arFields[iFieldName-1].fName = iFieldName;
41:     arFields[iFieldName-1].wDataLen = sizeof( uint32 );
42:     arFields[iFieldName-1].pBuffer = (void*)&(pRecord->m_nOther);
43:     iFieldName++;
44:
45:     arFields[iFieldName-1].fType = AEEDB_FT_DWORD;
46:     arFields[iFieldName-1].fName = iFieldName;
47:     arFields[iFieldName-1].wDataLen = sizeof( uint32 );
48:     arFields[iFieldName-1].pBuffer = (void*)&(pRecord->m_nCost);
49:     iFieldName++;
50:
51:     arFields[iFieldName-1].fType = AEEDB_FT_DWORD;
52:     arFields[iFieldName-1].fName = iFieldName;
53:     arFields[iFieldName-1].wDataLen = sizeof( uint32 );
54:     arFields[iFieldName-1].pBuffer = (void*)&(pRecord->m_nDueTime);
55:     iFieldName++;
56:
57:     arFields[iFieldName-1].fType = AEEDB_FT_DWORD;
58:     arFields[iFieldName-1].fName = iFieldName;
59:     arFields[iFieldName-1].wDataLen = sizeof( uint32 );
60:     arFields[iFieldName-1].pBuffer = (void*)&(pRecord->m_nDueMiles);
61:     iFieldName++;
62:
63:     return IDATABASE_CreateRecord( pIDatabase,
64:                                    arFields,
65:                                    Fld_LastField );
66: }
```

This is pretty boring stuff. Lines 1–11 define an enumeration of the fields in a record for RocketMileage, and the SaveRecord function on lines 13–66 creates and populates the fields of a database record (lines 21–61) and creates a new record with the fields.

 CAUTION   *Some QUALCOMM BREW handset implementations— typically those prior to BREW 2.0—have a bug and can't read or write* AEEDB_FT_DWORD *database fields. To work around this issue, if you experience crashes in your database code manipulating* AEEDB_FT_DWORD *fields, use the type* AEEDB_FT_BINARY *instead and treat your* DWORD *data as a four-byte binary blob of data.*

Using the IDBRecord Interface

Once you have a record—from IDATABASE_CreateRecord, IDATABASE_GetRecordByID, or IDATABASE_GetRecordNext—you can access individual fields using the IDBRecord interface.

If you want to obtain the record number of a specific record, you can do so using the IDBRECORD_GetID method, like this:

```
1: uint16 id = IDBRECORD_GetID( pIDBRecord );
```

You can then use the resulting ID in later calls to IDATABASE_GetRecordByID. You can remove a specific record by calling IDBRECORD_Remove:

```
1: IDBRECORD_Remove( pIDBRecord );
```

You can also update a record's fields using IDBRECORD_Update, which takes the same arguments as IDATABASE_CreateRecord. Unlike IDATABASE_CreateRecord, however, IDBRECORD_Update returns a BREW error code: SUCCESS if the operation completed successfully or an error code in the event of an error.

Most of the time, however, you use the IDBRecord interface to access specific fields of a single database record. To do this, you use the IDBRECORD_Reset and IDBRECORD_NextField functions to iterate over all the fields in a record, such as the function shown in Listing 7-3.

Listing 7-3. Iterating Over All of the Fields in a Database Record

```
 1: IDBRecord *pIDBRecord;
 2: AEEDBFieldType iFieldType;
 3: AEEDBFieldName iFieldName;
 4: uint32 iFieldLength;
 5: byte *pData;
 6: // Do something to initialize pRecord.
 7:
 8: IDBRECORD_Reset(pIDBRecord);
 9:
10: // While there are fields to examine...
11: while( IDBRECORD_NextField(pIDBRecord,
12:                            &iFieldName, &iFieldLength
13:                            ) != AEEDB_FT_NONE )
14: {
15:   // Get the contents of this field
16:   pData = IDBRECORD_GetField(pIDBRecord, &iFieldName,
17:               &iFieldType, &iFieldLength );
18:   if (!pData) break;
```

```
19:    // Cast *pData based on iFieldType and use it here.
20: }
21: IDBRECORD_Release( pRecord );
```

After resetting the record to point to the first field (line 8), this code iterates through each field of the current record using IDBRecordNextField, which returns the data type of the next field or returns AEEDB_FT_NONE if there are no more fields to examine.

You'll use this kind of a loop when you need to decode the serialized format of a database record, too. In that case, you'll use the field name in a switch statement to set each field of a C structure, such as the LoadRecord function shown in Listing 7-4.

Listing 7-4. Decoding a Serialized Record

```
1: CAppRecordPtr *LoadRecord( IDBRecord *pIDBRecord )
2: {
3:     AEEDBFieldType iFieldType;
4:     AEEDBFieldName iFieldName;
5:     CAppRecordPtr  *pResult;
6:     uint32 iFieldLength;
7:     byte *pData;
8:
9:     ASSERT( pIDBRecord );
10:
11:    pResult = MALLOC( sizeof( CAppRecord ) );
12:    if ( !pResult ) return NULL;
13:
14:    MEMSET( pResult, 0, sizeof( CAppRecord ) );
15:
16:      // Begin at the beginning
17:    IDBRECORD_Reset( pIDBRecord );
18:
19:      // While there are fields to examine...
20:    while( IDBRECORD_NextField( pRecord,
21:                   &iFieldName,
22:                   &iFieldLength
23:                      ) != AEEDB_FT_NONE )
24:    {
25:       // Get the contents of this field
26:       pData = IDBRECORD_GetField( pRecord, &iFieldName,
27:                   &iFieldType, &iFieldLength );
28:       if (!pData) break;
29:
```

```
30:     switch( iFieldName )
31:     {
32:       case Fld_EntryType:
33:         pResult->m_type = *((int16 *)(pData));
34:         break;
35:       case Fld_Time:
36:         pResult->m_nTime = *((uint32 *)(pData));
37:         break;
38:       case Fld_Miles:
39:         pResult->m_nMiles = *((uint32 *)(pData));
40:         break;
41:       case Fld_Other:
42:         pResult->m_nOther = *((uint32 *)(pData));
43:         break;
44:       case Fld_Cost:
45:         pResult->m_nCost = *((uint32 *)(pData));
46:         break;
47:       case Fld_DueTime:
48:         pResult->m_nDueTime = *((uint32 *)(pData));
49:         break;
50:       case Fld_DueMiles:
51:         pResult->m_nDueMiles = *((uint32 *)(pData));
52:         break;
53:       default:
54:         break;
55:     }
56:   }
57:
58:   return pResult;
59: }
```

There's nothing exciting here, either. The foundation of LoadRecord is the same while loop you saw in Listing 7-3, followed by a switch statement that uses each of the field names in turn to decide which element of the structure to fill (lines 30–55).

Overcoming Issues with the Database Interface

Using a database in your application isn't without challenges. Although it's convenient to be able to design a simple schema and store data without worrying about the representation of your data on the phone's file system, you must be aware of other issues that can arise.

The two most common issues when using the database interface are performance and data sorting. The first, performance, is an issue you can't do much about, but you need to be aware of its ramifications as you use databases. The second, data sorting, can cause problems for you when porting an application from another mobile platform or when designing an application that needs to present data you enter in a specific order.

Addressing Performance Issues

Today's handsets store files—including database files—on a file system stored in flash memory. Flash memory has many outstanding qualities including low cost, relatively low power consumption, and the ability to retain its contents once power is turned off. Unfortunately, it has two significant drawbacks: slow performance when writing data and a limited number of write operations on each memory cycle.

Because of how flash memory stores each bit of information, it's orders of magnitude slower to write to flash memory than it is to read from flash memory. Worse, because of how flash memory operates, you can write to each location only a set number of times—typically tens or hundreds of thousands of times—before a given memory location fails permanently and can no longer store a datum. Consequently, the drivers that provide the file system support on handsets work to ensure that, when making changes to files on the file system, the operations are spread evenly over the entire flash memory region so no specific memory location fails before any other. Of course, scattering bits on the file system to ensure that all memory locations receive on average the same number of write operations makes the file system implementation more complex—and thus slower.

There's little you can do directly to compensate for this performance issue in your implementation because the limitation is fundamentally a hardware and operating system one. That said, you can minimize the impact write performance has on your application by keeping records in memory for as long as they're likely to change and only writing them to the database when modifications are complete.

Sorting Database Entries

The QUALCOMM BREW database interface doesn't provide any mechanisms for ordering records, and there's no documented guarantee regarding the specific ordering of records or fields within a database. Consequently, if your application needs to provide sorted views of data in its database, it's up to you to manage how you sort records. This is at stark odds with other platforms such as the Palm

Powered platform, where you have access to a secondary database region that you can use to store record IDs sorted in a specific order.

Instead, you must do one of two things: either sort records on demand or keep a separate file of record IDs sorted in a specific order. Because of the hassles of keeping a file of record IDs in order—and the need to insert new record IDs in the middle of the list as you continue to keep the records sorted—I'm a big fan of sorting on demand.

One good way to do this is to create a sorted list of record IDs when you need to sort the database. As you'll learn in the next section where you see how Rocket-Mileage does this, it's really quite simple. Although it's not the most efficient way to sort a set of records, I'm partial to using an insertion sort: You simply iterate over the records in the database and create a linked list of record IDs sorted by whatever criteria you like as you iterate. Although not as efficient as more sophisticated algorithms such as a heap sort or Quicksort, it lets you load and sort database entries in one pass. Once you have a list of sorted record IDs, you can quickly obtain fields from a specific record using the `IDatabase` and `IDBRecord` interfaces because reading from the database is only marginally slower than reading information from main memory. Equally important, by sorting only the list of record IDs (rather than the records themselves), you use significantly less memory than if you loaded all of your records into main memory simply to create a sorted list.

Using a Database in a Real Application

Using a database in your application is almost as easy as you might expect from the material presented in this chapter. To help you with your efforts, this section shows you how you can use the database interfaces to store the mileage information you enter in RocketMileage.

Understanding the Schema

RocketMileage uses a database to store each vehicle maintenance event. Unlike a traditional desktop application, however, RocketMileage doesn't store *all* events; it stores only the most recent events for a specific kind of service. Doing this minimizes the amount of data storage the application uses and simplifies data management for application users. The database consists of records with the fields in Listing 7-5.

Listing 7-5. The Database Schema

```
 1: typedef enum _EMileageEntryType
 2: {
 3:   ME_Gas = 1,
 4:   ME_Oil,
 5:   ME_Tire,
 6:   ME_Tuneup,
 7:   ME_OtherService,
 8:   ME_Parking,
 9:   ME_Mileage,
10:   ME_Undefined
11: } EMileageEntryType;
12:
13: typedef struct
14: {
15:   EMileageEntryType m_type;
16:   uint32 m_nTime;
17:   uint32 m_nMiles;
18:   uint32 m_nOther;
19:   uint32 m_nCost;
20:   uint32 m_nDueTime;
21:   uint32 m_nDueMiles;
22: } CAppRecord, *CAppRecordPtr;
```

To track mileage, you don't need to keep every mileage event in a database; instead, you simply use the fact that the average mileage is simply the sum of the number of miles driven divided by the sum of the number of gallons of fuel consumed. You can keep these in the application's *preferences*, a special place each application can access that stores information not suited to either databases or files. The shell maintains a file of all the application's preferences, and when you delete an application on the handset, you also delete the preferences information for that application.

Accessing Application Preferences

Accessing the preferences is easy—far easier than using a database. To load your application's preferences, simply use the IShell method ISHELL_GetPrefs, which loads the preferences structure you provide for a specific class ID:

```
1: result = ISHELL_GetPrefs( GetShell( pThis ),
2:                           AEECLSID_OURS,
3:                           APP_PREFS_VERSION,
4:                           &appPrefs,
5:                           sizeof(CAppPrefs) );
```

ISHELL_GetPrefs takes as arguments an IShell interface, the class ID of the application whose preferences to fetch, the version number of the preferences to fetch, a region into which to copy the preferences, and the size of the preferences. The shell knows nothing about what's in the preferences structure, so you can put just about anything in there that makes sense for your application. It will return either SUCCESS if the application preferences were successfully copied to your structure or an error code in the event of a failure.

To set your application preferences, you simply use the corresponding method ISHELL_SetPrefs, which takes the same arguments:

```
1: result = ISHELL_SetPrefs( GetShell( pThis ),
2:                           AEECLSID_OURS,
3:                           APP_PREFS_VERSION,
4:                           &appPrefs,
5:                           sizeof(CAppPrefs) );
```

In RocketMileage, each time you enter a mileage record, the program updates the database with the information you've just entered, updates the sums of the miles traveled, and updates the fuel used in the application preferences. When you need to display mileage, you take the ratio of the two and then manually insert the decimal point at the right spot (because everything is stored as integers.)

 TIP   *Be sure to increment your application's preferences version every time you change your application preferences structure. QUALCOMM BREW uses that to replace and upgrade preference structures as they change. If you don't, your application can crash on handsets or the emulator because the data QUALCOMM BREW gives you won't be what you expect in your preferences structure!*

Serializing Records for the Database

The previous section showed you how you can load a record from the database into a C structure as well as how to save C structures as records in your database using StoreRecord and LoadRecord. These methods are completely functional but lack generality. For example, if you want to write another application, you have to completely rewrite them, even though the basic algorithm (iterating over record fields) remains the same.

In RocketMileage—and in the framework that accompanies the book—you can find two other ways to do the same thing. The first way is using macros that make it easy to initialize the contents of an AEEDBField structure for common data types, shown in Listing 7-6.

Listing 7-6. Macros to Initialize the Contents of an AEEDBField *Structure*

```
 1: #define DBStringField( pf, p, f ) \
 2:    (pf) ->fType = AEEDB_FT_STRING; \
 3:    (pf)->fName = (f); \
 4:    pf->wDataLen = (uint16)WSTRSIZE(wszString); \
 5:    pf->pBuffer  = (void*)(p);
 6:
 7: #define DBBlobField( pf, p, l, f ) \
 8:    pf->fType = AEEDB_FT_BINARY; \
 9:    pf->fName = f; \
10:    pf->wDataLen = (uint16)l; \
11:    pf->pBuffer  = (void*)(p);
12:
13: #define DBWordField( pf, p, f ) \
14:    pf->fType = AEEDB_FT_WORD; \
15:    pf->fName = f; \
16:    pf->wDataLen = sizeof(uint16); \
17:    pf->pBuffer  = (void*)(p);
18:
19: #define DBDWordField( pf, p, f ) \
20:    pf->fType = AEEDB_FT_BINARY /* AEEDB_FT_DWORD */; \
21:    pf->fName = f; \
22:    pf->wDataLen = sizeof(uint32); \
23:    pf->pBuffer  = (void*)(p);
24:
25: #define DBByteField( pf, p, f ) \
26:    pf->fType = AEEDB_FT_BYTE; \
27:    pf->fName = f; \
28:    pf->wDataLen = sizeof(byte); \
29:    pf->pBuffer  = (void*)(p);
```

These macros make it easier to write routines such as SaveRecord, but they don't really go far in making things any easier to reuse. Consequently, the functions DBFreezeRecord, DBThawRecord, and DBRecordField let you serialize database records or access all the fields or a specific field of a serialized record. These rely on two functions provided as part of a specific application (the AS_DBFieldFromDatabase and AS_DBFieldToDatabase functions), which provide access to each specific field in a record's C structure. Listing 7-7 shows the DBFreezeRecord function.

Listing 7-7. The DBFreezeRecord *Function*

```
 1: int DBFreezeRecord( CAppRecordPtr pRecord,
 2:                     AEEDBField **ppResult )
 3: {
 4:   AEEDBField *arFields;
 5:   AEEDBFieldName i;
 6:   AEEDBFieldType iFieldType;
 7:   uint16 iFieldLength;
 8:   byte *pData;
 9:   int sz;
10:   int result = SUCCESS;
11:
12:   ASSERT( pRecord && ppResult );
13:
14:   // Allocate our result buffer
15:   sz = Fld_LastField * sizeof( AEEDBField );
16:   arFields = (AEEDBField *)MALLOC(sz);
17:   if ( !arFields ) return ENOMEMORY;
18:   *ppResult = arFields;
19:
20:   // For each field, get the database representation
21:   for ( i = 1; i < Fld_LastField; i++ )
22:   {
23:     result = AS_DBFieldToDatabase( pRecord,
24:                                    i,
25:                                    &iFieldType,
26:                                    &pData,
27:                                    &iFieldLength );
28:     if ( result != SUCCESS ) break;
29:     arFields[i-1].fType = iFieldType;
30:     arFields[i-1].fName = i;
31:     arFields[i-1].wDataLen = iFieldLength;
32:     arFields[i-1].pBuffer  = (void*)(pData);
33:   }
```

```
34:
35:   if ( result != SUCCESS )
36:   {
37:     // Free the field array before exiting
38:     FREE( arFields );
39:     *ppResult = NULL;
40:   }
41:   return result;
42: }
```

This routine simply breaks apart the monolithic StoreRecord routine into two pieces: one in this routine that's responsible for iterating across all of the fields in the database record and the other piece, implemented in AS_DBFieldToDatabase, which converts a named field in the application's record into its representation for the database. The function returns a fully populated AEEDBField array describing the record, first created on lines 14–18, which you can use in calls to IDATABASE_CreateRecord or IDBRECORD_Update. Next, the routine simply iterates across all named fields in the database, converting each field from the record structure to a database field with the help of AS_DBFieldToDatabase.

For RocketMileage, the AS_DBFieldToDatabase function is just a big switch statement, as shown in Listing 7-8.

Listing 7-8. The AS_DBFieldToDatabase *Function*

```
1: int AS_DBFieldToDatabase( CAppRecordPtr pRecord,
2:                 AEEDBFieldName iFieldName,
3:                 AEEDBFieldType *piFieldType,
4:                 byte **ppData, uint16 *piFieldLength )
5: {
6:   int result = SUCCESS;
7:
8:   switch (iFieldName)
9:   {
10:     // For each field, set the field to the contents
11:     case Fld_EntryType:
12:       *ppData = (byte *)&(pRecord->m_type);
13:       *piFieldType = AEEDB_FT_WORD;
14:       *piFieldLength = sizeof( uint16 );
15:       break;
16:     case Fld_Time:
17:       *ppData = (byte *)&(pRecord->m_nTime);
18:       *piFieldType = AEEDB_FT_DWORD;
19:       *piFieldLength = sizeof( uint32 );
```

```
20:        break;
21:      case Fld_Miles:
22:        *ppData = (byte *)&(pRecord->m_nMiles);
23:        *piFieldType = AEEDB_FT_DWORD;
24:        *piFieldLength = sizeof( uint32 );
25:        break;
26:      case Fld_Other:
27:        *ppData = (byte *)&(pRecord->m_nOther);
28:        *piFieldType = AEEDB_FT_DWORD;
29:        *piFieldLength = sizeof( uint32 );
30:        break;
31:      case Fld_Cost:
32:        *ppData = (byte *)&(pRecord->m_nCost);
33:        *piFieldType = AEEDB_FT_DWORD;
34:        *piFieldLength = sizeof( uint32 );
35:        break;
36:      case Fld_DueTime:
37:        *ppData = (byte *)&(pRecord->m_nDueTime);
38:        *piFieldType = AEEDB_FT_DWORD;
39:        *piFieldLength = sizeof( uint32 );
40:        break;
41:      case Fld_DueMiles:
42:        *ppData = (byte *)&(pRecord->m_nDueMiles);
43:        *piFieldType = AEEDB_FT_DWORD;
44:        *piFieldLength = sizeof( uint32 );
45:        break;
46:
47:      // We probably shouldn't be here.
48:      default:
49:        result = EBADPARM;
50:        break;
51:    }
52:    return result;
53: }
```

The DBThawRecord function does simply the opposite, as shown in Listing 7-9.

Listing 7-9. Restoring a Serialized Record to Memory in DBThawRecord

```
1: int DBThawRecord( IDBRecord *pRecord,
2:                   CAppRecordPtr *ppResult )
3: {
4:   AEEDBFieldName iFieldName;
5:   AEEDBFieldType iFieldType;
```

```
 6:   uint16 iFieldLength;
 7:   uint16 iRecordID;
 8:   CAppRecordPtr pResult;
 9:   byte *pData;
10:   int result = SUCCESS;
11:
12:   ASSERT( pRecord && ppResult );
13:
14:   // Allocate our result
15:   pResult = MALLOC( sizeof( CAppRecord ) );
16:   if ( !pResult ) return ENOMEMORY;
17:   *ppResult = pResult;
18:   MEMSET( pResult, 0, sizeof( CAppRecord ) );
19:
20:   // Begin at the beginning
21:   iRecordID = IDBRECORD_GetID( pRecord );
22:   IDBRECORD_Reset( pRecord );
23:
24:   // Get the first field
25:   iFieldType = IDBRECORD_NextField( pRecord,
26:                                     &iFieldName, &iFieldLength);
27:
28:   // While there are fields to examine...
29:   while( result == SUCCESS &&
30:       iFieldType != AEEDB_FT_NONE )
31:   {
32:     // Get the contents of this field
33:     pData = IDBRECORD_GetField( pRecord, &iFieldName,
34:                               &iFieldType, &iFieldLength );
35:     if (!pData) break;
36:
37:     // Copy variable-length fields for storage
38:     if ( iFieldType == AEEDB_FT_BITMAP ||
39:         iFieldType == AEEDB_FT_BINARY ||
40:         iFieldType == AEEDB_FT_STRING )
41:     {
42:       byte *pTemp = (byte *)MALLOC( iFieldLength );
43:
44:       if ( !pTemp ) return ENOMEMORY;
45:       MEMCPY( pTemp, pData, iFieldLength );
46:       pData = pTemp;
47:     }
48:     result = AS_DBFieldFromDatabase( pResult,
49:                                     iFieldName, iFieldType,
```

```
50:                                          pData, iFieldLength );
51:    iFieldType = IDBRECORD_NextField( pRecord,
52:                                      &iFieldName, &iFieldLength);
53:   }
54:
55:    return result;
56: }
```

After allocating space for the new record on lines 14–18, the routine iterates across each field of the database record using IDBRECORD_Reset and IDBRECORD_NextField. For each field, the function copies database records that take a variable amount of space (lines 38–47) and then calls AS_DBFieldFromDatabase to convert those database fields and store them in the appropriate field of the application's C structure representation of the database.

Not surprisingly, AS_DBFieldFromDatabase is another switch statement, as shown in Listing 7-10.

Listing 7-10. The AS_DBFieldFromDatabase *Function*

```
1: int AS_DBFieldFromDatabase( CAppRecordPtr pRecord,
2:                             AEEDBFieldName iFieldName,
3:                             AEEDBFieldType iFieldType,
4:                             byte *pData, uint16 iFieldLength )
5: {
6:    int result = SUCCESS;
7:
8:    switch (iFieldName)
9:    {
10:     // For each field, set the field to the contents
11:     case Fld_unused:
12:       pRecord->unused = (uint16)*pData;
13:       break;
14:
15:     // We probably shouldn't be here.
16:     default:
17:       result = EBADPARM;
18:       break;
19:    }
20:    return result;
21: }
```

These four functions are handy when you need to examine the contents of an entire record, but in many cases that's overkill. For example, if all you want to do is to sort records by the time a next service is due, all you really need to access is the Fld_DueTime for each record. Later, you can use the sorted list of record IDs to determine the order in which to display information to the user. (The next section discusses exactly how to perform this sort.) Although you could certainly load each record from the database, extract all of the fields, find the value of the Fld_DueTime field, and then destroy the record, this is rather expensive. Instead, you can use the utility function DBRecordField to get a copy of the value of a specific field (see Listing 7-11).

Listing 7-11. Fetching a Specific Field from a Record

```
 1: int DBRecordField( IDBRecord *pRecord,
 2:                    AEEDBFieldName iFieldName,
 3:                    AEEDBFieldType *piFieldType,
 4:                    void **ppResult, uint16 *piFieldLength )
 5: {
 6:   AEEDBFieldType iFieldType;
 7:   AEEDBFieldName iThisFieldName;
 8:   byte *pData;
 9:
10:   ASSERT( pRecord && piFieldType && piFieldType &&
11:          ppResult && piFieldLength );
12:
13:   // Begin at the beginning
14:   IDBRECORD_Reset( pRecord );
15:
16:   // Get the first field
17:   iFieldType = IDBRECORD_NextField( pRecord,
18:                                     &iThisFieldName,
19:                                     piFieldLength);
20:
21:   // While there are fields to examine...
22:   while( iFieldType != AEEDB_FT_NONE )
23:   {
24:     // Is this the field we want?
25:     if ( iThisFieldName == iFieldName )
26:     {
27:       // Get the contents of this field
28:       pData = IDBRECORD_GetField( pRecord, &iFieldName,
29:                                   piFieldType, piFieldLength );
30:       if (!pData) break;
31:
32:       // Copy the contents to a new buffer
```

```
33:        *ppResult = (byte *)MALLOC( *piFieldLength );
34:        if ( !*ppResult ) return ENOMEMORY;
35:        MEMCPY( *ppResult, pData, *piFieldLength );
36:        return SUCCESS;
37:      }
38:      iFieldType = IDBRECORD_NextField( pRecord,
39:                                        &iThisFieldName,
40:                                        piFieldLength);
41:    }
42:
43:    return EBADPARM;
44: }
```

This routine iterates over all fields in the specified database record (lines 22–41), searching for a specific field (lines 25–37). If the routine finds it (lines 28–36), it extracts the field's value (lines 28–29) and makes a copy of the value (lines 32–35), which you can use as you see fit and free when you're finished.

Sorting Records for Display

As mentioned previously in the chapter, there's no support for keeping database records sorted in a specific order. Instead, it's up to your application to sort records on demand, such as when presenting a list of items to the user.

It's easy to keep a linked list of database record IDs and values of a specific field for use when sorting records. You can do this using a singly linked list and an insertion sort function that manages the linked list nodes (see Listing 7-12).

Listing 7-12. The Linked List Nodes and an Insertion Sort That Sorts Linked List Entries

```
1: typedef struct _Node
2: {
3:   struct _Node *m_pNext;
4:   void *m_pData;
5:   void *m_pMetaData;
6: } Node;
7:
8: typedef struct _NumericNode
9: {
10:   struct _NumericNode *m_pNext;
11:   uint32 m_nData;
12:   uint32 m_nMetaData;
```

```
13: } NumericNode;
14:
15: typedef int32 (PFNNODEORDER)( void *pThis,
16:                               Node *n1,
17:                               Node *n2 );
18: typedef int32 (PFNNUMERICNODEORDER)( void *pThis,
19:                                      NumericNode *n1,
20:                                      NumericNode *n2 );
21:
22: #define NodeLinkSorted ( pThis, head, n, fnSort, kind ) \
23: { \
24:   kind *_p = head; \
25:   while( _p->m_pNext && fnSort( pThis, n, _p ) > 0 ) \
26:         _p = _p->m_pNext; \
27:   n->m_pNext = _p->m_pNext; \
28:   _p->m_pNext = n; \
29: }
```

This listing defines two kinds of nodes for linked lists: Node, which stores pointers to list items (used, among other things, by the framework's state machine management code), and NumericNode, which stores unsigned long integers. The nodes have the same structure and field names, which is important because by doing it that way you can use the macro NodeLinkSorted to sort Node and NumericNode lists.

NodeLinkSorted takes five arguments: a pointer to your application's structure, the head of the list in which to insert a specific node, the node to insert, the function that provides comparison for nodes, and the type of node being used (either NumericNode or Node). The macro itself is about as close to making a C++ template using C and the preprocessor as you can get; it uses the incoming type to define a temporary variable used to iterate across the linked list (lines 25–26) until it finds the right place to insert the new node (lines 27–28) as indicated by the comparison function.

The comparison function is the same sort of comparison function you implement when using standard library utilities such as qsort on other platforms. For example, Listing 7-13 is a simple test routine used to reverse-sort by time entries in the database and dump them to the debugging log.

Listing 7-13. Testing the Sort Operation

```
1: typedef NumericNode DBRecordCache;
2: typedef NumericNode *DBRecordCachePtr;
3:
4: static int32 orderRecordsByTime( void *p,
```

```
 5:            DBRecordCachePtr n1,
 6:            DBRecordCachePtr n2 )
 7: {
 8:   int32 result = 0;
 9:   UNUSED( p );
10:   // Compare the two
11:   return n2->m_nMetaData - n1->m_nMetaData;
12: }
13:
14: static void sort( void *p )
15: {
16:   CAppPtr pThis = (CAppPtr)p;
17:   IDBMgr *pIDBMgr;
18:   IDatabase *pIDatabase;
19:   IDBRecord *pIDBRecord;
20:   DBRecordCachePtr pNode, pHead;
21:   AEEDBFieldType iFieldType;
22:   uint16 iFieldLength;
23:   uint32 *pt;
24:   CAppRecordPtr pRecord;
25:
26:   pHead = MALLOC( sizeof( DBRecordCache ) );
27:   if ( pHead )
28:   {
29:     MEMSET( pHead, 0, sizeof( DBRecordCache ) );
30:   }
31:   else return;
32:
33:   // Open the database
34:   if ( ISHELL_CreateInstance( GetShell( pThis ),
35:     AEECLSID_DBMGR, (void **)&pIDBMgr ) != SUCCESS )
36:     return;
37:   IDBMGR_Release( pIDBMgr );
38:   if ( !pIDatabase ) return;
39:
40:   // Add each record's ID to a list in the right order
41:   IDATABASE_Reset( pIDatabase );
42:   pIDBRecord = IDATABASE_GetNextRecord( pIDatabase );
43:
44:   while( pIDBRecord != NULL )
45:   {
46:     pNode = (DBRecordCachePtr)
47:       MALLOC( sizeof( DBRecordCache ) );
48:     if ( !pNode )
```

```
49:    {
50:      DBRecordCachePtr pTemp;
51:      pNode = pHead->m_pNext;
52:      while( pNode )
53:      {
54:        pTemp = pNode;
55:        pNode = pTemp->m_pNext;
56:        FREE( pTemp );
57:      }
58:      return;
59:    }
60:    pNode->m_nData = IDBRECORD_GetID( pIDBRecord );
61:
62:    DBRecordField( pIDBRecord, Fldf_Time,
63:                   &iFieldType, &pt, &iFieldLength );
64:    pNode->m_nMetaData = *pt;
65:    FREE( pt );
66:
67:    NodeLinkSorted( pThis, pHead, pNode,
68:                    orderRecordsByTime, DBRecordCache );
69:
70:    IDBRECORD_Release( pIDBRecord );
71:    pIDBRecord = IDATABASE_GetNextRecord( pIDatabase );
72:  }
73:  // Iterate across all the nodes.
74:  // Dump their contents to the debug log
75:  pNode = pHead->m_pNext;
76:
77:  while( pNode )
78:  {
79:    pRecord = NULL;
80:    pIDBRecord = IDATABASE_GetRecordByID( pIDatabase,
81:                              (uint16)pNode->m_nData );
82:    if ( pIDBRecord ) DBThawRecord( pIDBRecord, &pRecord );
83:    if ( pRecord )
84:    {
85:      DBGPRINTF("Type : %d", pRecord->m_type );
86:      DBGPRINTF("Time : %d", pRecord->m_nTime );
87:      DBGPRINTF("Miles: %d", pRecord->m_nMiles );
88:      DBGPRINTF("Cost : %d", pRecord->m_nCost );
89:      DBGPRINTF("Other: %d", pRecord->m_nOther );
90:      DBGPRINTF("Next (time) : %d", pRecord->m_nDueTime );
91:      DBGPRINTF("Next (miles): %d", pRecord->m_nDueMiles );
92:    }
```

```
93:    if ( pIDBRecord ) IDBRECORD_Release( pIDBRecord );
94:    if ( pRecord ) FREE( pRecord );
95:    pNode = pNode->m_pNext;
96:    }
97:    IDATABASE_Release( pIDatabase );
98:
99:    if ( pHead )
100:   {
101:     DBRecordCachePtr pTemp, pNode;
102:     pNode = pHead;
103:     while( pNode )
104:     {
105:       pTemp = pNode;
106:       pNode = pTemp->m_pNext;
107:       FREE( pTemp );
108:     }
109:   }
110: }
```

The comparison function (lines 4–12) simply establishes the order of two nodes by subtracting their values. As you can see from this function, you use the node's m_nData field to store a record's ID and the m_MetaData field to store the Fld_Time field of each record when ordering the records.

The sort routine sort begins (lines 26–31) by allocating the head of the linked list, which will be a dummy element that refers to the first node in the list. Next, it opens the database using the IDBMgr interface (lines 34–38). Then, for each record in the database (lines 44–72), the function creates a new node to hold that record's ID and Fld_Time information (lines 46–59, including the cleanup code if there's an out-of-memory error), gets the record's database ID (line 60) and Fld_Time datum (lines 62–65), and uses NodeLinkSorted to link the node into the list at the right location (line 67–68).

Once it has created the list, the remainder of the function walks across the linked list (starting with the first node, which is the node *after* the head, selected on line 75) with the while loop on lines 77–97. This code fetches the record interface for the node's database record by ID (lines 80–81) using IDATABASE_GetRecordByID, then gets the C structure representation of the record using the DBThawRecord function provided by the framework (line 82), and then dumps each field of the record to the debugging console (lines 83–92). Once it does this, it releases the record (line 93), frees the memory-resident representation of the record (line 94), and moves to the next node (line 95).

Finally, the routine releases the database (line 97) and the memory used by the sort list (lines 99–109) one node at a time.

Summary

You should remember the following key points after reading this chapter:

- QUALCOMM BREW provides a database interface that lets you store records consisting of multiple fields.

- The database implementation is best suited for storing multiple records of similarly structured data, and files are better for storing streams of data.

- There are three interfaces at your disposal for managing databases: IDBMgr, which lets you manipulate databases; IDatabase, which lets you manipulate a *specific* database; and IDBRecord, which gives you control over the contents of a specific record.

- When saving and loading records in a database, you must convert your memory-resident representation to and from an array of fields of type AEEDBField for the database interfaces.

CHAPTER 8

Drawing Graphics

THE **QUALCOMM BREW** platform provides you with a rich set of graphics Application Programming Interfaces (APIs) that you can use in your application. In previous chapters, you've seen just the tip of the iceberg: drawing text and simple bitmap graphics. It's time to delve deeper now and learn how you can use QUALCOMM BREW's graphics APIs to provide innovative user interfaces and vivid games.

This chapter reviews the three kinds of graphics QUALCOMM BREW supports: bitmaps, basic graphics primitives, and sprites. You've already learned a bit about using bitmaps in the SlideShow application, but there's a lot more you can do with them. With QUALCOMM BREW's graphics primitives, your applications can draw text, lines, and shapes in various colors, creating both static images and animations for applications such as games. For game developers, later versions of QUALCOMM BREW provide an interface to a simple sprite and tile engine, freeing you of much of the tedium when developing games. Because RocketMileage does little with graphics, this chapter illustrates these interfaces using a variety of code snippets and small sample applications.

Understanding QUALCOMM BREW Graphics Capabilities

A key feature of QUALCOMM BREW since its inception has been its graphics APIs. Initial market research by QUALCOMM and many wireless carriers revealed a huge market opportunity for games, and providing first-class support for graphics to help game developers was an obvious step in realizing QUALCOMM BREW's potential. Moreover, these same graphics APIs enable a host of other applications, such as location-based services, with maps and other diagrams.

The graphics APIs span several classes yet group functionality into three basic areas. The first, bitmap graphics, let you manipulate a bitmap image in a format such as the Windows BMP format, letting you copy the image to a region of the screen, transform the image, and so on. The second, graphics primitives, provides a vector-based approach to graphics, letting you construct a complex image using primitive graphics objects such as points, lines, arcs, circles, and ellipses. Finally, the third group of interfaces, implemented through the ISprite interface, provides a tile map for creating backgrounds and sprites to represent individual items in front of that background. Using the ISprite class, you can create scrolling maps and side-scrolling, two-dimensional graphics games, or you can use the same class to create innovative user interfaces for your application.

Over time, QUALCOMM has continued to improve its support for graphics, making QUALCOMM BREW arguably the best-of-breed platform for mobile graphics development. As a result, there are significant improvements in the graphics interfaces between the QUALCOMM BREW 1.0, 1.1, and 2.0 software releases; as a developer, you must recognize these differences when writing applications for specific handsets. It makes little sense, for example, for you to plan a game relying on the ISprite interfaces in QUALCOMM BREW 2.0 only to find that you're expected to release the game on the Motorola T720 handset running QUALCOMM BREW 1.1. Table 8-1 lists the graphics interfaces and in what version of QUALCOMM BREW you can find them.

Table 8-1. QUALCOMM BREW Graphics APIs and BREW Version

INTERFACE	PURPOSE	QUALCOMM BREW VERSION
IBitmap	Bitmap management	2.0
IDIB	Device-independent bitmaps	2.0
IDisplay	Simple display-based graphics functions	1.0, 1.1, 2.0
IFont	Font management (used by IDisplay)	2.0
IGraphics	Two-dimensional graphics primitives	1.0, 1.1, 2.0
ISprite	Sprite and tile management	2.0
ITransform	Bitmap transformations	2.0

Understanding QUALCOMM BREW Bitmaps

QUALCOMM BREW provides you with an interface to *blit*—copy—bitmaps to various parts of the screen. In QUALCOMM BREW 1.0, the bitmap interface was rudimentary. It consisted only of the single interface: IDISPLAY_BitBlt. You could use IDISPLAY_BitBlt to blit a Windows BMP file to the display using one of several copy modes, such as copying pixels from the source to the destination, binary-ORing the pixels from the source and destination to determine the new value of each pixel, binary-XORing the pixels from the source and destination to determine the new value of each pixel, and so on. (The various bit blit options are defined by the AEERasterOp enumeration, which you can find in the file AEEDisp.h.)

Using this bit blit operation requires two steps: converting an image into the handset's device-specific bitmap format from a Windows bitmap and then actually blitting the image to the display (see Listing 8-1).

Listing 8-1. Blitting to the Display

```
1: void *pBitmap, *pDeviceBitmap;
2: int xDest, yDest, cxDest, cyDest, xSource, ySource;
3: AEEImageInfo imageInfo = { 0 };
4: boolean bRealloc;
5:
6: // Assemble the bits as a Windows BMP for pBitmap
7:
8:
9: pImage = CONVERTBMP( pBitmap, &imageInfo, &bRealloc );
10: if ( pImage )
11: {
12:     IDISPLAY_BitBlt( GetDisplay(pThis),
13:         xDest, yDest,
14:         cxDest, cyDest,
15:         pImage,
16:         xSource, ySource,
17:         AEE_RO_COPY );
18:   IDISPLAY_Update( this->m_pIDisplay );
19: }
20: else
21: {
22:   DBGPRINTF("CONVERTBMP failed!!!");
23: }
24:
25: if ( bRealloc ) SYSFREE( pImage );
```

Starting with a bitmap in the Windows BMP format in the memory pointed to by pImage, the routine first converts the bitmap to the handset's native bitmap format using the function CONVERTBMP on line 9. This call is necessary because each handset manufacturer can choose to represent bitmaps in whatever format is best suited for its device. Because your application and QUALCOMM BREW don't have any knowledge about the format of the resulting bitmap, CONVERTBMP provides both with information about the resulting bitmap (in the AEEImageInfo structure imageInfo) and about whether you must free the resulting bitmap using the flag bRealloc. CONVERTBMP will first try to perform the bitmap conversion in place and, if that fails, will allocate memory from the system heap to store the converted bitmap.

If the conversion succeeds, CONVERTBMP returns a pointer to the device-specific bitmap, which you can use to blit to the screen using IDISPLAY_BitBlt (lines 12–17). This method takes a reference to the display, the rectangle on the screen that the bitmap will be copied to (defined by xDest, yDest, cxDest, and cyDest), the source bitmap (pImage), the top-right corner in the source bitmap (xSource, ySource) from which to blit, and the kind of bit blit operation to perform.

Once the bit blit is complete, the code must free the device-specific bitmap if it was allocated by CONVERTBMP. Because CONVERTBMP uses the system heap rather than the application heap to store the device-specific bitmap, you must use the SYSFREE function to free the bitmap (line 25).

Although the IDISPLAY_BitBlt function is simple, there's a lot you can do with it, as you can see from the plethora of successful games available on handsets running QUALCOMM BREW 1.0 and 1.1. A common trick to save memory is to store an application's icons, images, and tiles in a single large bitmap and then use IDISPLAY_BitBlt to extract specific images from the bitmap. Although more complex than keeping a slew of bitmaps within your application, it has the advantage of saving a tremendous amount of Random-Access Memory (RAM) because you eliminate the overhead of the image header for each of the separate images.

QUALCOMM BREW 2.0 has greatly enhanced bitmap capabilities by adding support for off-screen bitmaps in both handset-native and device-independent formats. Using the new IDisplay methods IDISPLAY_GetDeviceBitmap, IDISPLAY_GetDestination, and IDISPLAY_SetDestination, you can obtain or set a handle to the display's bitmap using the new IBitmap interface. The IBitmap interface provides you with methods to change the color value of a specific pixel, blit images into and out of the specified IBitmap instance, fill a rectangle in the bitmap with a particular color, and perform color conversions between the Red-Green-Blue (RGB) color space and the color space of the bitmap itself.

This off-screen bitmap support is best used for animations in which your application may need to perform a number of bit blit operations to update the position of several items between redrawing frames. When using a single bitmap—such as the one provided in QUALCOMM BREW 1.0 using IDisplay—you must take great pains to ensure that the drawing and bit blit operations happen quickly enough to prevent flickering. This is a challenge for developers on all platforms but can quickly become insurmountable on limited hardware such as wireless handsets. To prevent flickering, you use a technique known as *double-buffering* in which you use two separate buffers. For each frame update, you first do all of the drawing and blitting to an off-screen bitmap, and once the frame update is complete, blit the off-screen bitmap onto the on-screen bitmap. Doing this keeps updates to the screen to a minimum, avoiding flickering. (Double-buffering is available in QUALCOMM BREW 1.0 but only with the IGraphics interface.)

Another new interface in QUALCOMM BREW 2.0 is the ITransform interface. This interface provides two bitmap-specific methods: ITRANSFORM_TransformBitSimple and ITRANSFORM_TransformBitComplex. ITRANSFORM_TransformBitSimple lets you perform simple transformations on a bitmap, including rotation by 90-degree intervals, flipping around the x axis, and scaling by powers of 2 (changing the size of an image by 2, by 4, or by 8, or changing the size by 1/2, 1/4, or 1/8). ITRANSFORM_TransformBitComplex lets you pass a matrix defining a specific transformation, including arbitrary rotation and scaling.

Understanding QUALCOMM BREW Graphics Primitives

QUALCOMM BREW provides two interfaces for creating graphics primitives: IDisplay and IGraphics. The IDisplay interface, which you first encountered in the HelloWorld example at the beginning of this book, is available in all versions of QUALCOMM BREW and gives you the ability to draw text, filled and hollow rectangles, and horizontal and vertical lines to the display. Using this interface you can create many simple diagrams and user interface primitives such as buttons, but it's not really suited for more advanced tasks such as games, maps, or charts.

For more advanced graphics, you can use the IGraphics interface, available since QUALCOMM BREW 1.0. The IGraphics interface gives you more complex drawing operations than the simple ones provided by the IDisplay interface. In addition to the same basic features provided by IDisplay, the IGraphics interface provides additional shape-drawing capabilities, including the ability to draw points, ellipses, circles, arcs, triangles, rectangles, polygons, lines at any angle, and polylines (lines connecting multiple points). You can draw all of these as empty or filled regions in any color supported by the wireless handset. Unlike the simpler IDisplay interface, the IGraphics interface supports the notion of a *view port*. In other words, the handset's display is a movable window that shows a segment of a larger canvas. You can imagine the view port to be like a camera, showing just one segment of a larger screen. You can also control how each pixel is drawn to the canvas, setting a *paint mode* such as copy (pixel values are copied to the canvas), binary-OR or binary-exclusive-OR (pixel values are ORed or XORed with canvas pixel values to determine the drawn value), and so forth.

Understandably, using an IGraphics instance is a little more complicated than using an IDisplay instance. Generally, you should follow these steps:

1. Create an instance of IGraphics using ISHELL_CreateInstance.

2. Set the background color using IGRAPHICS_SetBackground.

3. Set the view port using IGRAPHICS_SetViewport.

4. Set the foreground color using IGRAPHICS_SetColor.

5. Set the fill color and fill mode if you're going to draw filled shapes using IGRAPHICS_SetFillColor and IGRAPHICS_SetFillMode. Like IGRAPHICS_SetColor, you may want to repeat this step more than once for each shape.

6. Set the paint mode using IGRAPHICS_SetPaintMode. Like the previous two steps, you can change the paint mode between drawing shapes.

7. Begin drawing using the functions IGRAPHICS_DrawPoint, IGRAPHICS_DrawLine, IGRAPHICS_DrawRect, IGRAPHICS_DrawArc, IGRAPHICS_DrawPie, IGRAPHICS_DrawPolygon, IGRAPHICS_DrawPolyline, and IGRAPHICS_DrawText.

8. Update the display to show the drawn shapes periodically as your program requires by calling IGRAPHICS_Update.

The sample code later in this chapter shows how to use the IGraphics interface in greater detail (see "Using the IGraphics Interface").

Understanding QUALCOMM BREW Sprite Operations

The final interface for graphics in QUALCOMM BREW, ISprite, lets you use sprite-based graphics for fast animation. Available only on handsets running QUALCOMM BREW 2.0 or beyond, this new addition is bound to enable game developers to create new and interesting games for the platform.

A *sprite* is a small bitmap with associated properties such as location, transparency, and an associated transformation to the bitmap that should be performed before the sprite is drawn. A *sprite engine*—such as the one implemented by the ISprite interface—manages drawing sprites in layers, giving the illusion of depth between sprites (often called *two-and-a-half dimensions* because an image composed with sprites has more depth than a traditional image) and the background, which is composed of *tiles* of individual, stationary bitmaps. You can have different-sized tiles and sprites, but all of your tiles and sprites for a given animation must be the same size. The ISprite interface supports sprites and tiles that are 8×8, 16×16, 32×32, and 64×64 pixels in size and that are color with or without transparent pixels. For each ISprite instance, your application can provide one set of background tiles and sprites to draw on four different layers, one on top of the other.

Designing an application that uses sprites requires you take the time to create three kinds of graphic resources:

- A set of tile bitmaps that portrays the background for your animation

- A set of sprite bitmaps that portrays each of the objects in your animation

- One or more *tile maps* that specify which tiles should be drawn in what positions on your animation's background

You store your tile and sprite images in independent bitmaps with the images for each sprite or tile ranging down in one long column in the bitmap, one image after the next. (For example, if you were using tiles of 8×8 pixels, your tile bitmap would be 8-pixels wide, with each tile following the other down the *y* axis.) You provide these bitmaps to the ISprite interface and refer to each tile or sprite by an index into the bitmap containing the item. For the first tile in your tile bitmap, for example, the index is 0; for the second, the index is 1, and so forth.

Your tile map is a little trickier. The tile map itself is a two-dimensional array of indexes into your tile bitmap. There's no standard BREW mechanism for storing a two-dimensional array of integers, so you have a number of choices depending on your application. If your background is random, you can create it on the fly in a memory region when your application starts. Otherwise, you can create tile maps as files—perhaps with a simple header that describes the *x* and *y* extents of the tile map and the specific tile bitmap to use—that contain a run of tile indexes. If the tile maps are sufficiently small, you might want to define them programmatically in your source code, perhaps as a structure in a header file that your application source code includes.

CAUTION   *Beware, however, the temptation to store your tile map in a global variable. Although this will work in the emulator, it will fail horribly on the handset because QUALCOMM BREW applications can't have global variables. Instead, you need to define your tile map as a series of instructions in source code that allocates a region of memory for the tile map and then fills each integer memory location in the region with a tile index.*

Once you design your sprites, tiles, and tile map to use the ISprite instance in your application, you must do the following:

1. Create an ISprite interface instance using ISHELL_CreateInstance.

2. Create a target bitmap onto which the ISprite interface will render the tiles and sprites. (You can do this using the IDisplay interface.)

3. Use the ISPRITE_SetDestination method to bind the bitmap to the ISprite interface.

4. Initialize the ISprite interface's tile buffer using the ISPRITE_SetTileBuffer method, passing it your bitmap of tiles.

5. Initialize the ISprite interface's sprite buffer using the ISPRITE_SetSpriteBuffer method, passing it your bitmap of sprites.

6. Draw your tile map using the ISprite interface's ISPRITE_DrawTiles method.

7. Draw your sprites using the ISprite interface's ISPRITE_DrawSprites method.

8. Blit the bitmap you created in step 2 to the display.

9. Perform whatever computations are necessary to update the locations of each sprite.

10. Redraw your sprites starting at step 7 and continue until you're done with your animation.

You'll see an example of using the ISprite method later in this chapter (see "Using the ISprite Interface").

Using the IGraphics Interface

The GraphicsSample application that accompanies this book shows you how to use the IGraphics interface to draw various shapes, as well as pan the view port around a drawing. This application is simple; all it does is draw a handful of random shapes to a canvas and let you scroll around the canvas. Figure 8-1 shows the GraphicsSample application in action.

Figure 8-1. The GraphicsSample application

The GraphicsSample application demonstrates the three key parts of using the IGraphics interface: initializing the interface and its view port, drawing to its canvas, and positioning the view port after drawing. Let's look at each of these in turn.

Initializing the IGraphics Interface

Using the GraphicsSample framework, the GraphicsSample interface uses a single state and keeps all of its data in its application data pointer (see Listing 8-2).

Listing 8-2. The GraphicsSample Application Data

```
1: typedef struct
2: {
3:    IGraphics *pIGraphics;
4:    uint16  cxCanvas, cyCanvas;
5:    uint16  x, y;
6:    uint16 arRandom[ NUMSHAPES * POINTSPERSHAPE ];
7: } CAppData, *CAppDataPtr;
```

You store the application's IGraphics instance—allocated in the AS_Init function, which you'll see next—along with the extents and center point on the canvas view port being displayed in this structure. You also keep a record of the shapes the application chooses to draw in arRandom, which you fill with random numbers to determine the kind, position, and size of each shape.

The AS_Init function creates the CAppData structure using MALLOC, creates an IGraphics instance, and initializes the extents and center points of the drawing canvas (see Listing 8-3).

Listing 8-3. Initializing the GraphicsSample Application

```
1: int AS_Init( CAppPtr pThis )
2: {
3:    CAppDataPtr pAppData;
4:    int result = EFAILED;
5:
6:    ASSERT( pThis );
7:
8:    // Create the application's global data here.
9:    pAppData = MALLOC( sizeof( CAppData ) );
10:
11:   if ( pAppData )
12:   {
13:     MEMSET( pAppData, 0, sizeof( CAppData ) );
14:
15:     // Set our canvas size
16:     pAppData->cxCanvas = VIEW_EXTENTS;
17:     pAppData->cyCanvas = VIEW_EXTENTS;
18:
19:     // Set the default view port position to
20:     // the center of the extents
21:     pAppData->x = pAppData->cxCanvas / 2;
22:     pAppData->y = pAppData->cyCanvas / 2;
23:
24:     SetAppData( pThis, pAppData );
25:     result = ISHELL_CreateInstance( GetShell( pThis ),
26:       AEECLSID_GRAPHICS,
27:       (void **) &(pAppData->pIGraphics) );
28:   }
29:
30:   return result;
31: }
```

The VIEW_EXTENTS constant is defined elsewhere and merely sets the size of the drawing canvas that you use with IGraphics. You use the cxCanvas and cyCanvas members of the application data structure to set the clipping region for the IGraphics instance.

The actual shape creation occurs when you first enter the main state in mainEntry (see Listing 8-4).

Listing 8-4. Creating Shapes

```
 1: static boolean mainEntry( void *p,
 2:                           EStateChangeCause change )
 3: {
 4:   CAppPtr pThis = (CAppPtr)p;
 5:   CAppDataPtr pData;
 6:
 7:   UNUSED( change );
 8:
 9:   ASSERT( pThis );
10:
11:   pData = GetAppData( pThis );
12:
13:   // Clear the display
14:   IDISPLAY_ClearScreen( GetDisplay( pThis ) );
15:
16:   // Decide what to draw.
17:   // We're going to get a shape, colors, and three coordinates
18:   // for each shape
19:
20:   // Get a buffer filled with random numbers
21:   GETRAND( (byte *)pData->arRandom,
22:            NUMSHAPES * 5 * sizeof( uint16 ) );
23:
24:   IGRAPHICS_Pan( pData->pIGraphics, x, y );
25:
26:   // Do some drawing
27:   mainDraw( pThis );
28:
29:   return TRUE;
30: }
```

After clearing the display (line 14), the routine fills the array member arRandom of the application's data pointer with random bytes using the GETRAND helper function (lines 21–22). This function, a replacement to the ISHELL_GetRand function available in early QUALCOMM BREW–enabled handsets, uses the system clock and other handset components to generate a sequence of pseudorandom bytes. Because it relies on the system clock, you shouldn't call this function more than once every few hundred milliseconds, or the results may not be sufficiently random. These random bytes will be used by mainDraw to determine what shapes will be drawn, as well as the shapes' positions, fills, and colors.

Next, on line 24, the routine centers the IGraphics view port in the middle of the drawing canvas. After that, the routine invokes the function mainDraw to draw the shapes specified in arRandom.

Drawing on the IGraphics Canvas

With the IGraphics context initialized and the shapes determined, it's time to draw the shapes on the canvas. The application invokes mainDraw in two places: initially in mainEntry and again whenever you move the view port with the directional pad (discussed in the next section).

Listing 8-5 shows the mainDraw function.

Listing 8-5. mainDraw

```
1: static void mainDraw( CAppPtr pThis )
2: {
3:   CAppDataPtr pData = GetAppData( pThis );
4:   uint16 iShape, i;
5:   IGraphics *pIGraphics = pData->pIGraphics;
6:   AEEClip clip = { 0 };
7:   AEETriangle triangle;
8:   AEERect rectangle;
9:   AEEEllipse ellipse;
10:  byte r, g, b, shape;
11:  boolean fill;
12:  uint16 *arRandom = pData->arRandom;
13:
14:  i = 0;
15:
16:  // Clear our canvas
17:  IGRAPHICS_SetBackground( pIGraphics, 255, 255, 255 );
18:  IGRAPHICS_ClearViewport( pIGraphics );
19:
20:  // Set our clipping region
21:  clip.type = CLIPPING_RECT;
22:  clip.shape.rect.x = 0;
23:  clip.shape.rect.y = 0;
24:  clip.shape.rect.dx = pData->cxCanvas;
25:  clip.shape.rect.dy = pData->cyCanvas;
26:  IGRAPHICS_SetClip( pIGraphics, &clip, 0 );
27:
28:  for ( iShape = 0; iShape < NUMSHAPES; iShape++ )
```

```
29:   {
30:      shape = (byte)(arRandom[ i++ ] % 3);
31:      r = (byte)(arRandom[ i++ ] % 255 );
32:      g = (byte)(arRandom[ i++ ] % 255 );
33:      b = (byte)(arRandom[ i++ ] % 255 );
34:      fill = (boolean)( ( arRandom[ i ] >> 8 ) && 0x1 );
35:
36:      // Set the fill color and mode for this shape
37:      IGRAPHICS_SetFillColor( pIGraphics, r, g, b, 0 );
38:      IGRAPHICS_SetFillMode( pIGraphics, fill );
39:
40:      // Add a random shape
41:      switch( arRandom[i] % 3 )
42:      {
43:        case 0:
44:          // Draw a triangle
45:          triangle.x0 = arRandom[ i++ ] % VIEW_EXTENTS;
46:          triangle.y0 = arRandom[ i++ ] % VIEW_EXTENTS;
47:          triangle.x1 = arRandom[ i++ ] % VIEW_EXTENTS;
48:          triangle.y1 = arRandom[ i++ ] % VIEW_EXTENTS;
49:          triangle.x2 = arRandom[ i++ ] % VIEW_EXTENTS;
50:          triangle.y2 = arRandom[ i++ ] % VIEW_EXTENTS;
51:          IGRAPHICS_DrawTriangle( pIGraphics, &triangle );
52:          break;
53:
54:        case 1:
55:          // Draw a square
56:          rectangle.x = arRandom[ i++ ] % VIEW_EXTENTS;
57:          rectangle.y = arRandom[ i++ ] % VIEW_EXTENTS;
58:          rectangle.dx = arRandom[ i++ ] % VIEW_EXTENTS / 4;
59:          rectangle.dy = arRandom[ i++ ] % VIEW_EXTENTS / 4;
60:          IGRAPHICS_DrawRect( pIGraphics, &rectangle );
61:          break;
62:
63:        case 2:
64:          // Draw an ellipse
65:          ellipse.cx = arRandom[ i++ ] % VIEW_EXTENTS;
66:          ellipse.cy = arRandom[ i++ ] % VIEW_EXTENTS;
67:          ellipse.wx = arRandom[ i++ ] % VIEW_EXTENTS / 4;
68:          ellipse.wy = arRandom[ i++ ] % VIEW_EXTENTS / 4;
69:          IGRAPHICS_DrawEllipse( pIGraphics, &ellipse );
70:          break;
71:      }
72:   }
```

```
73:
74:    // Update the display
75:    IGRAPHICS_Update( pIGraphics );
76: }
```

Functionally, this routine has four separate sections. In the first, it allocates all of its temporary variables (for clarity, there are a lot!) on lines 3–14. In the second, on lines 16–26, the routine initializes the IGraphics instance. In the third, on lines 30–38, the routine sets the drawing attributes for a specific shape. Finally, the switch statement on lines 41–72 determines whether to draw a triangle, rectangle, or ellipse, and then it sets the coordinates for the selected shape before drawing the shape.

The routine begins manipulating the IGraphics interface on line 16, where it first sets the background to white (with the values for red, green, and blue each 255), and then clears that portion of the canvas. Next, on lines 20–26, the routine sets the canvas's clipping region to the bounds defined in the application's data structure. The IGRAPHICS_SetClip method lets you select a variety of clipping shapes, including triangles and polygons. When you invoke IGRAPHICS_SetClip, you pass an AEEClip structure that contains a type field that describes the shape of the region to clip and a union shape that contains the coordinates of the clipping shape.

 TIP *Not all versions of QUALCOMM BREW support all clipping shapes, so it's best to check the API documentation when designing your graphics code to ensure that there's support for the clipping regions you desire on the handsets you're targeting.*

Next, for each shape to draw (line 28), the routine selects a shape using a random number in arRandom, followed by the red, green, and blue color values for the shape on lines 29–31. Finally, the routine uses a single random bit to determine whether the shape should be filled or empty.

The switch statement on lines 41–72 simply chooses a shape to draw, fills the structure for that shape with the shape's coordinates, and then draws the shape using the appropriate method of pIGraphics. Note, however, that different shapes denote their coordinates in different ways. For example, an AEERect structure denotes a rectangle by its *upper-left* corner, width, and height, and an AEEEllipse structure denotes an ellipse by its *center* coordinate and its major and semimajor axes.

The routine concludes on line 75 by updating the display with the call to IGRAPHICS_Update.

Positioning the View Port

The GraphicsSample routine lets you pan around the canvas to see the various
shapes that it draws. You do this using the directional pad on the handset, pressing
and holding the key in the direction you want to pan. In turn, the shell sends
the application EVT_KEY_PRESS, EVT_KEY_HELD, and EVT_KEY events, which the
application uses to determine when to start and stop panning. The event
handler AS_MainHandleEvent invokes the function mainHandleKey to process the
EVT_KEY_PRESS and EVT_KEY_HELD events and pan the view port around the canvas
(see Listing 8-6).

Listing 8-6. Handling Key Events for Scrolling

```
 1: static boolean mainHandleKey( CAppPtr pThis, uint16 wParam )
 2: {
 3:    boolean result = FALSE;
 4:    int dx, dy;
 5:    int32 newX, newY;
 6:    CAppDataPtr pAppData = GetAppData( pThis );
 7:
 8:    dx = dy = 0;
 9:
10:    switch( wParam )
11:    {
12:      case AVK_UP:
13:        dy = -( pThis->m_cy / 4 );
14:        result = TRUE;
15:        break;
16:      case AVK_DOWN:
17:        dy = ( pThis->m_cy / 4 );
18:        result = TRUE;
19:        break;
20:      case AVK_LEFT:
21:        dx = -( pThis->m_cx / 4 );
22:        result = TRUE;
23:        break;
24:      case AVK_RIGHT:
25:        dx = ( pThis->m_cx / 4 );
26:        result = TRUE;
27:        break;
28:    }
29:
30:    if ( result )
```

```
31:    {
32:        // Adjust the view port in the correct direction
33:        newX = pAppData->x + dx;
34:        newY = pAppData->y + dy;
35:
36:        // Pin scrolling within our canvas
37:        if ( newX < 0 ) newX = 0;
38:        if ( newY < 0 ) newY = 0;
39:        if ( newX > VIEW_EXTENTS ) newX = VIEW_EXTENTS;
40:        if ( newY > VIEW_EXTENTS ) newY = VIEW_EXTENTS;
41:
42:        pAppData->x = (uint16)newX;
43:        pAppData->y = (uint16)newY;
44:        IGRAPHICS_Pan( pAppData->pIGraphics,
45:                pAppData->x, pAppData->y );
46:        mainDraw( pThis );
47:    }
48:
49:    return result;
50: }
```

The initial switch statement (lines 10–28) simply determine what key you're holding down and sets the variables dx and dy to one-quarter the view port's size to determine how far to scroll. Next, if one of the four directional keys is held down (line 30), the routine calculates a new center point on the canvas and stores it in the variables newX and newY.

Next, the code tests the new coordinates to ensure that the center point is on the canvas using the four comparisons on lines 37–40 and setting out-of-bound points to the canvas extents as necessary. Then, it updates the application structure's notion of the center point on lines 42–43 and pans the view port to the new center point. Finally, it redraws the shapes on the canvas on line 46 by invoking mainDraw.

Invoking mainDraw is crucial because IGraphics doesn't store a record of the shapes you draw to its canvas, and it doesn't use a bitmap to represent its canvas. Because of the limited memory size of most wireless handsets, it'd be prohibitively expensive in many cases to do this, so you must track the shapes on your canvas that you might want to redraw later. Typically, using an array of shape selections, attributes, and points—much like in this example—is sufficient for many applications. Of course, you can store this data wherever it's most appropriate, either in memory or on the local file system.

Using Coordinates vs. Points

With QUALCOMM BREW providing an `AEEPoint` structure to represent points, you might wonder why all of the code in this section refers to points using raw integer coordinates, such as `newX` and `newY`, rather than a single `AEEPoint` structure `newPoint`.

To be honest, there's really no reason to pick one method over the other. Because I find it easier to follow code that uses explicit variables for each coordinate, I chose to write this code in that style as well. However, if you find it easier to think of points in terms of `AEEPoint` structures, go right ahead!

Using the ISprite Interface

To demonstrate the `ISprite` interface, you'll look at a simple game called *Neko to Nonezumi* (cat and mouse), which you can see in Figure 8-2.

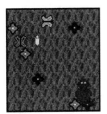

Figure 8-2. The Neko to Nonezumi game

The game itself is quite simple—too simple for all but toddlers probably, but that's okay because it's supposed to show you how to use the `ISprite` interface, not how to write a game! When the game starts, you use the directional pad to move the cat toward the mouse, catching the mouse by cornering it on the screen and hovering over it.

The application uses the `ISprite` interface to manage everything visible on the display: the cat and mouse, the two butterflies, and the grassy field dotted with flowers. Let's see how it works.

Defining the Tiles and Sprites

The application has four sprites (one cat, one mouse, and two different-colored butterflies) and three tiles. You can see all of them in Figure 8-3, where they're drawn by the application when you enable the DEBUG_SPRITES definition in AppStates.c.

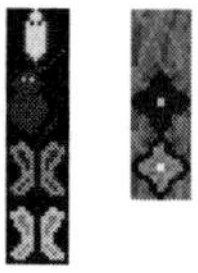

Figure 8-3. The sprite images (on the left) and tile images (on the right)

Each tile and sprite image is a separate bitmap in the application's BREW Archive (BAR) file. For consistency, you can number the sprite images starting from resource ID 5,000 and the tile images starting from resource 6,000.

As the application initializes, the AS_Init function loads each of the sprite and tile bitmaps and creates the sprite and tile buffers used by the ISprite interface with help from several helper functions (see Listing 8-7).

Listing 8-7. Loading Sprite and Tile Maps

```
 1: int AS_Init( CAppPtr pThis )
 2: {
 3:   CAppDataPtr pAppData;
 4:   int result = EFAILED;
 5:   uint16 arRandom[ 256  ];
 6:   int width, height;
 7:   IBitmap *pIBitmap;
 8:   ISprite *pISprite;
 9:
10:   width = 8;
11:   height = 8;
12:
13:   ASSERT( pThis );
14:
15:   // Create the application's global data here.
16:   pAppData = MALLOC( sizeof( CAppData ) );
```

```
17:
18:   if ( pAppData )
19:   {
20:     MEMSET( pAppData, 0, sizeof( CAppData ) );
21:
22:     // Get our sprite interface
23:     result = ISHELL_CreateInstance( GetShell( pThis ),
24:       AEECLSID_SPRITE,
25:       (void **) &(pAppData->pISprite) );
26:     pISprite = pAppData->pISprite;
27:
28:     if ( result == SUCCESS )
29:     {
30:       // Get a bag of random numbers
31:       GETRAND( (byte *)arRandom,
32:               256 * sizeof( uint16 ) );
34:
35:       // Initialize our sprites
36:       initSprites( pAppData->arSprites );
37:       result = loadSprites( pThis, &pIBitmap );
38:       if ( result != SUCCESS )
39:       {
40:         if ( pIBitmap ) IBITMAP_Release( pIBitmap );
41:         ISPRITE_Release( pISprite );
42:         return result;
43:       }
44:       ISPRITE_SetSpriteBuffer( pISprite,
45:                                TILE_SIZE_16X16,
46:                                pIBitmap );
47:       IBITMAP_Release( pIBitmap );
48:
49:       pIBitmap = NULL;
50:
51:       // Initialize our tile map
52:       result = initTiles( pThis,
53:         pAppData->arTileMap,
54:         width, height,
55:         arRandom );
56:       if ( result != SUCCESS )
57:       {
58:         if ( pIBitmap ) IBITMAP_Release( pIBitmap );
59:         ISPRITE_Release( pISprite );
60:         return result;
61:       }
```

```
62:        result = loadTiles( pThis, &pIBitmap );
63:        if ( result != SUCCESS )
64:        {
65:          if ( pIBitmap ) IBITMAP_Release( pIBitmap );
66:          ISPRITE_Release( pISprite );
67:          return result;
68:        }
69:        ISPRITE_SetTileBuffer( pISprite,
70:                                TILE_SIZE_16X16,
71:                                pIBitmap );
72:        IBITMAP_Release( pIBitmap );
73:
74:        // Set the destination
75:        result = createBitmap( pThis,
76:                                pThis->m_cx, pThis->m_cy,
77:                                &pIBitmap );
78:        if ( result != SUCCESS )
79:        {
80:          ISPRITE_Release( pISprite );
81:          return result;
82:        }
83:        ISPRITE_SetDestination( pAppData->pISprite, pIBitmap );
84:        pAppData->pIBitmap = pIBitmap;
85:
86:        // Stash aside our application globals
87:        SetAppData( pThis, pAppData );
88:      }
89:    }
90:
91:    return result;
92: }
```

The interesting bits start at line 23, where you create an instance of ISprite. If this succeeds, you stash a copy away in the local pISprite variable (to save typing and improve legibility in the printed listing) and proceed to get 256 random numbers using GETRAND. The routine then calls initSprites on line 36 (described next), which sets the position and other information for each sprite. After that, it calls loadSprites on line 37, which loads each of the sprite images and composites them on one big bitmap. After setting the sprite buffer using ISPRITE_SetSpriteBuffer on line 44, you release the sprite buffer's bitmap because it's now owned by the ISprite interface and will be freed when the interface is released. Lines 51–72 do the same for the tile map: They create an array of tiles in initTiles, load each of the tile images, composite them into a bitmap using loadTiles, and set the tile buffer using ISPRITE_SetTileBuffer. Next, you create the destination bitmap—where the ISprite instance blits all of the tiles and sprites—using the utility function createBitmap and set the destination bitmap for the interface using its ISPRITE_SetDestination method.

Initializing Sprites and Tiles

Each sprite is described by an instance of the structure AEESpriteCmd (see Listing 8-8).

Listing 8-8. Sprite and Tile Structures

```
 1: typedef struct {
 2:     int16 x;
 3:     int16 y;
 4:     uint16 unTransform;
 5:     uint8 unMatrixTransform;
 6:     uint8 unSpriteIndex;
 7:     uint8 unSpriteSize;
 8:     uint8 unComposite;
 9:     uint8 unLayer;
10:     uint8 reserved[5];
11: } AEESpriteCmd;
```

This structure stores the sprite's current position in the destination bitmap (lines 2 and 3), the transform to apply to the sprite image when blitting it to the bitmap (lines 4–5), the index into the sprite buffer to the image for the sprite (line 6), the size of the sprite (line 7), whether the sprite is opaque or has transparency data (line 8), and the layer into which the sprite should be placed. Several of these fields—unTransform, unSpriteSize, and unComposite—should be set using constants defined in AEESprite.h. The initSprites function called by AS_Init does what's shown in Listing 8-9.

Listing 8-9. Initializing the Sprites

```
1: static void initSprites( AEESpriteCmd *pSprites )
2: {
3:   pSprites[Sprite_Mouse].x = 32;
4:   pSprites[Sprite_Mouse].y = 32;
5:   pSprites[Sprite_Mouse].unTransform = 0;
6:   pSprites[Sprite_Mouse].unSpriteSize = SPRITE_SIZE_16X16;
7:   pSprites[Sprite_Mouse].unSpriteIndex = Sprite_Mouse;
```

```
 8:    pSprites[Sprite_Mouse].unLayer = 1;
 9:    pSprites[Sprite_Mouse].unComposite = COMPOSITE_KEYCOLOR;
10:
11:    pSprites[Sprite_Cat].x = 128 - 32;
12:    pSprites[Sprite_Cat].y = 128 - 32;
13:    pSprites[Sprite_Cat].unTransform = TRANSFORM_SCALE_2;
14:    pSprites[Sprite_Cat].unSpriteSize = SPRITE_SIZE_16X16;
15:    pSprites[Sprite_Cat].unSpriteIndex = Sprite_Cat;
16:    pSprites[Sprite_Cat].unLayer = 1;
17:    pSprites[Sprite_Cat].unComposite = COMPOSITE_KEYCOLOR;
18:
19:    pSprites[Sprite_Butterfly_Red].x = 32;
20:    pSprites[Sprite_Butterfly_Red].y = 128 - 32;
21:    pSprites[Sprite_Butterfly_Red].unTransform = 0;
22:    pSprites[Sprite_Butterfly_Red].unSpriteSize =
23:      SPRITE_SIZE_16X16;
24:    pSprites[Sprite_Butterfly_Red].unSpriteIndex =
25:      Sprite_Butterfly_Red;
26:    pSprites[Sprite_Butterfly_Red].unLayer = 3;
27:    pSprites[Sprite_Butterfly_Red].unComposite =
28:      COMPOSITE_KEYCOLOR;
29:
30:    pSprites[Sprite_Butterfly_Blue].x = 128 - 32;
31:    pSprites[Sprite_Butterfly_Blue].y = 32;
32:    pSprites[Sprite_Butterfly_Blue].unTransform = 0;
33:    pSprites[Sprite_Butterfly_Blue].unSpriteSize =
34:      SPRITE_SIZE_16X16;
35:    pSprites[Sprite_Butterfly_Blue].unSpriteIndex =
36:      Sprite_Butterfly_Blue;
37:    pSprites[Sprite_Butterfly_Blue].unLayer = 3;
38:    pSprites[Sprite_Butterfly_Blue].unComposite =
39:      COMPOSITE_KEYCOLOR;
40:
41:    pSprites[Sprite_Last].x = 0;
42:    pSprites[Sprite_Last].y = 0;
43:    pSprites[Sprite_Last].unTransform = 0;
44:    pSprites[Sprite_Last].unSpriteSize = SPRITE_SIZE_END;
45:    pSprites[Sprite_Last].unSpriteIndex = 0;
46:    pSprites[Sprite_Last].unLayer = 0;
47:    pSprites[Sprite_Butterfly_Blue].unComposite = 0;
48: }
```

The sprite array—stored within the application's data structure—consists of an AEESpriteCmd for each of the four sprites and a final entry with the unSpriteSize field set to the special constant SPRITE_SIZE_END, indicating the end of the sprite array. For all of the sprites except the cat's sprite, there are no transformations at first. However, the cat (because he's bigger than the mouse or the butterflies) has its unTransform field set to TRANSFORM_SCALE_2 so that the cat's bitmap is scaled to twice the size of the preset bitmap. All of the sprites are 16×16 pixels, as you can see from the unSpriteSize values of SPRITE_SIZE_16X16. (You could've used a sprite of size SPRITE_SIZE_32X32 and created a cat sprite that's 32 pixels on a side, but then you would've needed another sprite buffer bitmap to store it for the ISprite instance.)

Tiles, on the other hand, are represented using the AEETileMap structure (see Listing 8-10).

Listing 8-10. Initializing the Tiles

```
 1: typedef struct {
 2:     uint16 *pMapArray;
 3:     uint32 unFlags;
 4:     uint32 reserved[4];
 5:     int32 x;
 6:     int32 y;
 7:     uint16 w;
 8:     uint16 h;
 9:     uint8 unTileSize;
10:     uint8 reserved2[3];
11: } AEETileMap;
```

The first element of the structure, pMapArray (line 4), points to a memory region of unsigned words with each word containing information about a specific tile in a bit field, including:

- Its offset in the tile buffer

- Whether to rotate or flip the tile

- Whether the tile has transparency data

The x and y members (lines 5–6) specify the upper-left corner of the tile map on the destination bitmap. The w and h members (lines 7–8) specify the size of the bitmap, not in pixels or tiles, but using one of the MAP_SIZE constants defined in AEESprite.h. Tile maps can be any square whose side is a power of 2 between 2^0 (1) and 2^{10} (1,024).

CAUTION *Unpredictable things can happen if you specify sizes using these members without using these constants. In debugging this sample, I had a host of odd errors—from random crashes to peculiar-looking tile maps as the* ISprite *instance read off the ends of the* pMapArray *array. Another source of unpredictability are the* reserved *and the* reserved2 *fields. If you don't set them to 0, strange and terrible things can happen to your application.*

The AS_Init function calls the function initTiles to initialize the tile map (see Listing 8-11).

Listing 8-11. Filling the Tile Map

```
1: static int initTiles( CAppPtr pThis,
2:   AEETileMap *pTileMap,
3:   int width, int height,
4:   uint16 *pRandom )
5: {
6:   int i;
7:   uint16 *pTile;
8:   int flower = 0;
9:
10:   // Create the tile map array
11:   pTileMap->pMapArray = (uint16 *)
12:     MALLOC( width * height * sizeof( uint16 ) );
13:
14:   if ( !pTileMap->pMapArray ) return ENOMEMORY;
15:   // Now fill it
16:   pTile = pTileMap->pMapArray;
17:   for ( i = 0;
18:     i < ( width * height );
19:     i++ )
20:   {
21:     *pTile = *pRandom % 24;
22:     // Only 1 in 24 tiles has a flower (statistically speaking)
23:     if ( *pTile == 0 )
24:     {
25:       // Get another random bit to choose the tile
26:       if ( flower % 2 )
27:       {
28:         *pTile = Tile_Pink;
```

```
29:        }
30:        else
31:        {
32:          *pTile = Tile_Purple;
33:        }
34:        flower++;
35:      }
36:      else
37:      {
38:        *pTile = Tile_Grass;
39:      }
40:      pRandom++;
41:      pTile++;
42:    }
43:
44:    // Position the tile map on the destination bitmap
45:    pTileMap->x = 0;
46:    pTileMap->y = 0;
47:    pTileMap->w = MAP_SIZE_8;
48:    pTileMap->h = MAP_SIZE_8;
49:
50:    // The tiles are 16x16 pixels
51:    pTileMap->unTileSize = TILE_SIZE_16X16;
52:
53:    // No flags
54:    pTileMap->unFlags = 0;
55:
56:    // You MUST set these to zero, or bad things happen
57:    pTileMap->reserved[ 0 ] =
58:    pTileMap->reserved[ 1 ] =
59:    pTileMap->reserved[ 2 ] =
60:    pTileMap->reserved[ 3 ] = 0;
61:
62:    pTileMap->reserved2[ 0 ] =
63:    pTileMap->reserved2[ 1 ] =
64:    pTileMap->reserved2[ 2 ] = 0;
65:
66:    // Initialize the end-of-tile-map structure
67:    pTileMap++;
68:
69:    pTileMap->pMapArray = NULL;
70:
71:    return SUCCESS;
72: }
```

Whether you create your own tile map randomly or use a tile editor to create a tile resource that you load from a file in your application's download distribution or a Web server, the process is the same. This routine begins by allocating memory for the tile map (lines 11–12) and fails if the allocation fails (line 14). With the tile map in hand, you then walk across the tile map, randomly selecting a tile bitmap for each tile in the tile map (lines 17–42). Aesthetically the screen looks best with about one in 24 tiles showing a flower, so you use the random number allocated for each tile and the modulo function % (line 21) to determine whether the tile will contain grass (lines 37–39, if *pTile is 0) or a flower (lines 26–35). (Originally, I used another bit of the current tile's random number to choose the flower color, but I liked the idea of alternating colors better.)

The rest of the routine is straightforward bookkeeping. First, set the position and size of the tile map (lines 44–48), then set the size of each tile (line 51), don't wrap the tiles (line 54), and zero the reserved fields (lines 57–64). Next, on lines 67–69, you mark the end of the tile map array by setting the second tile map's pMapArray field to NULL.

Loading Sprites and Tiles

The loadSprites and loadTiles functions are responsible for creating the sprite and tile buffers used by the ISprite instance throughout the application. These functions make heavy use of the IBitmap interface. Because both functions are so similar, for brevity only loadSprites is discussed (see Listing 8-12).

Listing 8-12. Loading the Sprite Bitmaps

```
1: static int loadSprites( CAppPtr pThis, IBitmap **ppBitmap )
2: {
3:   IBitmap *pISpriteBitmap;
4:   int16 x, y, i;
5:   IBitmap *pBitmap;
6:   int result;
7:
8:   x = y = i = 0;
9:
10:  result = createBitmap( pThis,
11:                          16, 16 * Sprite_Last,
12:                          &pISpriteBitmap );
13:  if ( result != SUCCESS )
14:    return ENOMEMORY;
15:
16:  // Blit each of the sprites on to the bitmap buffer
```

```
17:    for ( i = Sprite_Mouse; i < Sprite_Last; i++ )
18:    {
19:      pBitmap = ISHELL_LoadResBitmap( GetShell( pThis ),
20:                                      APP_RES_FILE,
21:                                      RESID_SPRITE_BASE + i );
22:      if ( !pBitmap )
23:      {
24:        IBITMAP_Release( pISpriteBitmap );
25:        return ENOMEMORY;
26:      }
27:
28:      IBITMAP_BltIn( pISpriteBitmap, x, y, 16, 16,
29:                     pBitmap, 0, 0, AEE_RO_COPY );
30:      y+=16;
31:      IBITMAP_Release( pBitmap );
32:    }
33:
34:    *ppBitmap = pISpriteBitmap;
35:    return SUCCESS;
36: }
```

The function begins by creating the bitmap that will become the sprite buffer for the ISprite interface on lines 10–12 using createBitmap, which is discussed next. The bitmap created is 16-pixels wide and long enough to hold each of the sprite images one after the other down the bitmap.

Beginning with line 19, the function loads each sprite bitmap (via the loop that begins on line 17) using ISHELL_LoadResBitmap. This function returns a freshly instantiated IBitmap interface with a bitmap containing the desired image. With the sprite image for the current sprite stored in the bitmap instance pBitmap, the IBITMAP_BltIn method blits the image to the correct location in the sprite bitmap pISpriteBitmap on lines 28–29. This function takes the destination bitmap, the position (upper-left corner, width, and height) on the destination bitmap to place the image, the source bitmap, and the beginning point on the source bitmap. It also takes the mode to use when copying the source mode—in this case, AEE_RO_COPY—to do a pixel-by-pixel copy of the source bitmaps. With the current sprite's image copied to the sprite buffer, you bump the y coordinate to point to the location of the next image on line 30 and release the current sprite's IBitmap instance.

Once all of the bitmaps have been copied to the pISpriteBitmap, its pointer is copied to the result pointer *ppBitmap and the function returns.

At this point, it's worth taking a minute to look at the implementation of createBitmap. It's easy to create a new bitmap by using an IDisplay instance as a template, but because it's several lines of code, a utility function can do it for you (see Listing 8-13).

Listing 8-13. Loading the Tile Bitmaps

```
1: static int createBitmap( CAppPtr pThis,
2: int16 w, int16 h,
3: IBitmap **ppIBitmap )
4: {
5:   IBitmap *pIDeviceBitmap;
6:   IBitmap *pIBitmap;
7:   AEERect rect;
8:   int result;
9:
10:   result = IDISPLAY_GetDeviceBitmap( GetDisplay( pThis ),
11:                                      &pIDeviceBitmap );
12:   if ( result != SUCCESS )
13:   {
14:       return result;
15:   }
16:
17:   result = IBITMAP_CreateCompatibleBitmap( pIDeviceBitmap,
18:                                            &pIBitmap, w, h );
19:   IBITMAP_Release( pIDeviceBitmap );
20:   if (result != SUCCESS )
21:   {
22:     return result;
23:   }
24:
25:   SETAEERECT( &rect, 0, 0, w, h );
26:   IBITMAP_FillRect( pIBitmap, &rect,
27:                     IBITMAP_RGBToNative( pIBitmap, RGB_WHITE ),
28:                     AEE_RO_COPY );
29:
30:   *ppIBitmap = pIBitmap;
31:
32:   return SUCCESS;
33: }
```

This function begins by getting the display's device bitmap using the function IDISPLAY_GetDeviceBitmap and storing it in the pointer pIDeviceBitmap on lines 10–11. This bitmap is the bitmap used by the screen, so you make a new bitmap with the same color depth and new bounds using the method IBITMAP_CreateCompatibleBitmap on lines 17–18. This creates another bitmap using its interface as a template and the indicated width and height as the dimensions for the bitmap. You then release the display's device bitmap because you no longer need it and use IBITMAP_FillRect to fill the newly created bitmap with the color white, essentially erasing the bitmap (lines 25–28). Finally, you return the newly created bitmap in the pointer *ppIBitmap.

Drawing the Background and Sprites

The application first draws the background tile map and the sprite map when it enters the main state in mainEntry by calling mainDraw. The mainDraw function redraws the screen, updates the position of each of the sprites, and sets a timer to redraw the display a few milliseconds later (see Listing 8-14).

Listing 8-14. Drawing the Tiles and Sprites

```
1: static void mainDraw( void *p )
2: {
3:    CAppPtr pThis = (CAppPtr)p;
4:    CAppDataPtr pData = GetAppData( pThis );
5:    ISprite *pISprite = pData->pISprite;
6:    uint16 arRandom[ 3 ];
7:
8:    // Get a bag of random numbers
9:    GETRAND( (byte *)arRandom,
10:           ( 2 + 1 ) * sizeof( uint16 ) );
11:
12:    // Update the display
13:    mainDrawUpdate( pThis );
14:
15:    /*
16:       Figure out where things are going to move.
17:       Butterflies move every turn
18:       The mouse moves every two turns
19:     */
20:
21:    // Move the butterflies
22:    moveButterflies( pThis, arRandom );
23:
24:    // Move the mouse
25:    if ( pData->nTurn % 2 )
26:    {
27:      moveMouse( pThis, arRandom + 2 );
28:    }
```

```
29:
30:    // And do it again!
31:    pData->nTurn++;
32:
33:    ISHELL_SetTimer( GetShell( pThis ),
34:                     FRAME_DELAY_MSECS,
35:                     mainDraw, p );
36: }
```

This routine begins by allocating a pool of random numbers to determine where the various sprites should move on lines 9–10. Next, it redraws the tile map and sprites using mainDrawUpdate. Next, it determines where the butterflies (line 22) and mouse (lines 25–28) should move, and it updates the turn counter pData->nTurn. By using the turn counter, you can easily keep the mouse moving at a slower rate than the butterflies, giving all of the sprites a little extra character. Finally, it posts a timer with the shell to call the draw routine mainDraw again in FRAME_DELAY_MSECS.

The mainDrawUpdate function shows just how easy it is to use the ISprite interface once you set everything up (see Listing 8-15).

Listing 8-15. Updating the Screen Sprites

```
1: static void mainDrawUpdate( CAppPtr pThis )
2: {
3:    CAppDataPtr pData = GetAppData( pThis );
4:    ISprite *pISprite = pData->pISprite;
5:    IBitmap *pIDisplayBitmap = NULL;
6:    int result;
7:
8:    // Draw the tiles
9:    ISPRITE_DrawTiles( pISprite, pData->arTileMap);
10:
11:    // Draw the sprites
12:    ISPRITE_DrawSprites( pISprite, pData->arSprites );
13:
14:    // Update the display
15:    result = IDISPLAY_GetDeviceBitmap( GetDisplay( pThis ),
16:                                       &pIDisplayBitmap );
17:    if ( result == SUCCESS )
18:    {
19:      IBITMAP_BltIn( pIDisplayBitmap,
20:                     0, 0,
21:                     pThis->m_cx, pThis->m_cy,
22:                     pData->pIBitmap, 0, 0, AEE_RO_COPY );
```

```
23:
24:      IDISPLAY_Update( GetDisplay( pThis ) );
25:      IBITMAP_Release( pIDisplayBitmap );
26:   }
27: }
```

This function does three things: draws the tile map, draws the sprites, and then blits the ISprite instance's bitmap to the display. It redraws the tile map on line 9 using the method ISPRITE_DrawTiles. Next, it redraws the sprites on line 12 using the method ISPRITE_DrawSprites. (Obviously, you don't want to reverse the order of these function calls, or your tile map will overwrite your sprites.) Finally, it updates the display by getting the display's bitmap (lines 15–16) and invokes its IBITMAP_BltIn method to blit the ISprite instance's bitmap on to the device bitmap. Then it updates the display and releases the device bitmap (lines 24–25).

Moving Sprites

The various functions moveMouse, moveButterflies, and mainHandleKey are responsible for moving the mouse sprite, the butterfly sprites, and the cat sprite, respectively. In a more polished game, the moveMouse and moveButterflies routines could be quite complicated because they're the entry points for whatever game play artificial intelligence these characters require. In fact, for this application, they're quite simplistic and not particularly interesting.

The mainHandleKey routine, invoked by the main state's event handler when the EVT_KEY_PRESS and EVT_KEY_DOWN events occur, illustrates both sprite movement and handling user input (see Listing 8-16).

Listing 8-16. Moving Sprites While Handling Key Events

```
1: static boolean mainHandleKey( CAppPtr pThis, uint16 wParam )
2: {
3:    boolean result = FALSE;
4:    int dx = 0, dy = 0;
5:    int32 newX, newY;
6:    CAppDataPtr pData = GetAppData( pThis );
7:    uint32 now = GETTIMEMS();
8:
9:    // The user can only move every so often
10:   if ( now > ( pData->nTime + PLAYER_DELAY_MSECS ) )
11:   switch( wParam )
12:   {
13:     case AVK_UP:
14:         dy = -CAT_DELTA;
```

```
15:        result = TRUE;
16:        break;
17:      case AVK_DOWN:
18:        dy = CAT_DELTA;
19:        result = TRUE;
20:        break;
21:      case AVK_LEFT:
22:        dx = -CAT_DELTA;
23:        result = TRUE;
24:        break;
25:      case AVK_RIGHT:
26:        dx = CAT_DELTA;
27:        result = TRUE;
28:        break;
29:    }
30:
31:    if ( result )
32:    {
33:      // First determine the new position
34:      newX = pData->arSprites[ Sprite_Cat ].x + dx;
35:      newY = pData->arSprites[ Sprite_Cat ].y + dy;
36:
37:      PIN_X_COORD( pThis, newX );
38:      PIN_Y_COORD( pThis, newY );
39:
40:      pData->arSprites[ Sprite_Cat ].x = (uint16)newX;
41:      pData->arSprites[ Sprite_Cat ].y = (uint16)newY;
42:
43:      // Update the display
44:      //   don't wait until the next pass
45:      pData->nTime = now;
46:      mainDrawUpdate( pThis );
47:    }
48:
49:    return result;
50: }
```

The cat, being the largest animal on the playing field, also moves the slowest. To control how often the cat can move, this routine begins by checking the current system time in milliseconds (obtained on line 7 using the function GETTIMEMS, which is the QUALCOMM BREW function that replaces the method ISHELL_GetTimeMS available in early versions of QUALCOMM BREW) with the last time the player moved the cat (line 10), which is stored in the application data's nTime field.

If enough time has elapsed, a switch statement on lines 11–29 determines which coordinate of the cat's position should be adjusted based on what key you press by setting the dx and dy variables. Then, just as with the mainHandleKey function in GraphicsSample (discussed earlier in this chapter), you calculate the new coordinates for the cat sprite (lines 34–35) and ensure that the cat sprite will reside on the screen using the PIN_X_COORD and PIN_Y_COORD macros. After adjusting the cat's position so it remains on screen, you update the nTime field of the application data structure with the current time and invoke mainDrawUpdate to immediately redraw the screen.

The PIN_X_COORD and PIN_Y_COORD macros simply wrap the if statements you saw in GraphicsSample:

```
1: #define PIN_X_COORD( pThis, x ) \
2:    if ( x < 8 ) x = 8; else if ( x > 100 ) x = 100;
3: #define PIN_Y_COORD( pThis, y ) \
4:    if ( y < 8 ) y = 8; else if ( y > 100 ) y = 100;
```

These routines are a little overengineered because they take references to the application as well as the coordinate to pin, but with this interface, you can easily modify the code to pin objects to various coordinates without modifying the dependent functions.

Summary

The following are the key points you learned in this chapter:

- QUALCOMM BREW provides three kinds of graphics interfaces: bitmapped graphics, vector graphics through primitives, and sprite graphics.

- You use the IDisplay interface when you need to perform simple bitmap operations (such as bit blitting an image to the display) or simple vector-based graphics drawing.

- You can use the more advanced bitmap interfaces IDIB, IBitmap, and ITransform to perform other manipulations on bitmaps such as scaling.

- You can use the IGraphics interface to perform advanced vector graphics functions, including setting a view port to view the vector graphics you draw on the handset's canvas.

- You use the ISprite interface to manipulate a virtual world with a background of tiles and animated sprites.

Playing with Sounds

As a multimedia platform, QUALCOMM BREW wouldn't be complete without interfaces to play sounds. As with its graphics support, QUALCOMM BREW provides a handful of interfaces of increasing sophistication. These interfaces let your application play everything from simple tones to highly compressed yet rich sound samples encoded using technologies such as QUALCOMM PureVoice and MP3.

NOTE   *MP3 stands for Moving Pictures Expert Group Audio Layer 3.*

This chapter shows QUALCOMM BREW's sound interfaces—everything from the simplest, provided by the IShell interface, to the most advanced, provided by the ISoundPlayer interface. It also touches on the new IMedia interface, available in QUALCOMM BREW 2.0 and beyond, which unifies the presentation of multimedia data including sound and video content. To reinforce what you learn, the chapter uses the ISoundPlayer interface to add a background soundtrack and additional sounds to the sample game you saw in Chapter 8, "Drawing Graphics."

Representing Sound

As with other computing platforms, QUALCOMM BREW can manage sound data in a variety of formats. The simplest sounds—beeps, clicks, and the like—are available using the ISound interface directly from the handset's Read-Only Memory (ROM). In addition, handset vendors have the option of including support for additional sound formats, including the Music Industry Digital Interface (MIDI), Motion Picture Experts Group (MPEG), and QUALCOMM PureVoice (also known as QUALCOMM Code Excited Linear Predictive Coding, or QCELP).

Representing Sounds with MIDI

The MIDI file format has its beginnings in the MIDI standards of the mid-1980s, which allowed vendors of different kinds of electronic music instruments to interconnect instruments. The data formats quickly evolved to a file format that represents music as a series of notes played by musical instruments. Systems playing MIDI files use their own hardware and software to perform a best-effort emulation of the musical instruments and notes within the file, so although the MIDI format guarantees some fidelity regarding tempo and melody, a MIDI file played on two different instruments may sound different. Virtually all wireless handsets today ship with the ability to play MIDI files; in fact, most custom ring tones for handsets come as MIDI files.

MIDI is best used for representing fragments of songs with little memory, when the actual instrument sounds are less important than the tempo and melody. Because the file format supports representing specific instruments, tempo, notes, and rests, you can't use it for arbitrary sounds, such as speech or sound effects.

Representing Sounds with MP3

The German company Fraunhofer IIS developed the MP3 format to significantly decrease the amount of storage required for high-fidelity audio. The MP3 format uses *lossy* compression, which means the resulting compressed data contains less information than the original source. By discarding some information that's imperceptible to most listeners, MP3 files can compress audio data by up to a factor of 10 or 12 before you can hear a noticeable degradation in quality. Unlike MIDI, MP3 files represent the actual sound of the original source rather than just encoding the musical content, making it an exceptional choice for representing music, speech, and other audio data.

The exceptional compression characteristics of MP3 come with a computational cost, however. Most handsets today lack the hardware or processing power and software to be able to decompress MP3 files. Consequently, when selecting to encode the audio for your application with MP3, you should first check to be sure that your target hardware supports MP3.

Representing Sounds with QCELP

The Code Division Multiple Access (CDMA) wireless networks on which QUALCOMM BREW–enabled handsets operate use the QCELP format to carry the voice content of telephone calls. It's exceptionally well suited to compressing speech data and can represent telephone-quality voice data with a high degree of compression.

Unlike MIDI or MP3 files, which can be created using a myriad of music composition and recording applications, creating QCELP files requires a little-known tool. You use the QUALCOMM PureVoice converter to convert between Microsoft Windows WAV sound files and QCELP files.

Because QCELP is integral to the performance of a wireless handset, virtually every QUALCOMM BREW–enabled handset can play QCELP files. It's also a good choice for small sound samples, such as sound effects for games or small clips of music on handsets lacking MP3 support.

Understanding How to Play Sounds

The QUALCOMM BREW platform provides four interfaces to manage sounds, each offering increasing flexibility (and therefore complexity). Although for most applications you'll use either the ISoundPlayer interface or the IMedia interface, you'll see all four interfaces in this chapter so that you can make an educated decision when designing your application.

TIP   *The* IRinger *interface (introduced in Chapter 12, "Certifying Your Application") can also play sounds, but its interface for sound playback is identical to that offered by the* ISoundPlayer *interface.*

An important thing to remember as you read this chapter is that all sound playback is *asynchronous*—that is, playback begins after you invoke the appropriate method and continues in the background while your application executes. As a result, interfaces include methods to start, stop, and pause sound playback.

Using the Shell

The IShell interface, as you've seen throughout this book, is the grab bag of interfaces with methods that do a little of everything. This is true even of sound support. Using the ISHELL_Beep method, your application can play a number of different sounds. When you invoke this function, you pass a constant that indicates the type of tone the handset should play (see Table 9-1). Typically, the tones played are the same tones used by manufacturers within their on-board firmware applications.

Table 9-1. Sound Constants for Use with ISHELL_Beep

CONSTANT	PURPOSE
BEEP_OFF	Terminates a playing beep
BEEP_ALERT	Beep to alert the user
BEEP_REMINDER	Beep to remind the user
BEEP_MSG	Beep to indicate the arrival of a Short Message Service (SMS)
BEEP_ERROR	Beep to indicate an error condition
BEEP_VIBRATE_ALERT	Silent alert (vibration, indicator blinking, or the like) to notify the user
BEEP_VIBRATE_REMIND	Silent alert (vibration, indicator blinking, or the like) to remind the user

The ISHELL_Beep method is best used in two cases. In debugging your application, you can use various beep sounds to let you know when a particular segment of code is executing. It's not as robust as using the debugging log, but it has the advantage that you don't need to be tethered to your workstation to obtain debugging information when debugging on the handset. The second case is when your application provides functionality similar to the built-in applications and you want to mirror their user interfaces, especially the sounds they make.

Playing Tones

The ISound interface lets you adjust the handset volume, trigger the silent alert, and play a tone or a series of tones using the handset's speaker. Using the ISound interface, you access a handset manufacturer–specific database of sounds and play the sounds for an application-determined duration.

The interface includes the ISOUND_GetVolume and ISOUND_SetVolume methods, which let you set the sound playback volume on the handset. The volume returned is part of an AEESoundCmdData structure, which looks like this:

```
1:  typedef union
2:  {
3:    uint16 wVolume;
4:    uint16 wPlayIndex;
5:  } AEESoundCmdData
```

The ISOUND_PlayTone method plays a single tone, specified by an AEESoundToneData structure, which looks like this:

```
1:  typedef structure
2:
3:    AEESoundTone eTone;
4:    uint16 wDuration;
5:  } AEESoundToneData;
```

You specify the tone as a tone ID in the eTone field, and you specify the duration in milliseconds in the wDuration field. The eTone field can contain values from the AEESoundTone enumeration, which includes constants to specify tones such as those you hear when dialing a traditional phone, simple musical tones, and so on.

If you want to play a set of AEESoundTone tones in a series, you use ISound_PlayToneList. This function takes a pointer to a memory region filled with AEESoundToneData structures and the number of structures in the memory region. It plays each tone in turn as your application continues to execute.

While a sound is playing, you can stop the playback at any time by calling ISOUND_StopTone, which immediately stops any pending tone or tone list playback.

Your application may need to know the state of the ISound interface—say, to see if a specific tone is being played. To do this, you can register for notifications of the status from the ISound interface using ISOUND_RegisterNotify. This function takes a pointer to a function that the ISound interface periodically invokes with the status of the sound playback and takes a pointer to a block of data where you can store the application context or other function-specific data. The callback function must look like this:

```
1:  typedef void (* PFNSOUNDSTATUS)
2:  (
3:    void * pUser,
4:    AEESoundCmd eCBType,
5:    AEESoundStatus eSPStatus,
6:    uint32 dwParam
7:  );
```

The first argument your callback receives is the user data you pass to ISOUND_RegisterNotify. The second argument tells you the nature of the function call that triggered your notification function. The third argument indicates the status of the sound player and indicates whether the current operation is continuing, is finished, or has failed. Finally, the dwParam value is a pointer to an

AEESoundCmdData structure that tells your application the current volume (if the volume is being changed) or an index into the tone list that's currently playing.

Despite the flexibility of the ISound interface, it's not well suited to producing much besides the simplest of sound sequences because of the handset-specific nature of the AEESoundToneData lists. Unless you're in a position to write an authoring tool that lets you easily convert your sound data to AEESoundToneData structures, you're forced to compose these lists by hand. This, in turn, can be a laborious and error-prone process, and the results aren't even as flexible as a MIDI file.

Playing MIDI, MP3, and QCELP Sounds

Most of the time, you'll want to play your sound data using the ISoundPlayer interface, which lets you play sounds directly from a stream and monitor the playback process.

You can create an ISoundPlayer instance using one of two methods: in the traditional way using ISHELL_CreateInstance or by asking the shell for a handler of the sound file's MIME type using ISHELL_GetHandler. Once you create an instance of the interface, you can play sound in a memory region or a file, or you can point the player at a stream to play the sound. Note that if you use a stream, the interface *doesn't* perform streamed audio playback; instead, it reads the entire contents of the sound file into a buffer and then plays the buffer. (Thus, you can't use the ISoundPlayer interface to build a streaming audio player.)

You set the ISoundPlayer interface to the source of your sound data using either ISOUNDPLAYER_SetInfo or ISOUNDPLAYER_SetStream. When you use ISOUNDPLAYER, you pass a AEESOUNDPLAYERINFO structure with its eInput field set to either SDT_BUFFER or SDT_FILE and the pData field pointing to the buffer containing either the memory region or the filename. If you use ISOUNDPLAYER_SetStream, you simply pass the interface of the IAStream subclass with the audio data.

As with the ISound interface, you can register a function callback with ISOUNDPLAYER_RegisterNotify. This callback lets you know whether the sound is playing or paused, the nature of the requests made of the ISoundPlayer interface, and other information. You can also determine the duration of a sound by using the method ISOUNDPLAYER_GetTotalTime.

To actually play your sound, you call ISOUNDPLAYER_Play. Some sound types, such as MP3 and MIDI sounds, let you fast forward or rewind through the sound data programmatically, so you can select specific segments of a sound file or let users pick which segments of a sound file they want to hear. Similarly, with MIDI sounds, you can control the tempo and pitch of the playback. The ISoundPlayer interface includes these methods for controlling playback:

- ISOUNDPLAYER_Play: Begins or restarts the playback of the sound.

- ISOUNDPLAYER_Stop: Stops the playback of the sound.

- ISOUNDPLAYER_Rewind: Rewinds the playback by a specific number of milliseconds. (QCELP sound data doesn't support this.)

- ISOUNDPLAYER_FastForward: Fast forwards the playback by a specific number of milliseconds. (QCELP sound data doesn't support this.)

- ISOUNDPLAYER_Pause: Pauses the playback. (QCELP sound data doesn't support this.)

- ISOUNDPLAYER_Resume: Resumes the playback after you've paused it. (QCELP sound data doesn't support this.)

- ISOUNDPLAYER_SetTempo: Sets the tempo of a MIDI sound.

- ISOUNDPLAYER_SetTune: Sets the pitch level (in musical half-step instruments) of a MIDI sound.

Because of the computationally intensive nature of sound playback, you can have only one ISoundPlayer interface actually playing sound at once. You can, however, have more than one ISoundPlayer interface instantiated and prepared to play (within memory constraints), and switch between them at will.

The "Using the ISoundPlayer Interface in an Application" section of this chapter shows how you can use the ISoundPlayer interface to easily add sound to your application's user interface.

Playing Multimedia

Available in QUALCOMM BREW 2.0, the IMedia interface promises to unify multimedia management for both presentation and recording. This interface provides a simple way to present sound, animation, and even (if the hardware supports it) the playback of video or other content. Moreover, the interface has been designed so that you can also use it for recording content, such as operating a voice recorder or a camera on a camera-enabled handset.

NOTE *As this book goes to print, it's not clear which handset manufacturers will provide implementations to render specific kinds of media, such as animated images, MPEG video, and what have you. It's quite likely that the first uses of* IMedia *interfaces in your application will be to replace the* ISoundPlayer *interface or perhaps to use a developer extension that plays a specific kind of media, such as Mobile Scalable Vector Graphics (MSVG) or Synchronized Multimedia Integration Language (SMIL).*

After instantiating an IMedia interface—typically a subclass of IMedia that understands a specific media format—you must set its media using the IMEDIA_SetMediaData method, which can take data from a file, a memory region, or an ISource subclass (which you can create from an IStream subclass).

Once you've set the IMedia interface's media, you should set a status callback using the IMEDIA_RegisterNotify function. Your status callback function will receive regular invocations notifying it of status changes within the IMedia interface, including playback start, playback stop, and configuration changes (such as setting the size of the screen rectangle and the destination audio device or volume). Next, you configure the interface with multiple calls to IMEDIA_SetMediaParms, which lets you set the interface's screen bounds, volume, playback tempo, and playback pitch.

Once you configure the IMedia interface, you can begin playing the media using the following methods:

- IMEDIA_Play: Starts the media playback

- IMEDIA_Stop: Stops the media playback

- IMEDIA_Pause: Pauses the media playback

- IMEDIA_Resume: Resumes the media playback

- IMEDIA_Rewind: Rewinds the playback by the number of milliseconds you indicate

- IMEDIA_FastForward: Advances the playback by the number of milliseconds you indicate

The QUALCOMM BREW MediaPlayer sample that accompanies the Software Developer's Kit (SDK) provides an excellent introduction to using the IMedia interface.

Using the ISoundPlayer Interface in an Application

No game is complete without sound effects. To demonstrate the ISound and ISoundPlayer interfaces, the following sections show you how to add sound effects to the cat-and-mouse game you saw in the previous chapter.

The game uses sounds for two purposes: to provide a background MIDI track that plays throughout the game and to play a specific sound and vibrate the handset when the cat catches the mouse.

Adding Sound Interfaces to the Application

To start, add two fields to the application data structure to carry the ISound and ISoundPlayer interfaces, as shown in Listing 9-1.

Listing 9-1. The Application Structure

```
1: typedef struct
2: {
3:    ISoundPlayer *pISoundPlayer;
4:    ISound *pISound;
5:
6:    ISprite *pISprite;
7:    IBitmap *pIBitmap;
8:    AEETileMap  arTileMap[ TileMap_Last + 1 ];
9:    AEESpriteCmd arSprites[ Sprite_Last + 1 ];
10:
11:    int nTurn;
12:    uint32 nTime;
13: } CAppData, *CAppDataPtr;
```

These fields, pISoundPlayer and pISound (lines 3–4), store the interface to an ISoundPlayer instance and an ISound instance, respectively. You allocate these while the main state begins by making a call to the new function in Listing 9-2.

Listing 9-2. Allocating the ISoundPlayer *and* ISound *Instances*

```
1: static void mainMusicStart( CAppPtr pThis )
2: {
3:    CAppDataPtr pData = GetAppData( pThis );
4:
5:    // If these fail, it's OK.
6:    ISHELL_CreateInstance( GetShell( pThis ),
```

```
 7:    AEECLSID_SOUND, (void **)&pData->pISound );
 8:
 9:  ISHELL_CreateInstance( GetShell( pThis ),
10:    AEECLSID_SOUNDPLAYER, (void **)(&pData->pISoundPlayer ));
11:
12:  // Start the music playback
13:  mainMusicPlay( pThis );
14: }
```

Lines 6–10 in Listing 9-2 create instances of the ISound and ISoundPlayer interfaces. Because sound playback isn't crucial to game play, don't worry if these calls fail; instead, you can test for the existence of the desired interface before you use it.

Line 13 calls the new function mainMusicPlay to begin playing the background MIDI music.

Playing Background Music During Game Play

Playing music in the background is easy. You simply initialize an ISoundPlayer instance, tell it to play, and then restart the playback when it's done playing. You can do this with mainMusicPlay and mainSoundNotifyCallback. The playback begins in mainMusicPlay, as shown in Listing 9-3.

Listing 9-3. Starting the Playback

```
 1: static void mainMusicPlay( CAppPtr pThis )
 2: {
 3:   CAppDataPtr pData = GetAppData( pThis );
 4:
 5:   // It's OK if there's no sound player
 6:   if ( pData->pISoundPlayer )
 7:   {
 8:     ISoundPlayer *pISoundPlayer = pData->pISoundPlayer;
 9:     AEESoundPlayerInfo info = { 0 };
10:     int result;
11:
12:     // Set our data source
13:     info.eInput = SDT_FILE;
14:     info.pData = MUSIC_FILE;
15:
16:     result = ISOUNDPLAYER_SetInfo( pISoundPlayer, &info );
17:     /*
18:        or
```

```
19:      result =
20:      ISOUNDPLAYER_Set( pISoundPlayer, SDT_FILE, MUSIC_FILE );
21:      on earlier platforms such as 1.0.
22:    */
23:
24:    if ( result == SUCCESS )
25:    {
26:      // Set the notification callback
27:      ISOUNDPLAYER_RegisterNotify( pISoundPlayer,
28:        mainSoundNotifyCallback, pThis );
29:
30:      // Start the playback
31:      ISOUNDPLAYER_Play( pISoundPlayer );
32:    }
33:  }
34: }
```

As you can see, this is simple stuff. If the application has a valid interface to play the background MIDI (line 6), you first initialize the interface using ISOUNDPLAYER_SetInfo (lines 12–16) to play a sound file with the name MUSIC_FILE. MUSIC_FILE, defined in frameworkopts.h, points to a simple MIDI file.

NOTE   *On QUALCOMM BREW 1.0, the correct Application Programming Interface (API) to use is* ISOUNDPLAYER_Set. *See lines 19–20 of Listing 9-3 for an example.*

Next, the code registers a callback to receive notifications from the ISoundPlayer instance on lines 27–28. The instance will call mainSoundNotifyCallback at regular intervals, including when the MIDI finishes playing so you can restart the playback. Finally, if the initial ISOUNDPLAYER_SetInfo call succeeds, you begin the playback on line 31.

TIP   *On most versions of the QUALCOMM BREW Emulator, the sounds you play with the* ISoundPlayer *interface will only be heard if you play them from the file system. If you're playing your sounds from memory using* IMemAStream *and don't hear anything, don't panic. Instead, either store the sound in a file and play from the file or begin testing on the handset.*

The `mainSoundNotifyCallback` function looks for notifications that the playback has completed and calls `mainMusicPlay` to restart the playback in Listing 9-4.

Listing 9-4. Restarting the Playback

```
1: static void mainSoundNotifyCallback( void *p,
2:                                      AEESoundPlayerCmd    eType,
3:                                      AEESoundPlayerStatus eStatus,
4:                                      uint32 dwParam)
5: {
6:   CAppPtr pThis = (CAppPtr)p;
7:   CAppDataPtr pData;
8:
9:   if ( !pThis ) return;
10:  pData = GetAppData( pThis );
11:  if ( !pData ) return;
12:  if ( !pData->pISound && !pData->pISoundPlayer ) return;
13:
14:  if ( eStatus == AEE_SOUNDPLAYER_DONE )
15:  {
16:    mainMusicPlay( pThis );
17:  }
18: }
```

This routine begins with a number of guards (lines 9–12) to ensure that if the system invokes callback while the application is shutting down, the callback exits before accessing invalid data. After the guards, the function simply tests to see if the playback has completed (line 14) and restarts the playback with `mainMusicPlay` on line 16.

Eventually, all good things must come to an end. This is true for the background music, which stops playing when the main state exits. Listing 9-5 shows that the `mainMusicStop` function accomplishes this by releasing both of the sound interfaces.

Listing 9-5. Stopping the Background Music Playback

```
1: static void mainMusicStop( CAppPtr pThis )
2: {
3:   CAppDataPtr pData = GetAppData( pThis );
4:
5:   if ( pData->pISoundPlayer )
6:     ISOUNDPLAYER_Release( pData->pISoundPlayer );
```

```
 7:
 8:    if ( pData->pISound )
 9:      ISOUND_Release( pData->pISound );
10:
11: }
```

After releasing the sound interface on line 6, the playback stops, so there's no need for the application to use the ISOUNDPLAYER_Stop method.

Playing Sounds for Game Events

The mouse's movement is controlled by some simple logic in mouseMove (see Listing 9-6). To add sound, you simply add a segment of code that uses the mouse's distance from the cat to determine if the ISound instance should play a sound.

Listing 9-6. Controlling the Mouse's Movement

```
 1: static void moveMouse( CAppPtr pThis, uint16 *pRandom )
 2: {
 3:    CAppDataPtr pData = GetAppData( pThis );
 4:    int transform = 0;
 5:    int16 newX, newY;
 6:    int dx, dy, dx1, dy1;
 7:    int sY, sY;
 8:
 9:    // if the cat gets close to the mouse, we move.
10:    dx = pData->arSprites[ Sprite_Cat ].x -
11:      pData->arSprites[ Sprite_Mouse ].x;
12:    dy = pData->arSprites[ Sprite_Cat ].y -
13:      pData->arSprites[ Sprite_Mouse ].y;
14:    dx1 = dx > 0 ? dx : -dx;
15:    dy1 = dy > 0 ? dy : -dy;
16:
17:    // If we're really close, play a squeaky sound.
18:    if ( pData->pISound &&
19:     dx1 < MOUSE_TOO_CLOSE && dy1 < MOUSE_TOO_CLOSE )
20:    {
21:      AEESoundToneData tone = { 0 };
22:
23:      tone.eTone = AEE_TONE_REORDER_TONE;
24:      tone.wDuration = 500;
```

```
25:
26:     ISOUND_PlayTone( pData->pISound, tone );
27:     ISOUND_Vibrate( pData->pISound, tone.wDuration );
28:   }
30:
31:   ... continue with mouse movement logic
32: }
```

In this code, lines 10–13 calculate the *arithmetic distance* between the cat and the mouse. Unlike the distance formula—the square root of the sum of the squares—you learned in high-school math, this formula isn't as accurate, but it requires far less mathematical processing. This is an important point on QUALCOMM BREW–enabled handsets, both because this computation happens often and because QUALCOMM BREW has limited support for floating-point mathematics (addition, subtraction, multiplication, and division to be precise). Lines 14 and 15 calculate the absolute value of these distances.

Lines 18–19 verify that the application has a valid ISound instance and that the cat is sufficiently close to the mouse to warrant a sound. Line 21 allocates the tone variable that you'll use with ISOUND_PlayTone, and the following two lines select the AEE_TONE_REORDER_TONE (which sounds a little like a fast busy signal to play for one half of one second). Finally, the routine starts playing the sound and vibrating the handset using ISOUND_PlayTone and ISOUND_Vibrate on lines 26 and 27 before continuing with the mouse movement logic.

Summary

You should remember the following key points about playing sound and other multimedia with the QUALCOMM BREW interfaces:

- QUALCOMM BREW–enabled handsets can support sound media such as MIDI, QCELP, and MP3. However, not all handsets support all audio formats.

- All sound playback is asynchronous. If you need to monitor the status of sound playback, you must implement a function that the sound interface calls periodically to notify your application of the playback status.

- For simple sounds to alert the user or for sounds to debug application flow, you can use ISHELL_Beep or ISOUND_PlayTone to play a single tone.

- To play sound media such as MIDI, QCELP, and MP3, you can use the ISoundPlayer interface or, using BREW 2.0, the IMedia interface.

- Using either the ISoundPlayer interface or the IMedia interface, you can fast forward, rewind, pause, and resume the playback when playing sounds if the sound format supports it.

- The IMedia interface, available in QUALCOMM BREW 2.0, lets you play multimedia including animated images, sounds, and other rich multimedia such as MP4 video if the handset supports those data types.

CHAPTER 10

Networking Your Data

THE QUALCOMM BREW platform is a "connected" platform. In other words, it includes interfaces for performing Transmission Control Protocol/Internet Protocol (TCP/IP) networking, receiving Short Message Service (SMS), and, starting with QUALCOMM BREW 1.1, making Hypertext Transport Protocol (HTTP) requests—all over wireless networks. Moreover, the newest versions of the QUALCOMM BREW platform include support for Bluetooth, the popular personal area network standard. QUALCOMM BREW lets your application use Bluetooth to connect to nearby computing devices including wireless audio devices and handheld computers.

In this chapter, you'll learn about the most commonly used network interfaces, including the ISocket interface and the IWeb interface, and you'll see how to accept incoming SMS messages to trigger actions within your application. The chapter also touches on the new Bluetooth interfaces.

Choosing Wireless Network Options

With the QUALCOMM BREW platform's plethora of wireless connectivity options, it can be a challenge to pick which network and interfaces to use for transferring data to and from your application. The QUALCOMM BREW platform gives you several choices:

- Implementing TCP/IP networking via the INetMgr, ISocket, and IDNS interfaces, which lets you write client-side TCP/IP applications

- Implementing HTTP networking via the IWeb and IWebOpts interfaces, which lets you transfer data with Web servers using HTTP

- Receiving SMS messages to trigger actions within your application

- Implementing Bluetooth connectivity to audio devices and other computing devices

Choosing the ISocket Interface for TCP/IP Networks

Using the ISocket interface, you can implement virtually any client-side TCP network protocol, such as the Simple Mail Transport Protocol (SMTP) for delivering mail or the Post Office Protocol (POP) for downloading email.

The ISocket interface presents a streaming interface (see Chapter 6, "Streaming Data") to network sockets. The ISocket interface lets you open client-side sockets—that is, you can only create sockets that initiate outbound requests; you can't create a socket, listen on a port, and await client socket connections. Once the socket is open, you use it to read and write data from and to the remote host asynchronously by using callbacks when the interface is ready to receive or send data.

Working with raw sockets gives you great flexibility as an application developer, but it has some obvious drawbacks. For instance, your application must implement an entire Internet protocol, including all of the necessary error handling. In many cases, the reference implementations of these protocols are on platforms that have additional features, such as blocking sockets and multi-threading. As a result, implementing an Internet protocol takes a significant engineering investment. Worse still, if you choose to implement a protocol of your own design, you need to invest time in developing the server side of the protocol, including dealing with loading issues and the other intricacies of server development.

As a result, for most client-server applications that don't involve a legacy protocol, it's best to look elsewhere for network support. Specifically, look to the IWeb interface, which provides a robust HTTP client layer for applications that rely on remote Web servers to provide application-specific data.

Choosing the IWeb Interface for HTTP Transactions

Over the past several years, HTTP has grown from being a successful but single-purpose protocol that delivers text and multimedia data to clients to being a protocol that bears all kinds of data, from traditional Web content to back-end business-to-business and embedded-device data transactions using the Extensible Markup Language (XML) and other proprietary data payloads. Using an off-the-shelf Web server, such as the Apache Web server or Microsoft Internet Information Server (IIS), applications can use HTTP to transfer data across the Internet.

To facilitate interoperating with Web-based services, beginning in version 1.1, the QUALCOMM BREW platform includes a module that implements the client half of HTTP, including the ability to both send (using HTTP POST) and fetch (using HTTP GET) data, as well as examine the headers associated with a data transaction.

The IWeb interface provides a comprehensive interface to HTTP (including support for proxy servers, optional keep-alive connections, and other optional HTTP-related behavior) while remaining simple for the majority of transactions. To use the interface in its simplest form, you need only instantiate an interface and then provide the source Uniform Resource Locator (URL), a callback function for the result, and some simple options describing the request. The request proceeds asynchronously, and the interface invokes your callback with a structure containing status information about the request and an ISource instance, which gives you an interface to your data. In turn, you can read directly from this source or convert to a stream using the ISourceUtil interface's ISOURCEUTIL_AStreamFromSource method. Once you have a stream, you can pass the stream to interfaces such as IImage (see Chapter 5, "Interacting with the User") and ISoundPlayer (see Chapter 9, "Playing with Sounds"). You can also provide additional callbacks to receive notification of the network status and each of the incoming HTTP headers, but that's not required.

Beginning with version 2.0 of the QUALCOMM BREW platform, QUALCOMM has added support for Transport Layer Security (TLS), which is the new name for what was formerly Secure Socket Layer (SSL), with the ISSL interface. You can activate TLS support for your IWeb requests by asserting additional flags, but there's a hitch: Most handsets currently shipping don't yet support TLS. Moreover, the latest releases of the Software Developer's Kit (SDK) documentation indicate that the interface is defined and documented but not implemented, so it may be some time before you can take advantage of TLS in your application.

Choosing QUALCOMM BREW-Directed SMS for Application Notification

Because QUALCOMM BREW–enabled handsets can't listen on sockets for incoming connections, at first glance it seems that there's no way to have your application respond to outside requests. Fortunately, that's not true; by using SMS messages directed at your application (commonly called a *BREW–directed SMS message*, or just BDSMS), your application can receive an SMS message addressed to it and act on its contents, whether or not the application is running. For example, a BDSMS can awake your application and cause it to make a network transaction to download breaking news, or it can update your application's configuration in the event of back-end infrastructure changes. Some companies, such as M7 Networks, are developing products and services that incorporate BDSMS with games so that you can invite multiple players to play in a single game from your handset by launching an application that then uses a central server and BDSMS.

As you'll see in the section "Understanding BDSMS," using BDSMS is easy—in fact, *any* application can receive a BDSMS with little effort. It's more difficult, however, to incorporate BDSMS in your application from a business perspective because most wireless carriers don't let just anyone originate SMS messages on their network. Instead, they give only certain partners, commonly called *aggregators*, access to the servers that send SMS messages over their networks. As a result, when developing your application, you must work closely with the carriers that will distribute your application and obtain their help in identifying an aggregator you can use to access their networks when you need to send BDSMS messages.

Choosing Bluetooth for Personal Area Networking

The Bluetooth standard defines a multiple-node wireless network for replacing cables between closely coupled devices, such as laptop computers, cell phones, printers, user interface devices, and the like. Using Bluetooth-enabled devices, for example, you can use your handheld computer to place phone calls on your mobile phone and even access the Internet to read mail or browse the Web—all without making a physical connection between your mobile phone and your handheld computer.

The Bluetooth standard defines a set of *profiles*, each with specific capabilities. These capabilities include the ability to carry audio content between a remote audio device and a wireless handset, the ability to carry serial data between two devices, and the ability to share a Local Area Network (LAN) connection between a handheld computing device and a wireless access point.

Although no QUALCOMM BREW–enabled handsets yet include Bluetooth, starting with version 2.0, QUALCOMM BREW includes several interfaces for Bluetooth:

- You use the `IBTSDP` interface to perform device discovery and determine the names and capabilities of the other devices within range on the network.

- You use the `IBTAG` interface to interface with Bluetooth audio devices, such as headsets, activating or deactivating the audio channel that carries audio from the wireless terminal to the audio device.

- You use the `BTSIOPORT` interface to establish a connection to a remote Bluetooth serial port, such as one on a handheld computer, to exchange data.

Bluetooth is an excellent choice when you're creating an application that lets the mobile terminal talk with another device, such as to exchange contact/calendar information or pictures taken by a camera-enabled handset.

Understanding the Network Interfaces

Once you select the appropriate network interface for your application, you need to use the interface in your application. The following sections show in more detail how you can use each of the three kinds of network interfaces in your application.

Understanding the ISocket Interface

Of the three network interfaces, the ISocket interface (and its companion class, the INetMgr interface) is the most complex because it offers the greatest flexibility. At a superficial level, the ISocket interface resembles the Berkeley socket interface found under Unix, Linux, Mac OS X, and the Winsock interface in that the socket provides an entity to which you can write data and from which you can read data. However, it has a fundamental difference: All network input/output is asynchronous. As a result, you can't issue a request to read or write data unless the socket is in a state to do so.

This leads to a more complex, yet more flexible, application architecture. Because ISocket operations are asynchronous, you can perform additional operations while your socket is open, giving the impression that the networking occurs in the background. Moreover, by structuring your application as a state machine—with individual states for establishing the connection, reading data, and writing data—you can eliminate most of the added complexity.

Before you can use an ISocket instance, you must create it. Unlike most other classes, you can't use ISHELL_CreateInstance to create an ISocket instance; instead, you use the INetMgr class, which provides a set of interfaces to manage network interfaces. This interface includes methods to obtain a host's IP address given its host name using INETMGR_GetHostByName, obtaining the status of the network support on the handset using INETMGR_NetStatus, and obtaining an ISocket instance using INETMGR_OpenSocket. Using either the INETMGR_GetHostByName or INETMGR_OpenSocket calls results in the handset connecting to the network by establishing a wireless network connection and starting the handset's network stack.

In most applications, you'll want to establish a connection to a remote host using its host name, rather than its IP address, because you can change hosts on the server side while retaining the host name, but it's more difficult to do so and retain the IP address. Thus, when establishing an Internet connection, you should first obtain the IP address of the remote host using its host name. You do this using the INETMGR_GetHostByName function, which takes an INetMgr instance, a pointer to a structure that will store the resulting IP address, the remote host name, and a callback. The invocation looks like this:

```
1: void INETMGR_GetHostByName(INetMgr *pINetMgr,
2:                            AEEDNSResult *pres,
3:                            const char *psz,
4:                            AEECallback *pcb );
```

Unlike the other functions that require callbacks you've seen, this function requires an AEECallback structure, which is simply a structure that wraps both the callback function and application data in one structure:

```
1: typedef struct _AEECallback
2: {
3:   AEECallback *pNext;
4:   void *pmc;
5:   PFNCBCANCEL pfnCancel;
6:   void *pCancelData;
7:   PFNNOTIFY pfnNotify;
8:   void *pNotifyData;
9:   void *pReserved;
10: } AEECallback;
```

Rather than accessing the fields of this structure directly, it's best to use the CALLBACK_Init macro, like this:

```
1: CALLBACK_Init( cb, callbackFunction, pThis );
```

The macro CALLBACK_Init ensures that the callback function (callback-Function) will be called with the argument pThis, and the macro also initializes the parts of the structure responsible for managing cancelled callbacks.

The AEEDNSResult structure you pass to INETMGR_GetHostByName should be allocated in your application context because it must exist throughout the lifetime of the Domain Name Service (DNS) request. When your callback is invoked, the AEEDNSResult structure will contain the number of addresses obtained for the specific host in its nResult field and an array of nResult IP addresses for the desired host in its addrs field.

With the IP address of the remote host in hand, you can create a socket to make your connection using the INETMGR_OpenSocket method:

```
1: pThis->m_pISocket = INETMGR_OpenSocket( pThis->m_pINetMgr, AEE_SOCK_STREAM );
```

This creates a TCP socket.

This method returns an unconnected ISocket instance, which you connect to a remote host:

```
1: ISOCKET_Connect( pThis->m_pISocket,
2:                   nIPAddress,
3:                   HTONS(nPort),
4:                   (PFNCONNECTCB)callbackFunction, pThis );
```

This method takes the ISocket interface to connect, the remote network address, the remote port, the callback to invoke when the connection is complete, and a pointer to the data to pass the callback.

 TIP *You should be sure to use the* HTONS *macro to convert the port address to network byte order.*

Once the connection establishment is complete, the socket invokes your network callback, and you can begin reading and writing data. To do this, use the ISOCKET_Read and ISOCKET_Write methods, which take the socket, a pointer to the buffer of bytes to write, and the number of bytes to read or write. In return, these two functions provide the number of bytes actually read or written, or they provide an error code. Most errors indicate a communications error, and you should shut down the socket and perform whatever error handling your application requires (such as notifying the user and storing the data for a later transaction). If, however, one of these calls returns the error code AEE_NET_WOULDBLOCK, this indicates the operation can't proceed without blocking application flow, and you should retry later. To know when to retry the read or write, schedule a callback using either ISOCKET_Readable or ISOCKET_Writable, and the socket will invoke your callback when it can accept another ISOCKET_Read or ISOCKET_Write invocation. If at any time you need to cancel the callbacks, you can do so using ISOCKET_Cancel, which cancels both callbacks.

Once you're finished using the socket, you should close it using ISOCKET_Release. The handset's network stack will keep the underlying physical connection to the Internet via the wireless network for a short time so that multiple socket invocations don't require repeated connections to the network. If you will be performing operations with multiple sockets in sequence, you can adjust this time (called the *linger time*) using INETMGR_SetLinger, which takes the desired linger time as a time in milliseconds and returns the previously set linger time. In practice, you want to experiment to find the optimum linger time for your application, but a typical delay is around 30 seconds, which spans enough time for a user to perform another action that leads to initiating another network transaction without leaving the connection open unduly long.

To manage the asynchronous cycle of obtaining a remote IP address, reading and writing data, and managing errors, you can use multiple states within your application. Generally, you can create a state for each of the phases of a socket's life cycle:

- Creating the INetMgr instance, setting the linger time with INETMGR_SetLinger, and starting the IP address resolution using INETMGR_GetHostByName.

- Handling the resulting callback from INETMGR_GetHostByName, creating the socket using INETMGR_OpenSocket, and connecting the socket to the remote host using ISOCKET_Connect. This state can also release the INetMgr instance using INETMGR_Release.

- Reading data, invoked by ISOCKET_Readable.

- Writing data, invoked by ISOCKET_Writable.

- Closing the socket with ISOCKET_Release.

- Handling errors at any point with a specific error state that releases the socket and network manager and handles the specific error. You can determine the nature of the error using INETMGR_GetLastError and ISOCKET_GetLastError.

In conjunction with these states, you can maintain two buffers—one for output to the remote host and one for input from the remote host—and update application state based on the flow of your protocol as your application moves between its reading and writing states.

In a few circumstances, your network protocol may require that you use datagrams via the Unconnected Datagram Protocol (UDP), rather than TCP sockets, as described here. To do this, simply pass the AEE_DGRAM option to INETMGR_OpenSocket, and instead of using ISOCKET_Read and ISOCKET_Write, use ISOCKET_SendTo and ISOCKET_RecvFrom. Like ISOCKET_Read and ISOCKET_Write, when these interfaces block application execution, they return AEE_NETWOULDBLOCK, and you can schedule a callback using ISOCKET_Readable or ISOCKET_Writable.

Understanding the IWeb Interface

In principle, the IWeb interface is simple to use: You instantiate it, give it a URL and a callback, and await the response. In practice, however, using the interface can be significantly more complex depending on the options you want to include with the request.

The key to mastering the IWeb interface is understanding the options available to you when using the interface. Table 10-1 shows the various options, each of type WebOpt.

Table 10-1. IWeb *Interface Options*

OPTION	ARGUMENT	PURPOSE
WEBOPT_ACTIVEXACTIONS	uint32	This is the maximum number of allowed transactions; the interface handles overflow by enforcing queuing.
WEBOPT_CONNECTTIMEOUT	uint32	This is the connection timeout in milliseconds to pass to the underlying network socket.
WEBOPT_CONTENTLENGTH	uint32	This is the content length of object body in request or response.
WEBOPT_HANDLERDATA	void *	This is the pointer to application-specific data for the transaction callback.
WEBOPT_HEADER	char *	This is the pointer to a character string containing carriage return–separated and linefeed-separated HTTP headers.
WEBOPT_HEADERHANDLER	PFNWEBHEADER	This is the pointer to a callback to invoke with each HTTP header in the response.
WEBOPT_IDLECONNTIMEOUT	uint32	This is the idle timeout in milliseconds.
WEBOPT_METHOD	char *	This is the pointer to a character string containing the HTTP request type. The default is "GET".
WEBOPT_PROXYSPEC	char *	This is the pointer to a URL to a host to use as an HTTP proxy.
WEBOPT_STATUSHANDLER	PFNWEBSTATUS	This is the pointer to a callback to invoke periodically with transaction status.
WEBOPT_USERAGENT	char *	This is the pointer to a character string containing the user-agent string.

In most cases, the only header you're likely to want to change is the WEBOPT_METHOD header, which lets you specify the type of HTTP request. (For an in-depth overview of HTTP, see the World Wide Web Consortium's Request for Comment 2616.) The default value is "GET", which fetches a document from a remote server, but often you want to use "POST", which sends a block of remote data to the server instead. When doing so, you should also use WEBOPT_CONTENTLENGTH to indicate how large the block of data your application is sending to the server.

Perhaps more important, you can supply pointers to two additional callbacks: one invoked with each header the IWeb interface receives and one invoked periodically to provide your application with status notifications. You use the WEBOPT_HEADERHANDLER to supply a pointer to a callback function with this signature:

```
1:  typedef void (*PFNWEBHEADER)(void *pNotifyData,
2:                               const char *pszName,
3:                               GetLine *pglVal);
```

The first argument is the data you set using WEBOPT_HANDLERDATA; more than likely, it's your application pointer. The second argument is the name of the header (such as "Content-Type" or "Content-Encoding"). The last argument is a pointer to a GetLine structure, with the header's value stored in its psz field. (Your callback doesn't need to free either pszName or pglVal before it exits.)

Similarly, you can provide a status callback with the following signature:

```
1: typedef void (*PFNWEBSTATUS)(void *pNotifyData,
2:                              WebStatus ws,
3:                              void *pData);
```

The IWeb interface invokes this callback periodically throughout a transaction, including status about the transaction in the ws argument. The WebStatus field is an enumeration, with the values shown in Table 10-2.

Table 10-2. The WebStatus *Enumeration and Meanings*

VALUE	MEANING
WEBS_STARTING	The connection is starting.
WEBS_CANCELLED	The connection has been cancelled.
WEBS_GETHOSTBYNAME	The IWeb interface is determining the IP address of the remote host.
WEBS_CONNECT	The IWeb interface has connected.
WEBS_SENDREQUEST	The IWeb interface is sending the request.
WEBS_READRESPONSE	The IWeb interface is reading the response.
WEBS_GOTREDIRECT	The IWeb interface received a redirect to another URL.
WEBS_CACHEHIT	The IWeb interface found the desired content in its cache.

After creating an IWeb instance with ISHELL_CreateInstance, you use the IWEB_GetResponse method to start a Web transaction.

It takes the following arguments:

```
1:   IWEB_GetResponse( pIWeb,
2:                     (pIWeb, piWResp, pcbFunc, pszUrl,
3:                     ...
4:                     WEBOPT_END));
```

> **TIP**   *The extra set of parentheses when invoking* IWEB_GetResponse *is crucial because the function is actually a macro that condenses the options you specify.*

IWeb places the results of the request in the piWResp structure, which is a pointer to an IWebResp interface. Because of this, it's important you don't allocate this structure on your stack but instead place it somewhere in your application context. Otherwise, when the IWeb request finishes, it'll write to a variable that's now out of scope, corrupting the call stack. The callback function, pcbFunc, has this signature:

```
1:  void WebAction_GotResp( void *p )
```

where p points to the callback data you set using WEBOPT_HANDLERDATA. The pszURL argument points to the URL that the IWeb interface should fetch, and after that argument comes a comma-delimited list of WebOpt options and their arguments.

Once your callback returns, you can obtain the results of the transaction by calling the IWebResp interface's IWEBRESP_GetInfo method, which returns a WebRespInfo structure. It has the following fields:

```
1:  typedef struct
2:  {
3:    int nCode;
4:    ISource *pisMessage;
5:    long lContentLength;
6:    const char *cpszContentType;
7:    const char *cpszCharset;
8:    int32 tExpires;
9:    int32 tModified;
10: } WebRespInfo;
```

The result data is available through the pisMessage field, which is an ISource instance you can use or convert to an IStream using the ISOURCEUTIL_AStreamFromSource method. The nCode field stores the HTTP result code (such as 200 for a valid response), and the lContentLength contains the number of bytes (if known) in the response. You can obtain the content type using the cpszContentType field and the character set using the cpszCharset field. Finally, you can determine the data's expiry (for caching) and last-modified date using the tExpires and tModified fields.

Understanding BDSMS

Using BDSMS is strikingly easy. By addressing an SMS message to a specific class ID, the application receives an EVT_APP_MESSAGE event when the SMS message is received. Thus, all you need to do is format an SMS message correctly, and your application will receive the message. A BDSMS message looks like this:

```
1:  //BREW:classid:message
```

where classid is the class ID of the class to receive the message, and message is the message that QUALCOMM BREW will deliver to your application. Once QUALCOMM BREW detects the incoming BDSMS, it'll strip the leading part of the message and deliver message as a pointer to the memory region with its contents as the event handler's dwParam argument. Thus, all your application needs to do is include an event handler for EVT_APP_MESSAGE in its event handler and then access the contents of *dwParam to obtain the contents of the message.

Your application can receive BDSMS messages whether or not it's running. If your application isn't running, the shell will first invoke your AEEClsCreateInstance function to create an instance of your application and then send it the EVT_APP_MESSAGE event. You can either handle the message at that time (bearing in mind that your application is closed, and you can't perform any user interface interaction) or invoke ISHELL_StartApplet to launch your application to handle the message. If, on the other hand, your application is already running, it simply receives the EVT_APP_MESSAGE message as just another event to handle.

In the next chapter, you'll learn about other ways to handle SMS messages in general using the QUALCOMM BREW notification mechanism, such as how you can view the text of any incoming message.

Summary

The following are the key points you learned in this chapter:

- You can access raw sockets for client-side applications through the INetMgr and the ISocket interfaces.

- You use the IWeb interface to make HTTP requests of remote Web servers, including retrieving and posting data.

- You use BDSMS messages to send application-specific data. Your application receives this data packaged with an event, regardless of whether it's running.

CHAPTER 11

Controlling the Handset

DESIGNED TO MEET the needs of Original Equipment Manufacturers (OEMs) as well as application developers, the QUALCOMM BREW platform offers a bevy of interfaces you can use to control the handset directly or to access features traditionally controlled by handset OEMs, such as the built-in address book and ring tones.

This chapter presents a survey of these interfaces, including how to send and receive a Short Message Service (SMS) message, determine the handset's position, access the built-in address book and ringer control applications, manage your application's licensing, and initiate a voice call. Next, the chapter shows you how to package a segment of code as an *extension*, a component that presents the same kind of interface as a QUALCOMM BREW interface but that you can share between applications or sell to other developers. After reading this chapter, you'll have a good understanding of how to control the handset's native telephony functions and use them to create novel applications or add features to your existing application.

Understanding How You Can Control the Handset

You can control many aspects of handset operation, including sharing data between applications and sharing data between your application and specific OEM applications such as the address book and ringer application. This is a powerful feature of QUALCOMM BREW. With features and interfaces similar to high-end wireless handsets running the Palm Powered or Microsoft Pocket PC Smartphone platforms, you can create applications with unprecedented integration on handsets affordable to the majority of consumers today.

Accessing the Built-in Address Book

Wireless handsets include a built-in address book application that lets you store the names, phone numbers, and email addresses of contacts, which you can then use to make phone calls or to send an SMS.

The OEM address book is organized as a set of address book records. Each address book record is a set of address book record fields, a category designation, and an associated ID. Each field contains the data associated with that field, as well as an ID and a type. A record can only hold a single datum—if a record has two home phone numbers, for example, it will have two fields, one for each home phone number. The IAddrBook interface contains methods to access the address book itself, and the IAddrRec interface contains the methods to manipulate a specific record. Using these classes, you can create new records in the OEM address book, delete records, and modify individual fields in a specific record. You do this using an interface similar to the database interfaces you saw in Chapter 7, "Storing Data."

After creating an IAddrBook instance using ISHELL_CreateInstance, you iterate either across the categories of address book records using IADDRBOOK_EnumCategoryInit and IADDRBOOK_EnumNextCategory or across the records in the address book using IADDRBOOK_EnumRecInit and IADDRBOOK_EnumNextRec. The record iterator lets you iterate across all records in the database or search for a specific record that contains a specific field, a specific substring in one of its fields, or a specific record that belongs in a specific address book category. Once you begin the search using IADDRBOOK_EnumRecInit, you call IADDRBOOK_EnumNextRec repeatedly to obtain the records that match your search criteria. This method returns an instance of IAddrRec for each matching record or NULL if no more records match the search criteria you specified when calling IADDRBOOK_EnumRecInit.

With an IAddrRec instance in hand, you can obtain or change its category using IADDRREC_GetCategory and IADDRREC_SetCategory. To obtain a specific field, first use IADDRREC_GetFieldCount to obtain the number of fields in the record and then iterate across all of the fields using IADDRREC_GetField, which takes the IAddrRec instance and the index of the field to fetch, returning an AEEAddrField structure:

```
1: typedef struct
2: {
3:   AEEAddrFieldID fID;
4:   AEEAddrFieldType fType;
5:   void *pBuffer;
6:   uint16 wDataLen;
7: } AEEAddrField;
```

The first member, fID, is simply the field ID as an enumeration (with values such as WORK_PHONE or URL). The fType field is the data type used to store the string and is a constant, such as FT_STRING, that matches the data types defined by the database Application Programming Interfaces (APIs). The value of the field is stored in the memory region at pBuffer, and the size of the record's data is stored in wDataLen.

You can also add new fields by filling out an `AEEAddrField` structure and calling `IADDRREC_AddField`, or you can remove a field by specifying its index and calling `IADDRREC_RemoveField`. Once you change a field's contents, you should call either `IADDRREC_UpdateField` (to update a single field in a record) or `IADDRREC_UpdateAllFields` (to update an entire record).

If you want to add a field, you create an `IAddrRec` instance using the `IADDRBOOK_CreateRec` instance. This method lets you create a new address book entry in a specific category with the fields you specify. Once you create it, you can manipulate it just like any other `IAddrRec` instance or simply release it because the process of creating the record automatically adds it to the address book. If you need to remove a record, you can do so using the `IADDRREC_RemoveRec` method. To remove *all* records in the address book, use `IADDRBOOK_RemoveAllRecs`.

 TIP *These interfaces are only available in handsets running versions of the QUALCOMM BREW platform 1.1 and beyond and may not be available on all handsets. When creating an* `IAddrBook` *instance, be sure to check the return value and handle creation failures accordingly. Moreover, your application must have the Access to Address Book privilege set in its Module Information File (MIF) to be able to use these interfaces.*

Managing an Application's Licensing

A feature unique to the QUALCOMM BREW platform is its integrated support for managing *application licensing*—under what circumstances the application is allowed to run on the handset. The original licensing terms are set at the application's time of purchase and are automatically maintained by the platform on behalf of the application.

There are times, however, when you may want your application to assume responsibility for adjusting its licensing characteristics. A game, for example, might award additional free play beyond the number of plays purchased, or you may want to limit the features accessible in a demo release of the application. You can perform operations such as these using the `ILicense` interface, which lets you adjust an application's license count on the handset.

An application can have one of the following kinds of licenses:

- No expiration at all, indicated by AEELicenseType of LT_NONE

- A per-use license, indicated by AEELicenseType of LT_USES

- Application expiration on a specific date, indicated by AEELicenseType of LT_DATE

- Application expiration after a certain number of days of downloading, indicated by AEELicenseType of LT_DAYS

- Application expiration after a certain number of minutes of use, indicated by AEELicenseType of LT_MINUTES_OF_USE

You can determine which kind of license was purchased with the application using the method ILICENSE_GetInfo. If the application is licensed on a per-use basis, QUALCOMM BREW *doesn't* perform any license verification, and you should use ILICENSE_DecrementUsesRemaining and ILICENSE_IncrementUsesRemaining at appropriate times in your application to deduct or increase the number of times your application can be used (such as after completing a game, completing a game level, or downloading a Web resource). You can also set the number of uses using ILICENSE_SetUsesRemaining if you need to set it to a specific value.

Your application can also test to see under what terms the application was purchased and when it'll expire if it's using one of the other license mechanisms such as ILICENSE_GetPurchaseInfo, which returns not just the kind of license but the time (in seconds according to the handset's internal clock) at which the license will expire.

Using Telephony Features

Although this book has treated QUALCOMM BREW–enabled handsets as well-connected handheld computers, they're of course wireless handsets, complete with voice telephony features. The QUALCOMM BREW platform includes the ITAPI interface, which gives you access to a simple Telephony Application Programming Interface (TAPI) that lets you initiate a voice call, send an SMS message, obtain the text of an SMS message, get the handset's calling status, and get the caller ID information of an incoming call if it's available.

After creating an instance of ITAPI using ISHELL_CreateInstance, you can get the current state of the handset's telephony interface using the ITAPI_GetStatus method to which you pass the ITAPI instance and an empty TAPIStatus structure.

Upon return, this structure will be filled with information about the handset. The structure has the following fields:

```
 1: typedef struct
 2: {
 3:   char szMobileID[MOBILE_ID_LEN +1];
 4:   PhoneState state;
 5:   flg bData:1;
 6:   flg bDigital:1;
 7:   flg bRoaming:1;
 8:   flg bCallEnded:1;
 9:   flg bE911CallbackMode:1;
10:   flg bRestricted:1;
11: } TAPIStatus;
```

The szMobileID field provides the handset's mobile number, typically (but not always) the Mobile Directory Number (MDN) registered with the wireless carrier. The state field provides an indication of the handset's current state via an enumeration, indicating such things as whether the handset is offline, idle, originating a call, receiving a call, or in the middle of a call. The remaining flags indicate capabilities or handset states, as follows:

- The bData flag indicates whether the handset is making a data call.

- The bDigital flag indicates whether the handset is receiving digital coverage.

- The bRoaming flag indicates whether the handset is currently roaming on another network.

- The bCallEnded flag indicates if a call has just ended and is only set when your application receives this structure as part of a notification (discussed in the following section).

- The bE911CallbackMode flag indicates if the handset is in emergency 911 callback mode.

If a call is in place, you can obtain the telephone number of the remote side of the call using the ITAPI_GetCallerID field, which returns the corresponding telephone number as a string in an AECHAR buffer you provide. Typically, you can only do this when immediately originating a call (on suspend or resume) because your application can't run while a voice call is in operation.

You can also initiate a voice call using ITAPI_MakeVoiceCall, which suspends your application to make the voice call. When you invoke this method, the handset performs the following steps:

1. The handset displays a confirmation dialog box to the user.

2. When the user dismisses the dialog box, the shell sends the event EVT_DIALOG_END to your application.

3. Your application should redraw the screen with the contents visible prior to calling ITAPI_MakeVoiceCall.

4. If the user confirmed placing the call, the shell sends the event EVT_APP_SUSPEND to your application. Once your application handles the event, the handset will place the call.

5. When the call is complete, the shell sends the event EVT_APP_RESUME to your application.

6. Your application must resume and redraw the screen.

When you place a voice call, you can monitor its status using the ITAPI_OnCallStatus method, which registers a callback in your application that will be invoked when there are changes in call status, such as when the remote side has answered or disconnected. This method is the same as the ITAPI_OnCallEnd method.

To send an SMS message, use the ITAPI_SendSMS method, passing the contents of the SMS message and a callback that the shell will invoke periodically throughout the transmission of the SMS message. When you invoke this method, the handset does the following:

1. The handset begins the process of sending the SMS message.

2. The shell sends your application the EVT_APP_SUSPEND event.

3. The shell invokes the notification function you registered when calling ITAPI_SendSMS with the status of the message delivery.

4. The shell sends your application the EVT_APP_RESUME event.

Although your application's callback is invoked while your application is suspended, it's best to simply cache aside the status from the transaction and display it once your application resumes.

Finally, using ITAPI you can intercept any SMS message sent to the handset. Doing this requires that you register for *notifications* from the ITAPI class, either in your MIF or by calling ISHELL_RegisterNotify. Once you do so, each incoming SMS message generates an EVT_NOTIFY event to your application. This event includes an AEENotify structure, pointed to by the event's dwParam:

```
1: typedef struct
2: {
3:    AEECLSID cls;
4:    INotifier * pNotifier;
5:    uint32 dwMask;
6:    void * pData;
7:    AEENotifyStatus st;
8: } AEENotify;
```

The contents of the incoming SMS message are at the location indicated by pData. You can get at it using this (rather ugly) bit of casting code:

```
1:    AEESMSMsg *pSMS = (AEESMSMsg *)((AEENotify *)(dwParam))->pData;
```

The resulting structure AEESMSMsg isn't formally documented by QUALCOMM, so you probably shouldn't rely on its contents. A quick peek at the AEETAPI.h file shows its contents, which includes the sender's mobile number, the priority of the message, and the time at which the message arrived.

With the SMS message in hand, you can obtain its text representation using ITAPI_ExtractSMSText, which returns AEESMSTextMsg with the following members:

```
1: typedef struct
2: {
3:    uint16 nChars;
4:    char szText[1];
5: } AEESMSTextMsg;
```

Because the SMS message may contain both text and binary data on some networks, AEESMSTextMsg contains both the length of the SMS message as well as the data itself. (Note that szText isn't really a 1-byte array, but rather the message begins at &szText and continues past the end of the structure.)

The ITAPI interface can also send your application notifications of other telephony occurrences via status changes (which send your application a TAPIStatus structure at the notification's pData).

TIP *The* ITAPI *interface may not be available on some early handset models. When creating an* ITAPI *instance, be sure to check the return value and handle creation failures accordingly. Moreover, your application must have the TAPI privilege set in its MIF to be able to use this interface. Finally, not all versions of the QUALCOMM BREW platform support all methods, so check the AEETAPI.h file for the version of QUALCOMM BREW for which you're developing.*

Determining the Handset's Position

In the late 1990s, the Federal Communications Commission (FCC) passed a ruling (later known as the *E911 initiative*) that required all cell phones be able to provide their locations to emergency dispatch centers when calling 911 in order to help emergency response workers reach the scene of an emergency. Handsets shipping today all include this technology, called *gpsOne*; it uses a combination of Global Positioning System (GPS) and cellular network information to determine the wireless handset's position to within a few meters anywhere the handset has digital coverage.

The QUALCOMM BREW platform includes the IPosDet interface to obtain the handset's location, either by identifying the wireless carrier's sector (which can be used in carrier-specific applications) or by obtaining the handset's latitude, longitude, and elevation, along with its speed and direction if the handset is moving. (There's also the simpler-to-use ISHELL_GetPosition API, which returns a simple data structure to a callback method.) When integrated with Web-based services, this opens a new market for location-aware applications, such as those providing navigation, directory services, messaging, and gaming.

Using the IPosDet interface to obtain the handset's position is easy: You simply create an IPosDet interface using ISHELL_CreateInstance and call IPOSDET_GetGPSInfo. It'll return either SUCCESS or an error code, and then it'll invoke a callback you pass with the requested information. You must also pass a valid AEEGPSInfo structure, which will remain in scope until the shell calls your application callback (so don't allocate it on the stack). The AEEGPSInfo structure has the following fields you can examine in your callback function:

```
1: typedef struct _AEEGPSInfo
2: {
3:   uint32 dwTimeStamp;
4:   uint32 status;
5:   int32 dwLat;
```

```
 6:    int32 dwLon;
 7:    int16 wAltitude;
 8:    uint16 wHeading;
 9:    uint16 wVelocityHor;
10:    int8 wVelocityVer;
11:    AEEGPSAccuracy accuracy;
12:    uint16 fValid;
13:    uint8 bHorUnc;
14:    uint8 bHorUncAngle;
15:    uint8 bHorUncPerp;
16:    uint16 wVerUnc;
17: } AEEGPSInfo;
```

The dwTimestamp field contains the time in seconds in GPS time (since 1/6/1980) obtained. The status field indicates whether the request succeeded or failed. The dwLat and dwLon fields indicate the handset's position in degrees, with dwLat being in units of 180/2^25 degrees and dwLon being in units of 360/2^26 degrees. The wAltitude field specifies the altitude in meters, and the wVelocityHor and wVelocityVer indicate the velocity in quarter-meter units. The wHeading field indicates the current heading in 360/2^10 degrees, and the remaining fields indicate the uncertainty associated with the measurement. The most important field is the fValid field, which contains a union of flags indicating which of the fields (latitude, longitude, elevation, heading, and velocity) were actually measured. The data is returned as World Geodetic System 1984 (WGS-84) datum, so it's compatible with the most recent topographic data available.

TIP *The* IPosDet *interface may not be available on some early handset models. When creating an* IPosDet *instance, be sure to check the return value and handle creation failures accordingly. Moreover, your application must have the Access to Sector Information privilege set in its MIF to be able to use this interface. Finally, some carriers may not expose the handset's location information to the QUALCOMM BREW platform, and on these platforms, either the* IPosDet *interface can't be created or its methods will return obviously incorrect values.*

Managing Ringer Tones

The rich audio capabilities of the QUALCOMM BREW platform (see Chapter 9, "Playing with Sounds") aren't features of the QUALCOMM BREW platform itself but rather the underlying chipset provided by QUALCOMM. As a result, most handsets can play ring tones when receiving calls using the same audio types. To facilitate installing custom ring tones, the QUALCOMM BREW platform includes the IRingerMgr interface, which lets you install new ring tones on the handset.

Using the IRinger interface, you can do the following:

- Enumerate the various categories of ring tones on the handset.

- Enumerate the ring tones on the handset.

- Set the current ring tone.

- Create a new ring tone for use by the handset.

- Get a list of supported ringer types on the handset.

- Fetch information about a specific ringer.

- Play a specific ring tone.

To install a ring tone, you first want to make sure that the same ring tone isn't installed. To do this, you iterate over all the ring tones on the handset using the pair of functions IRINGERMGR_EnumRingerInit and IRINGERMGR_EnumNextRinger. The IRINGERMGR_EnumNextRinger returns a structure that describes the ringer:

```
1: typedef struct _AEERingerInfo
2: {
3:    AEERingerID id;
4:    AEESoundPlayerFile format;
5:    char szFile[MAX_FILE_NAME];
6:    AECHAR szName[MAX_RINGER_NAME];
7: } AEERingerInfo;
```

This structure includes the ringer's unique ID (id), the ringer's data format (format)—which is one of AEE_SOUNDPLAYER_FILE_MIDI or AEE_SOUNDPLAYER_FILE_MP3—the name of the file in which the ringer data is stored (szFile), and the human-readable name of the ringer (szName).

You can set the active ring tone by using IRINGERMGR_SetRinger or by passing the ring tone's ID. You can preview a specific ringer by using the IRINGERMGR_Play and IRINGERMGR_Stop methods. (There's also a more advanced playback interface, which resembles the ISoundPlayer interface you learned about in Chapter 8, "Drawing Graphics.")

Before installing a new ringer, you should check that the handset supports the format of the ringer. To do this, you can use the `IRINGERMGR_GetFormats` method, which provides an array of the formats that the handset supports. Once you're sure that the handset supports the format of the ring tone you want to install, simply call `IRINGERMGR_Create` with the data for the ring tone as a stream, its human-readable name, and its format. Of course, you can always remove a ring tone, too, using `IRINGERMGR_Remove` and passing the ID of the ring tone to remove.

TIP   *To use the `IRingerMgr` interface, your application must have the Write access to Ringer directory privilege set in its MIF.*

Sharing Code Between Applications

The QUALCOMM BREW platform provides developers with the ability to create *extensions*, which are similar in concept to shared libraries that can be used across multiple applications. An extension provides the same kind of interface as a native QUALCOMM BREW interface. It can be kept private to an application or shared among developers by being sold via the QUALCOMM BREW Delivery System, allowing developers to make money by selling value-added modules to other QUALCOMM BREW developers. For example, you might choose to offer an extension that implements a player for a specific media type or a new kind of user interface control. Your applications can use this extension, and, at your discretion, other developers can license your application, letting you make money when subscribers download their applications that use your extension. Most important, the entire extension model is hidden from wireless subscribers because extensions are transparently downloaded when they're needed by an application. Equally important, when you download several applications that require an extension, the extension itself only downloads once.

An extension is a module, just like an application. As such, it must inherit from the `IBase` interface, implementing the `AddRef` and `Release` methods, which are responsible for tracking and releasing the resources used by the extension. Coding an extension isn't much more difficult than writing an application, but it takes a little more time and a bit of a deeper understanding of the QUALCOMM BREW platform because you must implement the module's setup, teardown, and method dispatch table by hand.

Understanding the Life Cycle of a Module

When your application calls ISHELL_CreateInstance, the shell queries each module
with the desired class ID by calling its AEEClsCreateInstance function. This function
is a module's entry point, just as main is a traditional C program's entry point. In
previous chapters, you've seen the sample AEEClsCreateInstance, which typically
looks something like Listing 11-1.

Listing 11-1. The Genesis of a Module Such As an Application or an Extension

```
 1: int AEEClsCreateInstance( AEECLSID clsId,
 2:                           IShell *pIShell,
 3:                           IModule *po,
 4:                           void **ppObj )
 5: {
 6:   int result = EFAILED;
 7:   *ppObj = NULL;
 8:
 9:   if (AEECLSID_THEEXTENSION == clsId)
10:   {
11:     result = ExtensionCls_New( sizeof(Extension),
12:                               pIShell,
13:                               po,
14:                               (IModule **)ppObj);
15:     if ( result == SUCCESS )
16:     {
17:       result = Extension_Init( (void *) *ppObj );
18:       if ( result != SUCCESS )
19:       {
20:         Release( (IExtensionCls *)*ppObj );
21:       }
22:       return result;
23:     }
24:   }
25:   // Wrong class, _New or _Init failed
26:   return result;
27: }
```

This routine simply checks the incoming class ID against the module's ID
(line 9) and, if they match, creates a new instance of the module (lines 11–14) and
initializes its member variables (lines 15–23). Because all extensions are modules,
a module has the same entry point, too.

Defining the Extension Interface

For the applications you've seen throughout this book, the QUALCOMM-provided AEEAppGen.c file handles setting up your application's interface. This isn't so with an extension, where you must define the extension's interface by hand.

A module's interface is stored in a virtual function table (called a *vtable*), much like the virtual function tables used by C++. The first element of a module is a pointer that points to the module's vtable, which typically resides at the end of a structure defining the module. You can see this by looking at any of the interface definitions in the QUALCOMM BREW include files. For an extension, it looks like this:

```
1: struct _IExtensionCls
2: {
3:   struct _IExtensionClsVtbl *pvt;
4: };
5: typedef struct _IExtensionClsVtbl IExtensionClsVtbl;
6: struct _IExtensionClsVtbl
7: {
8:   uint32  (*AddRef)(IExtensionCls *);
9:   uint32  (*Release)(IExtensionCls *);
10:
11:   // Put your methods here.
12: };
13:
14: typedef struct _IExtensionCls IExtensionCls;
15: typedef struct _IExtensionCls IExtension;
```

This defines an extension with two methods, AddRef and Release. All extensions should implement these methods (in this order) to correctly implement the IBase interface. The IExtensionClsVtbl structure defines the extension's interface with two functions, and the extension itself consists of a pointer to IExtensionClsVtbl, which contains the addresses of those two functions.

This is a *public* definition of the extension interface. It's information you must share with other users of the extension because it describes how to call the methods provided by your extension. However, because dereferencing the functions in your extension's vtable using these structures is a messy and error-prone operation, it's best to provide macros to do this for users of your extension. For example:

```
1: #define IEXTENSION_AddRef(p)  \
2:   GET_PVTBL(p, IExtension)->AddRef(p)
3:
4: #define IEXTENSION_Release(p) \
5:   GET_PVTBL(p, IExtensionCls)->Release(p)
```

The QUALCOMM-supplied `GET_PVTBL` macro performs just the necessary skullduggery to obtain the address of the appropriate function in the extension's vtable:

```
1: #define GET_PVTBL(p,iname)       ((iname*)p)->pvt
```

Of course, your extension probably needs its own member variables and other such things, too. You do this by defining a *private* version of your extension structure, which has as its first element a pointer to the extension's vtable and, as its last element, the vtable itself. The extension member variables are sandwiched between the following:

```
 1: struct _Extension
 2: {
 3:   // note: this needs to be the first item in this structure
 4:   /// Virtual function table
 5:   IExtensionCls vtExtensionCls;
 6:
 7:   /// @name Member variables
 8:   //@{
 9:   /// References to us
10:   uint32      m_nRefs;
11:   /// copy of Shell pointer
12:   IShell     *m_pIShell;
13:   /// IModule interface pointer
14:   IModule    *m_pIModule;
15:   //@}
16: };
17: typedef struct _Extension Extension;
18: typedef struct _Extension *ExtensionPtr;
```

Within this extension's implementation, the extension itself is referred to as the structure `Extension`. It contains the extension's vtable (line 5), its reference count (line 10) used by `AddRef` and `Release` to track usage, the shell it's given on initialization (line 12), and its module (line 14). Because Extension's fields are a superset of IExtensionCls, the implementation of the extension can take a valid pointer to IExtensionCls and cast it to an Extension to obtain its private data. Moreover, because the format of the extension structure is kept private within the implementation of the extension, its members won't be available to users of the extension.

Initializing the Extension

At some point during initialization, you need to set up the extension's vtable as well as its private data. Typically, you do this during the invocation of AEEClsCreateInstance. I like to do this right away using a separate function, such as Extension_New, which performs roughly the same things as a C++ constructor does (see Listing 11-2).

Listing 11-2. Creating an Extension and Its vtable

```
 1: int ExtensionCls_New( int16 nSize,
 2:                        IShell *pIShell,
 3:                        IModule *pIModule,
 4:                        IModule **ppMod)
 5: {
 6:   ExtensionPtr pThis = NULL;
 7:   VTBL(IExtensionCls) *modFuncs;
 8:
 9:   // validate parameter(s)
10:   if(!ppMod || !pIShell || !pIModule)
11:   {
12:     return EFAILED;
13:   }
14:
15:   *ppMod = NULL;
16:
17:   // Allocate memory for the object
18:   if(nSize < sizeof(Extension)) nSize += sizeof(Extension);
19:
20:   pThis = (ExtensionPtr)
21:     MALLOC(nSize + sizeof(IExtensionClsVtbl));
22:
23:   if (NULL == pThis)
24:   {
25:     return ENOMEMORY;
```

```
26:    }
27:
28:    /* Allocate the vtbl and initialize it.
29:       Note that the modules and apps must not
30:       have any static data.
31:       Hence, we need to allocate the vtbl as well.
32:    */
33:    modFuncs = (IExtensionClsVtbl *)((byte *)pThis + nSize);
34:
35:    //Initialize individual entries in the VTBL
36:    modFuncs->AddRef      = AddRef;
37:    modFuncs->Release     = Release;
38:    // ... Add your vtable here.
39:
40:    // initialize the vtable
41:    INIT_VTBL(pThis, IModule, *modFuncs);
42:
43:    // initialize the data members
44:    pThis->m_nRefs       = 1;
45:    pThis->m_pIShell     = pIShell;
46:    pThis->m_pIModule    = pIModule;
47:
58:
49:    // Add References
50:    ISHELL_AddRef(pIShell);
51:    IMODULE_AddRef(pIModule);
52:
53:    // Set the pointer in the parameter
54:    *ppMod = (IModule*)pThis;
55:
56:    return AEE_SUCCESS;
57: }
```

This function shows a lot about how an extension—or even your application—is initialized behind the scenes, so let's take it a line at a time and see what it does. It begins with the size of the extension, a reference to the instantiating shell, a valid module pointer, and a pointer into which to place the newly allocated module that will be the extension. Line 7 uses the QUALCOMM-supplied macro VTBL to declare a pointer to the extension's vtable, which you later fill with pointers to the extension's public methods.

Lines 10–13 do the usual validation of arguments because if any of these pointers are invalid for any reason, the handset will crash trying to create the extension—a very bad thing. Next, you determine how much space to allocate (lines 18–21) and allocate it. You need enough space for the extension structure itself (including its private variables on line 18), along with the extension's vtable (line 21), which will piggyback on the end of the allocated Extension structure. Lines 23–26 perform more error checking and return with an error code signaling an out-of-memory condition if necessary.

Next, on line 33, you calculate the location of the vtable by finding the end of the Extension structure you just allocated and storing the value in modFuncs. On the subsequent lines 34–38, you assign each of the vtable's members to a pointer to a public function, such as AddRef or Release. A real extension would probably have several more functions, all of which would be assigned to the vtable here. Once the vtable has been populated, you use the QUALCOMM-provided macro INIT_VTBL on line 41 to finish initializing the vtable and then initialize the data members common to all extensions (the reference count, shell pointer, and module pointer, on lines 44–46). After that, you increment the reference counts for the incoming IShell and IModule interfaces on lines 50–52 in case your caller frees them while the extension still needs them. Finally, you return the newly created extension on lines 54–56.

Implementing the Extension's Methods

Because all extensions must implement the IBase interface, the AddRef and Release methods are a good example of how to implement the methods for an extension. You've already seen how to create the public interface functions and initialize the entries for these methods in the extension's vtable in the preceding sections; Listing 11-3 shows the implementation of the extension's AddRef method.

Listing 11-3. The Extension's AddRef Method

```
 1: static uint32 AddRef( IExtensionCls *p)
 2: {
 3:   ExtensionPtr pThis = (ExtensionPtr)p;
 4:   // validate parameter(s)
 5:   if (!pThis)
 6:   {
 7:     return 0;
 8:   }
 9:   return (++(pThis->m_nRefs));
10: }
```

On line 3, you cross-cast the public version of the extension—which consists of only the pointer to the vtable and the vtable—to the private version of the extension, which has all of its member variables. Next, on lines 5–8, you validate the incoming pointer and then on line 9 you return the updated reference count.

The Release method, shown in Listing 11-4, is a little trickier because it must undo all of the allocations performed by the Init method you saw in Listing 11-2.

Listing 11-4. The Extension's Release Method

```
1: static uint32 Release(IExtensionCls *p)
2: {
3:   ExtensionPtr pThis = (ExtensionPtr)p;
4:
5:   // validate parameter(s)
6:   if (!pThis)
7:   {
8:     return 0;
9:   }
10:
11:   // Manage our reference count.
12:   pThis->m_nRefs--;
13:
14:   if (pThis->m_nRefs != 0)
15:   {
16:     return pThis->m_nRefs;
17:   }
18:
19:   // Ref count is zero. Release memory.
20:   Extension_Free(pThis);
21:
22:   // Release interfaces
23:   if (pThis->m_pIShell)
24:   {
25:     ISHELL_Release(pThis->m_pIShell);
26:   }
27:
28:   if (pThis->m_pIModule)
29:   {
30:     IMODULE_Release(pThis->m_pIModule);
31:   }
32:
33:   FREE_VTBL(pThis, IModule);
34:
35:   // Free the object itself
```

```
36:    FREE( pThis );
37:
38:    return 0;
39: }
```

The Release method should *only* free the extension if the reference count
reaches zero, so lines 12–17 decrement the reference count and return if there are
still other objects using the extension. Next, on line 20, you call the Extension_Free
function, which would free any member variables allocated in the extension's
Extension_Init function. After that, lines 23–31 release the IShell and IModule
instances, respectively. Line 33 frees the extension's vtable using the QUALCOMM-
provided macro FREE_VTBL, and line 36 frees the object itself. Finally, on line 38, you
return the object's reference count—which is now 0.

Summary

In this chapter, you learned several ways to control the handset, including the
following:

- Using the IAddrBook and IAddrRec interfaces to access the OEM address book

- Using the ILicense interface to manage an application's per-use license
  count

- Using the handset's ITAPI interface to place voice calls, determine the
  handset's phone number, and receive and send SMS messages

- Using the IPosDet interface to determine the handset's position

- Using the IRingerMgr interface to install a new ring tone, enumerate the ring
  tones on the handset, and remove a ring tone

- Sharing code you write in extensions with other applications or other application developers

CHAPTER 12

Certifying Your Application

THE MOST IMPORTANT part of your application's development is its distribution: If it never makes it to market, you'll never have the opportunity to recoup the development costs, let alone revel in the knowledge that others are using your application. (Or perhaps it's the other way around….) Unlike most other platforms, where once you finish an application it's up to you to test, package, and distribute it, the QUALCOMM BREW platform has a stringent validation process known as *TRUE BREW* certification to ensure your application is of the highest quality before it reaches the hands of consumers. Once your application receives TRUE BREW certification, QUALCOMM works with you to establish a pricing plan and make your applications available to carriers. It then distributes royalties for application sales to you.

This chapter shows why you need to validate your application, as well as the process by which you obtain certification prior to distributing your application. You'll see how to package your application for certification, as well as the most common reasons why applications don't pass certification on the first attempt. Finally, the chapter closes with a brief discussion on pricing your application and working with carriers to distribute your application.

Validating Your Application

Testing is a crucial part of the development cycle of any QUALCOMM BREW application. Not only does QUALCOMM require a high standard of quality—validated by the third-party certification program maintained by National Software Testing Labs (NSTL)—but carriers insist upon it. Consumers have high expectations regarding the stability and quality of their wireless handsets, and fielding support calls from customers is an expensive prospect for wireless carriers. Consequently, you must ensure that your application is of the highest quality and then submit it to NSTL for third-party testing before making it available to consumers.

Performing Functional Tests

The TRUE BREW certification process provided by NSTL is to ensure software validity, not functionality. As NSTL validates your application, it doesn't directly test application functionality, except to ensure that if you claim a feature is available then it's actually available. Although NSTL notifies you if it finds an obvious functional flaw, it doesn't specifically test for functional defects. Consequently, you're still responsible for providing basic quality assurance for your application.

Thus, an obvious part of your software development cycle should be ensuring that your application functions in the manner that it's designed to perform. In many ways, this is really the standard software quality testing that you'd perform on any application, and it includes several types of testing:

- Inspection—either via formal code reviews, peer reviews, or team-style programming such as eXtreme Programming (XP)—helps catch defects at their source before they turn into application defects.

- Unit testing by developers ensures that each component of the application is high quality and doesn't bring defects into the completed application.

- Integration testing ensures that no defects arise when integrating individual components of the application.

- Executing test suites with your application ensures that regular operations perform as expected. Ideally, test suites are designed by individuals removed from the development process, and they're executed in completion several times throughout the application development.

- Regression testing ensures that once a bug is fixed, it stays fixed. Your organization should track software failures and their causes and periodically retest the application with test cases drawn from the database of defects to ensure that no problems re-emerge.

- Ad-hoc testing by engineers, testers, and other stakeholders helps you evaluate your application's stability in real-world scenarios prior to deployment.

- Automated testing through the QUALCOMM BREW Grinder and Shaker tools lets you simulate heavy (if random) application use on both the emulator and handset, helping track down difficult-to-find defects pertaining to boundary conditions such as missed events, overfilled text input fields, and the like.

Of course, it's up to you and your organization to determine how best to meet the challenge of functional testing. There's a wealth of good literature about software testing, and most of it draws the same conclusion: There's no silver bullet to creating defect-free code. Instead, you should rely on a bevy of different testing methodologies and tests to validate the functionality of your application.

Performing Validation Tests

What NSTL does provide, however, is software validation testing—that is, checking that your application doesn't violate the integrity of the wireless handset or the wireless network. This is a crucial part of application verification, not just to meet wireless carrier requirements and uphold consumer expectations but because most developers simply don't have the necessary experience at the outset to adequately validate their own applications.

The testing that NSTL performs isn't a secret; in fact, you can see the list of tests it performs in *Application Developer's TRUE BREW Test Guide: Requirements and Test Cases*, available at the QUALCOMM BREW extranet (`http://www.qualcomm.com/brew/`). Broadly speaking, these tests are divided into the following categories:

- **Application packaging**: The application includes the necessary files and documentation to execute correctly. The application has the necessary privileges and class dependencies set in its Module Information Files (MIFs), and only those privileges necessary to run are asserted.

- **Application functionality**: The application performs the basic operations described in the documentation without disruption or loss of data.

- **Application licensing**: If the application uses the `ILicense` interface, it does so in accordance with the documentation for changing its license count. Similarly, if the application uses the `ILicense` interface to determine whether the application is in a demonstration mode, both the licensed and demonstration modes operate as described in the documentation.

- **Application storage**: The application correctly handles its storage requirements, including boundary conditions such as a lack of sufficient dynamic or persistent storage.

- **Application stability**: The application doesn't reset or interfere with the stability of the wireless handset.

- **User interface**: The application meets the user interface requirements set by QUALCOMM.

- **Verification testing**: The application can be successfully installed and removed via the over-the-air distribution system and by the user. The application meets the requirements regarding the number of files in use and correctly handles boundary conditions when being installed or removed.

The best way to ensure that your application passes TRUE BREW certification by NSTL on the first pass is to thoroughly read *Application Developer's TRUE BREW Test Guide: Requirements and Test Cases* and add its tests to the suite of tests you use to verify your application. In conjunction with defensive programming—to catch errors on the handset when they occur—and regular peer reviews of your code, you'll be on a good footing to pass certification the first time.

Documenting Your Application

Although the QUALCOMM BREW platform doesn't provide a mechanism for obtaining end user manuals for QUALCOMM BREW applications, most carriers require user manuals to help their support staff in fielding questions about your application. (Most wireless carriers will handle first-tier support for your application, escalating only more difficult questions to your organization for clarification or rectification.)

At a minimum, your user manual should include a summary of your application's purpose, a section showing a typical use case walking the reader through how to use your application, and sections detailing each of your application's major features. You may not need to hire a technical writer to create the documentation because QUALCOMM BREW applications are typically small. Often an engineer with help from someone skilled in marketing can do the first pass at the user manual. Moreover, screen shots can often clarify awkward prose, so consider using an ample number of screen shots to substitute for lengthy procedural listings and awkward prose.

Submitting Your Application for Certification

Once you're confident your application is ready for certification—you've performed adequate functional testing and exercised the application using the validation test suites—it's time to package and submit your application for certification. In a sense, this is the point of no return: Once you submit your application to NSTL, you can no longer make changes to it. After being certified by NSTL,

QUALCOMM works with you to provide the files to wireless carriers. If you need to make a change, you must start the certification process again.

To submit your application for certification, you must package your application, sign it using the QUALCOMM BREW AppSigner, and submit it via the Web to NSTL. Once NSTL completes certifying the application, it'll contact you with the results of the testing, indicating that you've passed, or it'll provide you with a description of the tests that the application failed.

For more information on signing the application and determining the testing tier (and the corresponding price) that applies for your application, see the QUALCOMM BREW extranet for more information.

NSTL uses both the handset build and the emulator build of your application to perform its testing. Consequently, when submitting your application, you must include the application as both a Dynamically Linked Library (DLL) for the QUALCOMM BREW Emulator under Microsoft Windows as well as the Module (MOD) file for the emulator. You must also include your user documentation and an application specification, available from the QUALCOMM BREW extranet.

To package your application, follow these steps:

1. Create an empty directory. Within this directory, create three directories, named WIN, ARM, and DOC.

2. In the WIN directory, place the release build of your application's DLL, the MIF, an optional BAR file, and any other required data files.

3. In the ARM directory, place the release build of your application's MOD file, the MIF, an optional BAR file, and any other required data.

4. In the DOC directory, place the application specification, along with any other required documentation, such as the user guide required by many carriers. You should name the application specification *appname*_spec.doc, where *appname* is the name of your application. Similarly, name the user manual *appname*_mnl.doc. For other naming conventions, see the QUALCOMM BREW extranet.

5. Launch the QUALCOMM BREW AppSigner application.

6. From the main window, click Select Application. The Browse for Folder window appears.

7. Select the folder containing the MOD file you want to sign. You'll be prompted with a list of files in that directory.

8. Choose the BAR, MOD, and MIF files in the ARM directory by checking the box in the Include in Signing column of the list.

9. For each file in the list, if it's changed after the application is installed on the device, check the box in the Gets Modified column of the list. Note that files that change after installation on the handset are automatically signed as well.

10. Click the Add Signature button.

11. Enter your developer name in the dialog box that appears.

12. The VeriSign Personal Trust Agent dialog box appears. Enter your username and password for your VeriSign profile, and click Next. The VeriSign notarization server will process your request over the Internet, which may take a few moments.

13. The QUALCOMM BREW AppSigner application compresses your application directory.

14. Go to `https://www.nstl.com/nstl/index.htm` and fill out the form to submit your application for certification.

 TIP *Be sure to check the latest documentation on the QUALCOMM BREW extranet when signing your application to be sure that none of these steps have changed since the book's publication.*

Failing Certification: The Top Five Ways to Fail

It's easy to pass certification—if you follow the instructions carefully and perform adequate testing of your application before you submit your application for certification. Unfortunately, because it's easy to miss a step, the following are some of the common mistakes developers make.

Mispackaging Your Files

The initial steps in NSTL certification are automated, and if you don't follow the steps in preparing your submission package, fail to sign your application, omit a file, or include debug instead of release versions of your application, your application will fail certification almost immediately.

A related problem that often occurs, especially to first-time developers, is to forget to place a human-readable version number somewhere in your application, such as on the splash screen or from an About screen available from the main menu or a configuration menu.

Including Undocumented Functions or Documented Functions That Don't Work

Applications with undocumented Easter eggs—functionality that's hidden from the user and not documented—or functionality described in the user documentation that doesn't exist will guarantee failure.

One of NSTL's primary responsibilities is to help protect carriers from deploying applications that could potentially cause problems with their network. Obviously, one way to deploy a malicious application is to make a Trojan horse—an application that pretends to be useful but in fact does something quite the contrary. To eliminate this possibility, NSTL and carriers have a firm policy that all features must be documented.

In a similar vein, carriers want to ensure that your application does what you claim it'll do. Although NSTL doesn't do functional testing *per se*, it will fail an application that claims to perform a function that isn't actually implemented.

Failing to Handle Suspend and Resume Operations

QUALCOMM BREW–enabled handsets aren't just a computing platform; they're a wireless communications tool. Voice and data communications are the platform's top priority, and your application must gracefully yield to their needs. The suspend and resume feature of the QUALCOMM BREW platform is one way that the platform ensures that the telephony and data features are available anytime they're needed.

If your application can't successfully handle the EVT_APP_SUSPEND and EVT_APP_RESUME events or crashes the handset when these events occur, your application will fail certification.

Incorrectly Using the Clear Key

By convention, the Clear key provides the user with a way to back up to the previous step in an application—in any application. This is the firmest user interface guideline mandated by QUALCOMM, and it's rigorously enforced by QUALCOMM, NSTL, and the carriers. Be sure your application uses the Clear key for this single purpose, and you're more likely to pass on your first submission.

Failing to Handle File System Errors

If your application uses files on the file system, be sure your application handles cases where either the file system is full or the maximum number of files on the file system has been exceeded. NSTL provides a test application (available at the QUALCOMM BREW extranet) to help you ensure your application correctly meets these boundary conditions.

Pricing and Promoting Your Application

Once your application receives TRUE BREW certification, you can supply a pricing plan via the QUALCOMM BREW extranet. This pricing plan should take into account not just your business model but the following as well:

- The relative prices and availability (subscription, one-time fee, or limited number of uses) of competing applications

- The price range of other similarly featured applications available

- The pricing guidelines set by the carriers that will distribute your application

Most carriers—and vendors—obviously prefer a subscription model because it meshes well with consumers' expectations as a line item for a service on their cellular phone bill and provides your company with recurring revenue.

Once you set a pricing plan for your application, QUALCOMM makes your application available to individual carriers. Most carriers have an additional certification program, but the carrier certification program is generally far easier to pass than the TRUE BREW certification program.

Although QUALCOMM makes your application available to carriers, it behooves you to make contacts with the marketing and product managers responsible for QUALCOMM BREW applications at the wireless carrier companies that will distribute your application. Most are happy to help promote your application because they share in the revenue your application generates on their network.

Summary

In this chapter, you learned the following:

- The importance of functionally verifying your application because although TRUE BREW certification ensures that an application correctly interoperates with the wireless handset and wireless network, it doesn't test the functionality of your application *per se*

- How to package your application for submission to NSTL for TRUE BREW certification prior to delivery to QUALCOMM for distribution

- How to avoid the most common failures when submitting your application for certification

Index

Numbers and Symbols